3 9 35 0003

S0-BSD-913

DATE DUE

DEC 1 6 1999	
APR 0 9 2001	
MAY 0 8 2001	
APR 2 5 2007	
OCT 0 7 2013	

DEMCO, INC. 38-2931

LABOR AND HUMAN RESOURCES SERIES

LABOR STRUGGLE IN THE POST OFFICE:
From Selective Lobbying to Collective Bargaining
John Walsh and Garth Mangum

MASS IMMIGRATION AND THE NATIONAL INTEREST
Vernon M. Briggs, Jr.

Mass Immigration

and the

National Interest

Vernon M. Briggs, Jr.

M.E.Sharpe Inc.

Armonk, New York • London, England

SCCCC - LIBRARY
4601 Mid Rivers Mall Drive
St. Peters, MO 63376

WITHDRAWN

Copyright © 1992 by M. E. Sharpe, Inc.
80 Business Park Drive, Armonk, NY 10504

All rights reserved. No part of this book may be reproduced in any form without permission from the publisher, M. E. Sharpe, Inc.

Available in the United Kingdom and Europe from M. E. Sharpe, Publishers, 3 Henrietta Street, London WC2E 8LU.

First printing 1992

Library of Congress Cataloguing-in-Publication Data

Briggs, Vernon M.
 Mass immigration and the national interest / Vernon M. Briggs Jr.
  p. cm. — (Labor and human resources)
 Includes bibliographical references and index.
 ISBN 1-56324-170-6 — ISBN 1-56324-171-4 (pbk.)
 1. United States—Emigration and Immigration—Government policy—History.
 2. Alien labor—United States—History. 3. Labor Market—United States—History. I. Title. II. Series.
 JV6493.875 1992
 325.73—dc20   92-16927
                                                             CIP

Printed in the United States of America
The paper used in this publication meets the minimum requirements of the American National Standards for Information Sciences—Permanence of Paper for Printed Library Materials, ANSI Z 39.48—1984.

MV   10 9 8 7 6 5 4 3 2 1

Contents

List of Tables and Figures

Acknowledgments

In the process of completing this project, I have benefited from the use of excellent research facilities and from the assistance of a number of people. Among these were the staff and materials provided by the Franklin D. Roosevelt Presidential Library at Hyde Park, New York and the Catherwood Library at Cornell University in Ithaca, New York.

Likewise, officials of the U.S. Immigration and Naturalization Service, the U.S. Bureau of the Census, and the U.S. Department of State were very helpful in answering questions and, when possible, providing data that was requested. They, of course, are not in any way responsible for my interpretations of the information they provided.

I am also appreciative of the support provided during the Summer of 1991 by the Center for Advanced Human Resource Studies at the School of Industrial and Labor Relations at Cornell University.

Finally, I am deeply grateful for the professional work provided by Chris Smith and Jo Poole who faithfully prepared the numerous drafts of this manuscript.

V. M. B.

ONE

A Brief Perspective

Entering the final decade of the twentieth century, the United States finds itself once more in the throes of a protracted period of mass immigration. Without any public expectation as to what was to occur or participatory public debate over its anticipated merits, the level of immigration slowly began to rise during the mid-1960s; it accelerated in the 1970s; it soared in the 1980s; and, as a consequence of the significant statutory, judicial, and administrative actions taken during that decade, the phenomenon is now institutionalized as a fact of life for the 1990s. Indeed, unless specific policy interventions are invoked to reverse course, it will remain a feature of U.S. society for the indefinite future.

As a concept, the term "mass immigration" implies as its chief characteristic the quantitative size of the annual inflow of foreign-born persons into both the population and labor force of the United States. But also implicit in the usage of the term is disregard for the human capital characteristics of those who enter—especially in relation to the prevailing economic trends and social stresses at work within our nation.

In a world divided into nation states, immigration is a discretionary act of government. Its regulation is linked directly to any nation's claim to sovereignty over a particular land area. Thus, in the case of the United States, the federal government has, since 1891, preempted the exclusive right to determine all matters regarding immigration. The dynamo that has generated the revival of mass immigration since the mid-1960s, and has perpetuated its existence, is the immigration policy set at the national level by the U.S. government.

The entry of foreign-born persons into the U.S. population and labor force has not been a market-driven phenomenon. To the contrary, mass

1

immigration has been the inadvertent consequence of the design and implementation of the separate components of the nation's immigration policy and an appalling indifference by policymakers to the unexpected consequences of their actions. Specifically, the policy components are those that pertain to legal immigrants, illegal immigrants, refugees, asylees, and foreign workers temporarily permitted to work in the United States (i.e., "nonimmigrant workers" in the parlance of immigration law). Collectively, they constitute the mass immigration phenomenon of the current era.

But, regardless of the reasons for specifically admitting or indifferently permitting the entry of persons from foreign countries for permanent or temporary residence into the United States, all such individuals must support themselves by their own work or that of others. Hence, there are economic consequences associated with their presence, whether intended or not. As the scale of immigration has become larger, it follows that its economic effects on the labor market also have proportionately increased.

It is prevailing public policy that determines both the size and the composition of each of the aforementioned component groups. As such, it is these policies—and not the foreign-born persons themselves—that raise the question of congruence of mass immigration with the national interest. The foreign-born entrants are only responding to the opportunities afforded by prevailing public policy.

To be sure, the occurrence of mass immigration is not without precedents. At various times in the nation's past, it has been a significant characteristic of the U.S. economy. The nation's political structure that has postulated such ideals as freedom, equality under the law, and a toleration of diversity has long appealed to persons from all corners of the globe. Thus, as the immigration history of the nation clearly shows, there has never been any problem in attracting would-be immigrants when the nation thought it needed them. But historical and economic circumstances change. What is both necessary and positive in its effects at one time, may not be so at another time. Too much of modern economic analysis is ahistorical in its quest to interpret labor market happenings. But, with respect to immigration, an appreciation of historical circumstance is key to understanding the policies that govern the scale and shape the composition of the immigrant flows occurring at any given time. Thus, while the basic questions pertaining to the nation's immigration policy remain the same—how many immigrants should be admitted? what criteria should be used to choose who is admitted? how should the policy be enforced? what are the anticipated effects on the economy and the domestic labor force of immigration?—the answers will often be different.

As will be shown, the United States did not embark on its post-1965 course of mass immigration with any forethought. It was not the product of careful design or public debate. Nonetheless, mass immigration is, in the 1990s, an integral part of the matrix of forces that are transforming the U.S. labor market. The issue for study is not whether immigration itself is good, bad, or neutral in its effects. Rather, it is whether at this stage of this nation's economic development, mass immigration is consistent with the national interest in the 1990s. Is there a different role that immigration policy should play? If so, what is it?

In terms of sheer numbers, the 1980s witnessed the largest infusion of foreign-born persons for permanent settlement in the history of the United States. Barring any significant attempts to render U.S. immigration policy accountable for its economic consequences or to strengthen the enforcement of extant laws, immigration in the 1990s should surpass the record levels of the 1980s. Noting this trend, an international team of social science scholars who had been commissioned by three of the largest corporations in the United States (American Express, Sun Oil, and Bristol-Myers) to study contemporary U.S. society, concluded their comprehensive study in 1986 by observing that "America's biggest import is people."[1] The report further stated that "at a time when attention is directed to the general decline in American exceptionalism, American immigration continues to flow at a rate unknown elsewhere in the world."[2]

While it is true that the rapid pace of the independence movements in Eastern Europe in the late 1980s and the breakup of the Soviet Union in the early 1990s may result in a significant increase in immigration to Western European nations, such a development, should it occur, will not represent a circumstance parallel to the experience in the United States.[3] For in Western Europe, mass immigration is not being encouraged. Should it actually materialize, it will be despite significant obstacles imposed by most Western European governments.[4] Moreover, many of these governments actively seek to discourage any aspirations for permanent settlement in those who do come.[5] In this same vein, Japan too has taken strong steps to prevent virtually any immigration and to discourage those who do come from settling there.[6] In contrast, mass immigration to the United States has become an accepted feature of prevailing public policy and permanent settlement is the usual consequence even in those circumstances when the entry of foreign-born persons is a direct contravention of specific dictates of the existing law.

The Immigration Acts of 1924 and 1965

Historically, of course, mass immigration was a significant feature of American life throughout much of the nineteenth century and the early part of the twentieth century. The outbreak of World War I in Europe in 1914 sharply reduced the supply of immigrants while strong domestic opposition favoring restrictions was gathering force within the United States. When, in the postwar period, mass immigration from Europe showed signs of resuming, it was nipped in the bud by a series of legislative enactments capped by the Immigration Act of 1924. With popular support from virtually every influential quarter of society, that law imposed the nation's first numerical restriction on immigration. That action, in concert with the changing domestic and international events over the next forty years, brought a cessation to mass immigration. Besides, the essentially "open border" of the pre-1914 era had been appropriate to the frontier expansion and land acquisition phase of our nation's economic development which had come to an end by the 1920s. Although immigration continued after 1924, its scale was sharply reduced and the composition of the immigrant stream was significantly altered.

For the first time then, the nation had to turn inward and focus on tapping domestic reserves of underutilized groups to meet its employment needs. It was also time for the nation to commence the process of incorporating the racial and cultural components of the new society produced by mass immigration. The three successive waves of mass immigration that had occurred during the nineteenth and early twentieth centuries had added both size and greater diversity to the combination of English colonists, African slaves, and native Indians that comprised most of the nation's original population at the time of its birth in 1776. By the 1920s, the world's first multi-racial, -religious and -ethnic society had been produced. Whether such a diverse collection of people could be melded together to produce a competitive and productive labor force remained to be demonstrated. To a significant degree, that same question is more relevant in the 1990s—now that mass immigration has been revived—than it was in the 1920s when mass immigration was curtailed.

The immediate effect of the cessation of mass immigration in the mid-1920s was the release of the significant surplus of domestic labor that resided—largely in poverty—in the nation's rural sector. Mass immigration up until World War I had served to provide a growing urban labor force for the expanding nonagricultural industrial sectors of the North and West. When the scale of immigration was restricted in 1924, rural workers and their families were finally afforded an opportunity to compete for the broad array of urban jobs that industrialization had produced. The rural South, in particular, proved to be an especially large human reservoir that was released to become new urban job seekers. The black population, which had been overwhelmingly concentrated in the rural South as the direct legacy of slavery, was finally provided a chance to seek nonagricultural economic opportunities elsewhere. The vast majority of rural workers and family members, however, who migrated to urban areas once mass immigration stopped were native-born whites who had also been confined to the limited employment horizons of rural labor markets in all parts of the nation.

Before a new equilibrium could be established between urban and rural labor markets, the U.S. economy was beset by the depression decade of the 1930s which had temporarily disrupted the adjustment process. It remained, therefore, for the actual involvement of the United States in World War II to provide the momentum needed to prod the nation to address the human resource development needs of its diverse labor force. Under both the economic pressures exerted by the achievement of full employment, and the external political and military threats to the nation's actual survival, unprecedented public and private policies were initiated. Not only were significant steps taken to develop the employment potential of the nation's labor force in general but major policy initiatives were also undertaken to open job opportunities for minorities, women, youth, the disabled, and older workers in occupations and industries that, hitherto, had been closed to them. Without access to a supply of immigrants, many employers had no choice but to recognize that equal employment opportunity was not only consistent with the nation's ideals but was also a condition for its immediate survival. The first significant steps in this direction were taken in this era and, as subsequent events would reveal, there could be no turning back.

But the move to end mass immigration in the 1920s sought to do more than simply reduce the supply of immigrants. It also embodied specific social objectives. It sought to affect future racial and ethnic composition of the small flow of immigrants who were permitted to enter by specifying who still could be admitted and who could not. Indeed, the popular name for the Immigration Act of 1924 was the "National Origins Act." Thus, the legitimate concerns of a sovereign nation to exercise some control over the number of foreign-born persons it admits for citizenship purposes, as well as the reasonable concern that any government must exercise to protect the economic welfare of its domestic labor force from the adverse effects of unlimited competition, became entangled with racist attitudes and discriminatory actions.

Ironically, the Immigration Act of 1924 had the effect of setting in motion forces that would ultimately contribute to the significant reduction of past patterns of discrimination within the country while simultaneously erecting new discriminatory barriers with respect to the nation's external relations with the rest of the world. Such a paradoxical posture could not prevail for long.

It took the organized civil rights movement of the 1950s and early 1960s to complete the assault on all aspects of discrimination within U.S. society. This movement culminated its activities with the passage of historic legislation in 1964 (regarding public accommodations and employment), in 1965 (regarding voting rights), and in 1968 (regarding fair housing). Although the impetus for these new laws was primarily directed toward redressing the discriminatory legacy borne by black Americans, the legislation broadened rights protection beyond race to include national origin, gender, religious belief, and color. In subsequent years, federal protections have been extended to include coverage on the basis of age, disability, and alienage. But what is often overlooked in reviewing the evolution of civil rights legislation is that the pathbreaking laws of the 1960s were enacted at a time when immigration levels were sharply restricted. With regard to the employment implications of these laws, the assumption was that they would not only terminate future discriminatory practices but that they would also be accompanied by other human resource development policies designed to redress the past denial of opportunities for victim groups by preparing them for jobs. In the short run, this is, in fact, what did occur. Unprecedented federal legislation was adopted in the mid-1960s pertaining to education, training, health, housing, community development, and poverty prevention. With unemployment declining in the mid-1960s, it was assumed that the newly protected groups—blacks in particular—would soon become qualified to fill the available jobs that a tightening labor market was providing.

As for the external manifestation of discrimination that was embodied in the nation's existing immigration law, it was only natural that it too—in this period of heightened domestic concern over civil rights—would be a target for reform. And it was. But the immigration reform movement at the time did not include any plans for significantly raising the overall level of immigration. It was focused entirely on purging the immigration statutes of the explicit racism inherent in the national origin admission system. Every presidential administration since that of Harry Truman in the late 1940s through to that of John Kennedy in the early 1960s had sought to accomplish that feat. It was President Lyndon Johnson who did it. He successfully pressed for passage of the immigration reform package that had been drafted by President Kennedy and his advisors only months before his assassination.[7] What happened afterwards, with respect to immigration, was entirely unanticipated. The enactment of the Immigration Act of 1965 set in motion forces that, over the years that followed, accidentally triggered the renewal of the mass immigration experience.

There was no general shortage of would-be workers in the United States in the 1960s when the immigration legislation was drafted, debated, and passed. The nation was at war in Vietnam—a condition that had temporarily contributed to a declining unemployment rate—but it was not expected that the war would be long or that low unemployment would prevail once the increased military expenditures associated with the military buildup had passed.[8] Moreover, the postwar "baby-boom" had just reached the stage in 1965 when it was pouring an unprecedented number of new job seekers into the labor market—a process that would continue unabated for the next fifteen years before gradually tapering off in the 1980s.

How is it, then, that mass immigration could have been inadvertently renewed by a reform movement that did not seek such an objective? The explanation rests with what David North and Marion Houstoun have aptly described as "negative intent."[9] That is to say, "those interested in reforming the immigration law were so incensed with the ethnocentrism of the laws of the past that they spent virtually all of their energies seeking to eliminate the country-of-origin provisions, and gave very little attention to the substance or long-range implications of the policy that would replace them."[10] As a consequence, the Immigration Act of 1965 abolished the national origins system and replaced it with an admission system primarily designed to reunify adult family members with adult relatives who already lived in the United States. This admission system had strong political support in Congress because it satisfied the private and personal interests of those citizens who themselves had been recent immigrants. For under the national origin system, it was this constituency who were likely to have close relatives who were still citizens of other nations. It was also viewed by other special interest groups as a way to perpetuate the old national origins systems but under a guise more politically acceptable. Thus, the satisfaction of political concerns replaced the pursuit of social ends as the key element of the nation's immigration admission system.

The Immigration Act of 1965 did contain some provisions for using immigration policy as a means of meeting the economic needs of the nation that had been introduced in 1952 by the Immigration and Nationality Act. Namely, there were opportunities to admit some immigrants who already possessed skills and who had work experiences that were in short supply in the nation's labor market. But these provisions of the Immigration Act of 1965 were clearly secondary; a far smaller number of people could be admitted on such a basis. Also, the Immigration Act of 1965 provided for the first time since immigration had become a subject of regulation, a formal route for certain refugees to be admitted on the basis of humanitarian concerns.

Unfortunately, the qualifications for being a refugee were restricted to only those persons faced with persecution from nations to which U.S. foreign policy was opposed (that is, those in Communist-dominated nations) rather than those confronted with persecution *per se*. Hence, even this aspect of the law was designed primarily to serve political priorities.

This legislation was also important for what it did not do. Specifically, it failed to specify any effective measures to enhance the enforcement of its new provisions. Its supporters did not foresee the imminent explosion of illegal immigration that quickly ensued in the years after its passage.

Although the Immigration Act of 1965 did provide for a modest increase in legal immigration, its enactment marked the beginning of the "fourth wave" of mass immigration. The increase in the level of immigration occurred, in part, because the Act's provisions provided for such an outcome but mostly because the statute set in motion processes that its provisions proved unable to control. Also, the lack of effective deterrence in the Act invited mass abuse—an outcome that policymakers for many years chose to ignore.

Immigration Policy Gone Awry

Within a decade of the passage of the Immigration Act of 1965, it was clear that immigration policy had gone awry. Immigration reform was again placed on the national agenda. In 1978, Congress established the Select Commission on Immigration and Refugee Policy (SCIRP). It was created to study the effects of what had transpired over the preceding thirteen years and to make recommendations for changes. Appointed by President Jimmy Carter, this sixteen-member commission, chaired by the Rev. Theodore Hesburgh (who was President of Notre Dame University at the time and who had formerly been Chairman of the U.S. Civil Rights Commission) issued its comprehensive report in 1981.[11] It stated that immigration was "out of control"; that the nation must accept "the reality of limitations"; and that "a cautious approach" should be taken in the design of any reform measures.

In the wake of the SCIRP report, Congress enacted three major immigration statutes. They were the Refugee Act of 1980, the Immigration Reform and Control Act of 1986, and the capstone of the statutes, the Immigration Act of 1990. In part, each of these laws embraces some of the specific recommendations put forth by SCIRP. But each statute has also gone well beyond SCIRP's recommendations. As a consequence, the overall effect of these laws has been to ignore the "cautious approach" and the modest proposals suggested by the Select Commission. The result has been to dramatically raise the already high levels of immigration to even higher plateaus. Indeed, a 1991 study by the Urban Institute concluded that these statutory changes "have reaffirmed the United States' role as the principal immigrant-receiving nation in the world."[12] The same report found it "remarkable" that policymakers enacted the Immigration Act of 1990 "with the nation poised on the brink of a recession and a war in the Persian Gulf" and at a time "when other industrialized countries are making theirs [i.e., their immigration policies] more restrictive."[13]

The reason that Congress could take such "remarkable" expansionary actions—others would say they are a "retreat from reality"—is that immigration policy has been allowed to develop without any regard as to its economic consequences.[14] It is an area of public policymaking that has been captured by special interest groups with private agendas that simply ignore any concern for the national interest. The Select Commission specifically warned of their growing influence and it rejected their myopic appeals. As its report unequivocally stated, "the Commission has rejected the arguments of many economists, ethnic groups, and religious leaders for a great expansion in the number of immigrants and refugees."[15] It went on to say that "this is not the time for a large-scale expansion in legal immigration—for resident aliens or temporary workers."[16] But the warnings of the Select Commission proved to be of no avail as Congress, in the 1980s, elected to appease these and other political interest groups. The consequence is that immigration policy remains essentially a political instrument largely untouched by the economic environment in which it is applied.

In the meantime, new issues have arisen that are especially vulnerable to political manipulation and which neither the Select Commission nor Congress envisioned. In particular, the issue of mass asylum requests has proven to be especially susceptible to political manipulation. At times, it has been the Executive branch of government that has twisted asylum policy to benefit one group over another. At other times, it has been Congress that has exhibited partiality in its actions. But always there are special interest groups who have learned to join forces to lobby for each other's goals, usually with utter disregard for the national interest as to the outcome.

If immigration were insignificant in its size and if the human capital characteristics of those entering were consistent with contemporary labor market needs, there would be little reason to worry about the consequences of such a politically-driven policy. But neither condition is present. The scale of immigration, in all of its diverse forms, is without precedent and mass immigration reemerged just as the nation's labor market entered a period of radical transformation.

The Issue of Labor Market Transformation

On the labor demand side of the U.S. labor market, there are new forces at work associated with the nature and pace of technological change; the expansion of international competition; shifts in consumer spending preferences; and the prospective effects of substantial reductions in national defense expenditures. Collectively, these forces are reshaping the nation's occupational, industrial, and geographic employment patterns. Employment in most goods-producing industries and in many blue-collar occupations is declining, while it is increasing in most service industries and many white-collar occupations. Regional employment trends are extremely unbalanced, with growth generally more pronounced in urban (but not in central cities) than in rural areas and particularly strong in the Southeast and Southwest and weak in the Midwest and Prairie regions.

On the labor supply side of the labor market, the nation's labor force has been growing in size at a pace far faster than all of its major industrial competitors combined and without precedent in its own history. Of even greater significance has been the rapid changes in its composition.   The fastest growing segments of the labor force are women, minorities, and immigrants.   Women in general and minorities in particular (with the possible exception of Asian Americans) have had fewer opportunities to be trained, educated, or prepared for the occupations that are predicted to increase most in the coming decade. They are disproportionately concentrated in occupations and industries already in decline or most vulnerable to decline in the near future. As for immigrants, with human capital attributes playing such a minor role in the determination of eligibility to enter, it is not surprising that George Borjas, in his 1990 assessment of the economic impact of immigration, found that "the more recent immigrant waves have less schooling, lower earnings, lower labor force participation and higher poverty rates than earlier waves had at similar stages of their assimilation into the country."[17]   Nor should it be surprising to learn that the use of welfare assistance by immigrants has also been found to be higher than that of earlier waves of immigrants.[18]

When Congress, in the 1960s, embarked on the course of adopting a politically driven immigration policy that essentially neglects economic considerations, few people recognized that the country was entering a phase of fundamental economic change. Even after the new employment trends became evident in the 1980s, the congressional committees responsible for designing immigration policy essentially ignored them.

By definition, immigration policy can influence the quantitative size of the labor force as well as the qualitative characteristics of those it admits. Currently, there is little synchronization of immigrant flows with demonstrated needs of the labor market. With widespread uncertainty as to the number of immigrant workers who will enter in any given year, it is impossible to know in advance of their actual entry how many foreign-born people will annually join the U.S. labor force. Moreover, whatever skills, education, linguistic abilities, talents, or locational settlement preferences most immigrants and refugees possess are largely incidental to the reason they are legally admitted or illegally enter.

The labor market effects of the politically driven immigration system are twofold. Some immigrant and nonimmigrant workers have human resources endowments that are quite congruent with labor market needs, and some are desperately needed because of the appalling lack of attention paid by policymakers to the adequate preparation of citizens for the emerging job requirements of the labor market. But most do not have needed skills. The majority must seek employment in declining sectors of goods-producing industries or low-wage sectors of the expanding service sector. Such immigrants—especially those who have entered illegally—are a major reason for the revival of "sweat shop" enterprises and the upsurge in the child labor violations reported in the nation's urban centers. The existence of such Third World working conditions in many cities is nothing for the nation to be proud of, regardless of whether these immigrants actually displace citizen workers in exploitive work situations.

Unfortunately, many citizen workers who are among the urban working poor or the urban underclass are also to be found in many of the same declining occupations and industries. A disproportionately high number of these citizens are minorities—especially the young people and women. The last thing these citizen groups need is more competition from immigrants for the declining number of low-skill jobs that provide a livable income or for the limited opportunities for training and education that are available to low-income workers. Moreover, the flooding of low-wage labor markets with unskilled immigrant workers renders hollow the political rhetoric at the national level that there is any serious public concern for their well-being.

As matters now stand, the U.S. economy does not face any prospect of a labor shortage *per se*. What it does confront is a shortage of *qualified* labor. In this case, the appropriate remedy is to address the evolving problems of a mismatch between the skills of the citizen workforce and the emerging skill and education requirements of the workplace. The real need is for an expanded national human resource development policy for citizen workers, not for a continuing increase in immigrants who are admitted mainly without regard to their human capital attributes. Indeed, even in those cases where legitimate labor shortages exist, immigration should never be relied upon to completely fill such voids. First recourse should be to retrain and reeducate unqualified workers and to relocate unemployed and underemployed qualified workers. As the Commission on Workforce Quality and Labor Market Efficiency warned in its 1989 report to the U.S. Secretary of Labor, "by using immigration to relieve shortages, we may miss the opportunity to draw additional U.S. workers into the economic mainstream."[19] It went on to state that public policy should "always try to train citizens to fill labor shortages," although it acknowledged that, in some circumstances, "it may be necessary to draw on foreign workers more heavily than we do today."[20] What is needed is a more selective and flexible immigration policy than currently exists.

Thus, for the first time in this country's history, its extant immigration policy is inconsistent with the national interest. How this quandary developed and what alternatives there are for changes are the substance of what follows.

Notes

1. Oxford Analytica, *America in Perspective* (Boston: Houghton-Mifflin, 1986), p. 20.

2. Ibid.

3. Judith Miller, "Strangers at the Gate: Europe's Immigration Crisis", *The New York Times Magazine* (September 15, 1991), pp. 32-37; 49; 80-81; and 86.

4. E.g., see John Tagliabue, "Germany Wins Europe's Backing for Tougher Controls on Migrants", *New York Times* (November 1, 1991), p. A-6; William Schmidt, "Britain Proposes Curbs on Refugee Flows", *New York Times* (November 2, 1991), p. A-3; Stephan Kinzer, "Swiss Voting Results Reflect Anti-Immigrant Mood", *New York Times* (October 27, 1991), p. A-11; Alan Riding, "France Imposes a Tighter Political Refugee Policy", *New York Times* (February 14, 1991), p. A-11; and Craig R. Whitney, "Europeans Look for Ways to Bar Door to Immigrants" (December 29, 1991), p. A-1 and A-8.

5. E.g., see James M. Markham, "Minorities in Western Europe: Hearing 'Not Welcome' in Several Languages," *New York Times* (August 6, 1986), p. A-6; see also, Miller, op. cit. and Whitney, op. cit.

6. E.g., see James Sterngold, "301 Chinese Expelled by Japan", *New York Times* (December 20, 1989), p. A-12 and Steven Weisman, "New Indignities for Refugees in Japan," *New York Times* (October 24, 1989), p. A-3; and James Sterngold, "Japan Curbing Foreign Workers," *New York Times* (December 12, 1989), p. A-6.

7. Ira Mehlman, "John F. Kennedy and Immigration Reform," *The Social Contract* (Summer, 1991), pp. 201-206.

8. For a review of labor force issues in the 1960s, see Charles C. Killingsworth, "The Fall and Rise of the Idea of Structural Unemployment," proceedings of the 31st meeting of the Industrial Relations Research Association, presidential address (Madison, WI: Industrial Relations Research Association, 1978), pp. 1-13.

9. David S. North and Marion F. Houstoun, *The Characteristics and Role of Illegal Aliens in the U.S. Labor Market: An Exploratory Study* (Washington, D.C.: Linton & Company, Inc., 1976), p. 5.

10. Ibid.

11. Select Commission on Immigration and Refugee Policy, *U.S. Immigration Policy and the National Interest* (Washington, D.C.: U.S. Government Printing Office, 1981).

12. Michael Fix and Jeffrey S. Passel, *The Door Remains Open: Recent Immigration to the United States and a Preliminary Analysis of the Immigration Act of 1990* (Washington, D.C.: The Urban Institute, 1991), p. 1.

13. Ibid., p. 9.

14. Vernon M. Briggs, Jr., "Immigration Policy: Political or Economic?" *Challenge: The Magazine of Economic Affairs* (September-October, 1991), pp. 12-19.

15. Select Commission ..., op. cit., p. 7.

16. Ibid., p. 8.

17. George Borjas, *Friends or Strangers: The Impact of Immigration on the U.S. Economy* (New York: Basic Books, Inc., 1990), p. 20. See also the similar findings in Barry Chiswick, "Is the New Immigration Less Skilled Than the Old?" *Journal of Labor Economics* (April 1986), pp. 192-196.

18. Borjas, op. cit., Chapter 9. See also George Borjas and Stephen J. Trejo, "Immigrant Participation in the Welfare System," *Industrial and Labor Relations Review* (January, 1991), pp. 195-211.

19. Commission on Workforce Quality and Labor Market Efficiency, *Investing in People: A Strategy to Address America's Workforce Crisis* (Washington, D.C.: U.S. Department of Labor, 1989), p. 32.

20. Ibid.

TWO

Immigration Policy:
A Determinant of Economic Phenomena

There are two ways to study the economic effects of immigration on the population and labor force of the United States. One approach is to study the determinant of the immigration phenomenon itself and the other is analyze the consequences of immigration. In principle, the two approaches should come to the same conclusions. But in a social science such as economics, it is not possible to do the clinical research in a controlled laboratory environment as is typical in the physical and natural sciences. Thus, when studying an important economic issue, it is often impossible to identify and to isolate all of the key variables that influence its actual effects. Even when important variables are specified, there are often gross deficiencies in the quality of the data available for analytical purposes. This precludes adequate measurement from taking place. Hence, there is no certainty that the different approaches to the study of a complex subject like immigration will produce complementary conclusions. On those occasions when they do, the confluence adds strength to the findings of both approaches.

Measuring Consequences: The Standard Approach

As with most economic issues, the more popular methodological approach is to the study the consequences of a particular economic phenomenon. This methodology ignores the search for explanation amidst the complex forces of historical circumstances over time and of institutional practices

15

at any given time, all of which influence what takes place at a particular moment of investigation. It is an *ex post* approach that only becomes feasible *after* the particular events have occurred. By examining only consequences, the causes are ignored in favor of a focus on what the empirical data reflect about what seems to have happened. Impact is what matters. Within that approach, research would typically focus on such issues as the effect of immigrants on wages, employment, unemployment, labor force participation, and the use of social services. The impact approach seeks only to measure quantitatively what it can while carefully avoiding any comment about how to interpret the causitive factors.[1] This does not mean, of course, that impact research does not find its way into policy debates. It does. The research is picked up by special interests groups, if it is consistent with their predilections, and used to support their advocacy position. If the findings are contrary to their goals, the studies are simply ignored by proponents while being cited by opponents.

The strength of the study of consequences depends primarily on the quality and the availability of the relevant data. When it comes to the study of immigration, the gross inadequances of the existing data virtually always render this methodology vulnerable to skepticism about the strength of its findings. For no matter how elaborate the design of the econometric model, or how sophisticated the statistical techniques used to extract meaning, the data cannot be tortured to confess to information that is not there. This does not mean that some researchers will not try. But to most scholars who work in the immigration field, attempts to draw conclusive findings from the use of available statistical sources can breed only a sense of humility, not confidence, about what insights can be safely drawn.

Data Limitations: A Brief Comment

Without diverting to a lengthy discussion about the severe limitations plaguing the extant data for the study of immigration, a few brief cautions are necessary.[2] The bulk of the available data on immigrants is collected for administrative purposes. It flows from the administration of the immigration statutes by the Immigration and Naturalization Service (INS) of the U.S. Department of Justice. When a congressional committee sought in 1978 to study the mounting effects of immigration on the U.S.

population, it initially sought to tap this data. To its chagrin, it soon concluded that "despite these long established data collection programs, immigration-related data are still deficient in scope, quality, and availability" and it concluded that "immigration statistics are particularly inadequate as tools for policy analysis."[3] In this same vein, the Panel on Immigration Statistics of the National Research Council, after conducting an exhaustive study of immigration statistics in 1985 (subtitled *A Story of Neglect*), found that:

> Immigration for some reason is the Cinderella of the federal statistical system. In essence, a history of neglect has afflicted the record keeping concerning one of the most fundamental process underlying the development of American society.[4]

The alternative to administrative data are data on the foreign-born population that are drawn from the decennial Census. In conducting its ten-year headcount of the population, the Census counts not only citizens but also permanent resident aliens and all citizens of any foreign country, regardless of their immigration status, who live in the United States at the time.[5] The counting of the foreign-born in the Census, however, is restricted only to those persons who are asked to complete the long form of the Census. The long form was given to about 17 percent of the nation's housing units in 1990, and was distributed on the basis of a variable-rate sample. This means that a larger proportion of the households living in small governmental units received the long form to complete than did households living in large governmental units. The goal of this sampling procedure is to increase the reliability of data in small population areas while, admittedly, reducing somewhat the quality of data collected in large population units. As will be indicated later, the foreign-born population is not randomly distributed across the nation but, rather, is highly concentrated in a few large governmental units (i.e., in the central cities of metropolitan areas). This means that the methodology used by the U.S. Census Bureau virtually guarantees that the official measures of the foreign-born population are underreported. Furthermore, the actual published data on the foreign-born is based on a 5 percent sample of the data that is collected from tabulating the long forms. It is this sample information that comprises the public use data file that is used by scholars who study the impact of immigration on U.S. society.

Between the decennial Census counts, there are no regular interim measures of the monthly or yearly experiences of the foreign-born as there are for other personal characteristics of subgroups (e.g., age, gender, or race) of the population and labor force. There have been some periodic supplemental sample studies conducted by the Census Bureau of the aggregate foreign-born population as part of the regular *Current Population Survey* (CPS). Referred to as a postcensual estimate, these special "add-on" questions to the CPS are done on an irregular basis (it was done about once every two years in the 1980s) depending on the availability of funds by either INS or the Census Bureau. The CPS monthly sample is the best methodology yet devised for keeping abreast of changing population and labor force trends between Census counts but it too is ill-suited for collecting data on the foreign-born. The monthly CPS samples about 56,000 households in the entire nation that are selected from designated enumeration areas designed to reflect certain features of the nation's population distribution (e.g., the rural to urban population).   The foreign-born is not one of the criteria used to establish these areas. Once the areas are defined (they do not cover the entire United States), a random sample is drawn. But, as previously indicated, the foreign-born population is definitely not randomly distributed. Hence, the CPS is not an ideal source of information for the foreign-born yet it is all that is available between Census counts.

In addition to the inadequacy of data collection methods used to measure the foreign-born population, it is also likely that there is a significant statistical undercount of the foreign-born population due to the existence of a sizable illegal immigrant population. These persons seek to avoid any contact with governmental officials. The Bureau of the Census acknowledges the general undercount problem with its decennial data—not only of illegal immigrants but especially of certain other subgroups of the population.[6]

Those most likely to be missed are low-income working aged males from minority groups. As a consequence, the Census Bureau has developed a procedure designed to estimate how many people in certain groups or in certain communities have been missed. This feat is accomplished through the use of the Post-Enumeration Survey which consists of a detailed recounting of 5,000 randomly selected census blocks across the nation. For the 1990 Census, the undercount produced by the survey was estimated to be about 2.1 percent (or about 5.3 million people).[7] The 1990 Census missed a greater percentage of the U.S. population than did the 1980 Census and for "the first time in modern census history, the coverage rate did not improve over the previous Census."[8] There is no way to know if the mounting illegal immigration population contributed to the data backslide. For unlike other data groupings that flow from the Census, there is no identifying question concerning the respondent's legal status, thus no discrete population figure exists. Hence, there is no accurate way to determine an estimate of the undercount of illegal immigrants.

The Bureau of the Census has made a crude estimate of the number of illegal immigrants it believes were counted in the 1980 Census.[9] It placed the number at 2,057,000 persons. Unfortunately, due to budget cuts during the Reagan Administration, the INS data on registered permanent resident aliens used to make this comparison with the 1980 Census count are no longer available. Consequently, comparable estimates for the years since 1980 will no longer be possible. Other approaches, however, are being attempted.[10] But the critical concern for present purposes is not with those illegal aliens who have been counted but, rather, with the many others who were not. While no one knows what that figure is, it is believed by most observers to be substantial.[11]   The acknowledged presence of this shadow population and shadow labor force renders all published data on the foreign-born automatically suspect. For as David North and Marion Houstoun have noted about the size of the illegal immigrant population, there is a "discrepancy between the *de jure* and the *de facto* immigration policy" of the United States and "this gap is widening."[12]

In short, whenever conclusions are reached that are based on the use of Census data, they must always be understood to be substantial underestimates of the "real" dimensions of the foreign-born population. Furthermore, there is no way for the statistical analysis used in econometric impact studies that purport to assess the immigrant experience to be precise under these circumstances.

The Issue of Emigration

Another quandary that confounds efforts to assess adequately the impact of immigration is the issue of emigration. There has been no official data on emigration published by the INS since 1957. The reason that the data collection was terminated was that the data's reliability had been seriously questioned. Unlike most nations, the United States does not exercise any departure controls over people who wish to leave the country. Such data had to be estimated. The estimates were criticized because, when citizens and permanent resident aliens do leave, they seldom give up their citizenship or residency rights. Some of those who leave for extended periods of time later decide to return. In other cases, people emigrate after they have finished their working years. These emigrating retirees would affect the *population* statistics of the United States but they would not affect the *labor force* statistics since they have already quit working; under those circumstances, it makes no difference whether they reside within or outside the United States. Consequently, there is no way to know how to measure emigration or to interpret its labor market consequences.

As will be discussed in Chapter 3, emigration was believed to be relatively high during the periods of mass immigration in the nineteenth and early twentieth centuries. The widespread assumption accounting for this is that, since the number of immigrant men (especially single men) greatly exceeded the number of immigrant women, these same men often emigrated back to their families after achieving a certain amount of money or capital in the United States. But there is reason to believe that the mass immigration that began in the mid-1960s and continues to the present time has evidenced considerably less emigration because the number of women, children, and adult parents entering the United States together with adult male immigrants greatly exceeds that of earlier periods. As will be indicated in Chapter 6, this pattern suggests that, since 1980, more family immigrants are coming to the United States for permanent settlement than ever before. Hence, their subsequent emigration is less likely.

One long-term study of emigration that covered the years from 1900 to 1980 revealed that about one-third of all immigrants who entered the United States over this period subsequently left.[13] But an INS estimate made in 1990 of the emigration rate for immigrants admitted during the period 1975 to 1979 showed it to be 11.4 percent.[14] This lower rate may confirm that emigration rates are declining or it may mean that it is simply too early to determine the actual emigration rate for such a recent cohort of immigrants. Unfortunately, the data needed to continue these critical data estimates beyond 1980 are no longer collected. They were the victims of 1981 budget cuts. While there is good reason (indicated above) to believe that the emigration rate since 1980 is lower than that of the pre-1980 era, there is absolutely no way to know for certain. All that can be said is that there is some degree of annual emigration of both foreign-born persons and native-born persons which is not taken into account in any of the published immigration-related data series. The lack of emigration data is but another example of the huge data gap that plagues attempts to adequately assess the impact of immigration.

An Alternative Approach: Studying the Determinants of Economic Phenomena

William Baumol, who is a former President of the American Economic Association, has decried the chronic imbalance in economic research on critical issues that relies only on *ex post* data manipulation but which largely ignores the effort to "to derive understanding from the explicit study of institutions and history."[15] There is an alternative approach to focusing only on measuring the consequences of particular economic actions. It is to examine what Baumol has called "the substance of economic phenomena."[16] This approach does not deny the merits of quantifying consequences but it forces attention upon understanding what it is that actually causes a particular economic occurrence. In certain circumstances—the study of immigration being one—explaining the determinants may be more useful than merely measuring consequences. By focusing on understanding the causes of this economic phenomena, it is possible to anticipate how events affect subsequent consequences. If the focus is only on measuring consequences, one obtains findings without substantive indications of what led to those outcomes or what changes might produce alternative results. The limitations of such analyses are succinctly conveyed in the candid comments by George Borjas after he completed his comprehensive examination in 1990 of the aggregate effects of recent immigrants on the U.S. economy. He concluded his study by stating that "I do not know what our immigration policy should be."[17] There are few other areas of contemporary concern where historical influences and institutional practices have jointly played a more determining role in shaping economic consequences than in the area of immigration. Understanding how the "fourth wave" of mass immigration came into being and what maintains its momentum is crucial to any attempt to assess its compatibility with the emerging national interest. This study will pursue this less traveled road.

The Paramount Role of Public Policy

With regard to immigration, the phenomenon that has spawned and perpetuated the "fourth wave" of immigration is easy to identify. It is the relevant public policy exercised by the federal government. In the modern era of sovereign nation states, each with their established geographical borders, immigration has become a discretionary act of national governments. Foreign-born persons can legally enter the territory of another nation for the purpose of permanent settlement or to work only if they are specifically admitted. Otherwise, their entry is illegal and can only occur if there is governmental indifference to those who enter surreptitiously or who violate the terms of properly issued visas by not leaving when their visas expire. Public policy determines how many foreign-born persons are admitted and under what circumstances. In this instance, therefore, the relevant economic phenomena to study are the component parts of the nation's overall immigration policy. This is not to say that all forms of public policy represent economic phenomena. Rather, it is to argue that immigration is a special case whereby public policy itself is the catalyst for determining what actually transpires. Immigration policy does not reflect what is happening. It is the institutional arrangement that actually sets the level and shapes the character of subsequent market consequences. By the same token, the immigration policy that exists at any given time is significantly influenced by the historical context out of which it has evolved.

Although many types of public policy are complex, few are as difficult to comprehend as immigration policy. Indeed, immigration policy is often compared only to the internal revenue codes in terms of the intricacies of its multiple provisions. At its core, of course, are the statutory provisions set forth by Congress. These legislative enactments often are intended to serve multiple purposes. The product is influenced by both the historical circumstances that generate the need to enact the legislation and by the consensus-building processes imposed by a political forum functioning in a free society. Once passed, the actual implementation of these statutes is affected by the institutional capacities and practices of the federal agency in the executive branch of government that is charged exclusively with its administration. In this instance, it is the Immigration and Naturalization Service (INS) of the U.S. Department of Justice. Lastly, of course, there is the role of judiciary whose rulings are generally intended to resolve disputes over legal meanings and procedural applications. But, as will be seen, it too can sometimes create new policies.

Just as public policy brought a cessation to mass immigration in the 1920s, it was public policy that revived mass immigration in the 1960s, and it is public policy that continues to drive the phenomenon in the 1990s. It will also be public policy that will determine how long the "fourth wave" continues and what effects it exerts on the nation's economy, population, and labor force. As Napoleon once said, "policy is destiny."

Unlike the other major influences that are impinging on the size and composition of the contemporary U.S. labor force—such as the growing labor force participation of women (especially mothers with children); or the declining labor force participation rates for men over the age of forty-five; or the demographic effects associated with the progressive move-ment of the "baby boom" generation within the nation's population distribution; or the labor force implications of the differences in fertility rates between racial and ethnic groups—immigration is a policy-driven activity. It is no accident that the United States has stood alone for two decades among other advanced industrial nations in its annual admission of mass numbers of immigrants for permanent settlement. Immigration is the one element of a nation's labor supply that is a direct consequence of governmental choice—not a necessary or inevitable state of affairs. Indeed, all other major industrialized nations have conscientiously chosen not to follow this path at this stage of their economic development.

The Advantage of the Policy Approach

As will be revealed in the later chapters, there is an emerging general consensus between those who measure economic consequences and those who study immigration policy as a manifestation of economic phenomena as to what are the effects that "fourth wave" of immigration is having on the U.S. economy. The rough congruence is comforting because it lends some strength to the credibility of the research findings by both camps even though the methodological approaches are vastly different. It means that those who saw in advance where specific immigration policies were leading have found their views confirmed by those who waited to see what actually happened.

Nonetheless, the public policy approach has a fundamental advantage that the outcome approach does not. The way that immigration data are produced by the Bureau of the Census is in aggregate form. All persons who are foreign-born are lumped together. No distinction is made among the various entry possibilities: legal; illegal; refugee; asylee; nonimmigrant specifically permitted to work; nonimmigrant on visitor- or tourist-visa. With regard to the labor market, however, there are significant differences in the human capital characteristics between those who enter via each route. Accordingly, different local labor markets and different labor force segments of the native-born population may be affected in ways that are totally ignored by looking at only aggregate characteristics. In aggregate data, the positive benefits of certain policies can be canceled out by the negative effects of other policies. Under such circumstances, the aggregation of data on the foreign-born produces an average picture of a reality that does not actually exist. Accordingly, one could easily conclude that no policy changes are needed when, in fact, considerable gains could be achieved from expanding one policy component and contracting another. The public policy approach, therefore, has the clear advantage of being able to generate recommendations as to what immigration policy should be if it is, in fact, to serve the national interest under conditions of constant change. Given the economic environment of the 1990s, it is essential that all components of immigration policy be in step with the broader transformation processes that are restructuring the nation's labor market.

Studies that rely exclusively on the use of aggregate data cannot identify which elements of immigration policy should be expanded, contracted, abandoned, or left alone. By focusing on the role of public policy, on the other hand, the differential components individually become the object of attention. As conditions change it is possible to identify which policy elements should be altered in response to such dynamics.

In the process of examining how each of these components contribute to the overall immigration flow, policy-oriented research also produces data. It is, however, far less systematic. Such studies produce particularistic data about specific immigrants groupings—such as refugees, or illegal immigrants—or about effects of the presence of immigrants in certain industries, occupations, and geographic areas. Given the highly concentrated geographic nature of immigration, however, specific studies are much more likely to provide insight into the nature of the immigration phenomenon than are data collected and analyzed about the foreign-born as a whole.

The Perplexing Issue of Immigration Policy
and the Study of Economics

Of all the multiple issues that fall within the domain of the study of economics, none evinces less agreement among economists than does the issue of the role of immigration. As a consequence, most economists have purposely chosen to neglect the topic. Indeed, Henry Simons, a pioneer advocate at the University of Chicago of the benefits of free market economics, has frankly written that "as regards immigration policy, the less said the better."[18] He explained:

> Wholly free immigration, however, is neither attainable nor desirable. To insist that a free trade program is logically or practically incomplete without free migration is either disingenuous or stupid. Free trade may and should raise living standards everywhere .... Free immigration would level standards, perhaps without raising them anywhere.[19]

Milton Friedman, certainly the most well-known member of the "Chicago School" of economics, seems to have taken to heart Simons' advice to say as little as possible about immigration. Friedman is known to share Simon's identical views on the necessity of governments in free societies to have restrictive immigration policies.[20] But in his best known books, he either totally ignores the role of government to set immigration policy in free market economies, or he only briefly acknowledges the immigration experience of the United States with no mention of government's paramount role in this area. It is startling in *Capitalism and Freedom*, where Friedman specifically states what he sees to be the role of government in a free society, that there is absolutely no mention of immigration policy.[21] Likewise, in *Free to Choose*, references are made only to the positive adjustment experience of a few immigrants at the turn of the twentieth century.[22] Many of the benefits to U.S. workers in general, and black workers in particular, that Friedman attributes to capitalism in the time periods examined by these books only occurred because of the restrictive immigration policies that were in effect in the United States from the mid-1920s through the mid-1960s. But there is hardly a word concerning the entire subject of immigration in these heralded books on free market economics. Likewise, the praise in *Free to Choose* that is heaped upon Margaret Thatcher for the free market policies she championed as Prime Minister of Great Britain during the 1980s does not mention the highly restrictive immigration policy that she helped to put in place during her tenure and which still remains in effect. Britain, for instance, abandoned the principle of *jus soli* (i.e., "the right to soil") in 1983 which had been in place for seven hundred years and which is still in effect in the United States. No longer does British citizenship accrue merely from the fact that a person is born on British soil.

Another noted member of the economics faculty at the University of Chicago, Melvin Reder, has observed that "free immigration would cause rapid equalization of per capita income across countries accomplished mainly by leveling downward the income of the more affluent .... I resist this proposal."[23] Indeed, Reder, who is a specialist in labor economics, was the author of one of the most perceptive articles yet to be written on the topic of immigration policy and its labor market effects. Writing in 1963, just before the events that would trigger the beginning of the "fourth wave" of mass immigration commenced, Reder warned: "In short, a greater flow of immigration will injure labor market competitors with immigrants; these are, predominately, Negroes, Puerto Ricans, unskilled immigrants presently able to enter the country, and native rural-urban migrants (Negro and White)."[24] He also noted that employment and income opportunities of "secondary earners," such as "married women, youth, and aged persons" would be adversely affected by substantial increases in immigration.[25]

As a consequence, mass immigration "would slow the approach toward distributional equality within the United States."[26] He observed that substantial progress had been made toward improving the income position of the poor both in the U.S. and the other "Western democracies" as the result of the "deliberate state action" to restrict immigration "during the past twenty-five years to fifty years."[27] Reder further notes that these national benefits that occurred over the years when immigration was restricted probably contributed to international inequality in income distribution. Nevertheless, he concluded with the following powerful observation about U.S. immigration policy:

Consequently, our immigration policy inevitably reflects a kind of national selfishness of which the major beneficiaries are the least fortunate among us. We could not *completely* abandon this policy, even if we so desired.[28]

Other voices in economics have taken the polar opposite view. *The Wall Street Journal*, for instance has editorialized for the total elimination of border restrictions on those persons from other lands who wish to live and work in the United States: "If Washington still wants to do something about immigration, we propose a five word Constitutional Assessment: "There shall be open borders."[29]

In the same camp is Julian Simon (not to be confused with the aforementioned Henry Simons). While not calling for the entire abandonment of immigration restraints, he has called for "greatly increased immigration" above and beyond the already high levels legislatively in place for the 1990s.[30] Simon does not bother with any theoretical paradigms to rationalize his views. He does not seek to understand the historical development of immigration or to delve into any of the institutional intricacies that have resurrected mass immigration over the past two decades. He starts with his conclusion that, whatever the immigration level is at present, it is insufficient. The level should be significantly higher. He does not include refugees or asylees as immigrants in most of his statistical data and he totally ignores the labor market presence of nonimmigrant workers. Nor is there any recognition of the sizable undercount of illegal immigrants in the data he uses. For these reasons, all of his data greatly underestimate what is already happening. There is no concern in his work for any adjustment difficulties that citizen workers might be experiencing under present conditions, or any worry about what distributive effects would occur if he had his way and even higher levels of immigration occurred. As he said in 1991, "it is important to focus on the long-run situation rather than the little blips" that may occur in the short run.[31]

Virtually every economic benefit one can imagine is foreseen if only more immigrants are admitted. He claims that the rate of technological advance will be spurred; business will be able to hire more workers; retirees of the "baby boom era" will have more workers to support them; tax revenues will rise; the nation will be more competitive; the image of the United States will be enhanced; and more people will be able to enjoy the "blessings of life in the United States." In essence, mass immigration is described as having only benefits and, if he sees any costs, he does not indicate them.

There are also economists who argue for mass immigration in a more reasonable way. One is John Kenneth Galbraith, who envisions it as part of a broader strategy to reduce poverty in the world.[32] He does not contend that mass immigration is a panacea for solving the dilemma of the extensive variations on the standards of living that separate the advanced and the less economically developed nations of the world. But he does believe that immigration should be a vital factor in any global strategy to reduce income inequality in the world. Jagdish N. Bhagwati shares Galbraith's concern for the use of immigration policy for humanitarian concerns to help underdeveloped countries. But he also believes that the United States will confront a general shortage of labor in the early twenty-first century that large-scale immigration now could help to alleviate.[33] Bhagwati's proposals are not very specific and it is not clear how the entry of large numbers of unskilled workers from less developed nations would meet what appears to be an emerging shortage of highly trained workers coexisting with a growing surplus of poorly prepared citizen workers in the United States.

The aforementioned perspectives are not meant to be a definitive review of all of the views pertaining to the role of immigration in a free market economy. They are intended to be representative of the range of perspectives on this vital yet contentious policy issue. Hopefully, what follows will contribute to the ongoing discourse of this subject which too often has been secluded from careful scrutiny.

Notes

1. For another example of the use of this approach, see Robert LaLonde and Robert Topel, "Immigrants in the American Labor Market: Quality, Assimilation, and Distributional Effects," *American Economic Review* (May, 1991), pp. 297-302.

2. For a discussion of the data limitations, see Vernon M. Briggs, Jr., *Immigration Policy and the American Labor Force* (Baltimore: Johns Hopkins University Press, 1984), pp. 6-10 and 131-137.

3. U.S. Congress, House Select Committee on Population, *Legal and Illegal Immigration to the United States* (Washington, D.C.: U.S. Government Printing Office, 1978), p. 48.

4. National Research Council, Panel on Immigration Statistics, *Immigration Statistics: A Story of Neglect* (Washington, D.C.: U.S. Government Printing Office, 1985), p. 3.

5. John C. Keane, "Statement of the Director of the Bureau of the Census before the Subcommittee on Governmental Processes of the

Committee on Governmental Affairs of the U.S. House of Representatives" (September 18, 1985), p. 5 [xerox copy material].

6. Peter Passell, "Can't Count on Numbers," *New York Times* (August 6, 1991), p. A-1 and A-14.

7. "Statement" of L. Nye Stevens, Director of Government Business Operations Issues, U.S. Bureau of the Census, before the Subcommittee on Government Information and Regulation, Committee on Governmental Affairs, U.S. Senate (June 19, 1991), p.1 [Xerox copy material].

8. Ibid., 11.

9. Jeffrey S. Passel, "Estimating the Number of Undocumented Aliens," *Monthly Labor Review* (September 1986), p. 33.

10. See Karen A. Woodrow, "Undocumented Immigrants Living in the United States," *Proceedings*, American Statistical Association (August 1990), pp. (not yet available).

11. See, for example, the extensive discussion of the undercount issue in Elizabeth Bogen, *Immigration in New York* (New York: Praeger Publishers, 1987), Chapter 4.

12. David S. North and Marion Houstoun, *The Characteristics and Role of Illegal Aliens in the U.S. Labor Market* (Washington, D.C.: Litton & Company 1976), p. 30.

13. Robert Warren and Ellen Percy Kraly, *The Elusive Exodus: Emigration from the United States* (Washington D.C.: Population Reference Bureau, 1985).

14. U.S. Immigration and Naturalization Service, "Emigration from the United States," Statistics Division Bulletin #5 (April 1990), p. 2.

15. William J. Baumol, "Sir John Versus the Hicksians, or Theorist Malgre Lui," *Journal of Economic Literature* (December, 1990), p. 1715.

16. Baumol, op cit.

17. George J. Borjas, *Friends or Strangers: The Impact of Immigration on the U.S. Economy*, (New York: Basic Books, 1990), p.220.

18. Henry C. Simons, *Economic Policy for a Free Society* (Chicago: University of Chicago Press, 1948), p. 251.

19. Melvin W. Reder, "Chicago Economics: Permanence and Change," *Journal of Economic Literature* (March, 1982), p. 31.

20. Ibid.

21. Milton Friedman, *Capitalism & Freedom* (Chicago: University of Chicago Press, 1962), Chapter 2.

22. Milton Friedman and Rose Friedman, *Free to Choose* (San Diego: Harcourt Brace Janovich, Publishers, 1990), pp. 35-36.

23. Reder, op. cit, p. 31.

24. Melvin W. Reder, "The Economic Consequences of Increased Immigration," *The Review of Economics and Statistics* (August 1963), p. 227.

25. Ibid.

26. Ibid., p. 229.

27. Ibid., p. 230.

28. Ibid., [empuasis is in the original].

29. "The Re-Kindled Flame," *Wall Street Journal* (July 3, 1989), p. 6.

30. Julian L. Simon, "The Case for Greatly Increased Immigration," *The Public Interest* (Winter 1991), pp. 89-103. See also Julian Simon, *The Economic Consequences of Immigration* (London: Basil Blackwell, 1989).

31. Robert Reinhold, "In California, New Talk About a Taboo Subject," *New York Times* (December 3, 1991), p. A-20.

32. John Kenneth Galbraith, *The Nature of Mass Poverty* (Cambridge: Harvard University Press, 1979), pp. 136 ff.

33. Jagdish N. Bhagwati, "U.S. Immigration Policy: What Next?" in *Essays on Legal and Illegal Immigration*, edited by Susan Pozo (Kalamazoo: W.E. Upjohn Institute for Employment Research, 1986), p. 117; See also Jagdish Bhagwati "Behind the Green Card," *The New Republic* (May 14, 1990), pp. 31-39.

THREE

Creating a Nonagricultural Labor Force: The Original Role of Mass Immigration

Throughout its first 133 years as an independent nation (1788-1921), there were no limits on the number of immigrants who could enter the United States each year. It was the period when the combination of a political and military revolution (from Britain); land purchases (from France, Spain, Mexico, and Russia); boundary negotiations (with Britain); war (with Mexico and Spain); unilateral annexation (of the Hawaiian Islands); and land treaties accompanied by the physical relocation of the native "Indian" population established all of the land boundaries that presently constitute the United States. But setting the political jurisdiction was easier than enforcing the boundaries as barriers to entry. Throughout most of this critical period of nation-building, the vastness of the land area relative to the actual population of adult citizens meant that there was little that could be done to keep people out. For most of the period, there was little inclination on the part of public policymakers even to try. It was a time of industrial growth and development as well as geographical expansion that was characterized by frequent shortages of all categories of labor—skilled, semiskilled, and skilled; educated and illiterate; English speaking and non-English speaking.

The expanding amount of "free land" available for settlement throughout most of the nineteenth century also meant that it was difficult to keep significant portions of the native-born population from moving westward. Land in this era was often equated with opportunity. Therefore, when industrialization began—slowly before the Civil War but rapidly during the war and afterward—the growing need for a nonagricultural workforce created a demand for labor that the supply of immigrant workers was intended to fill. With some notable exceptions, it would take a generation or so for most of the immigrants to accumulate the funds and the knowledge to move inland for purposes only of settlement, even if they were inclined to do so. A disproportionate number of the immigrants of the nineteenth century were single men for whom family life only came much later, if at all. For most immigrants, the life as a settler on formerly public lands was not a viable option. Moreover, by 1890, the era of free land was essentially over as the frontier had virtually disappeared and with it went any rural settlement option that might have existed for subsequent immigrant streams.

The Exceptions to Voluntary Immigration

To be sure, not all of the people who populated the country during this critical period had voluntarily affiliated. Three groups in particular require special mention: the Indians; the Mexican heritage population; and the blacks.

The Indian Heritage Population

The most obvious of those who did not immigrate, of course, were the native people that Christopher Columbus had earlier misnamed as *los Indios*, or the Indians. The word was subsequently applied to all of the indigenous inhabitants of the Americas and has remained in use ever since. In the sixteenth century when the Europeans first arrived in the portion of the land mass of North America that would later become the United States, it is estimated that somewhat less than one million Indians inhabited the entire area. The North American Indians had not developed the structured and highly organized civilizations of some of the Indians of Central and South America. Some of the North American tribes were nomadic, but most were settled in particular regions where they lived communally off the land and wildlife. From the initial contact with Spanish explorers and missionaries in what would later become the Southwest to the extended subsequent encounters in later years with explorers, trappers, traders, and settlers from England, Spain, France, Holland, and Sweden in the remaining regions, the Indian population began to decline. The combination of the introduction of diseases for which the Indians had no immunities, of alcohol for which they had little tolerance, and of the consequences of numerous violent conflicts that quickly ensued from the clash of cultures between themselves and the settlers extracted an enormous human toll.

From the Indians, the colonists learned much. For example, they learned how to grow indigenous vegetables like corn and how to use plants with medicinal and narcotic properties like tobacco. Although there were numerous good faith efforts by early colonists to establish friendly relations and to convert some Indians to Christianity, "it proved impossible for the two races to live peacefully side-by-side."[1] There was no concept of private ownership of land in the Indian culture while the principle was fundamental to the culture of the English colonists. Consequently, as the white settlers cut down forests and expanded their land under cultivation, they reduced the area in which the Indians could hunt and fish. When Indian chieftains permitted settlers to use their hunting grounds, they soon found that the land was being cleared, fenced, and treated as their private property. Thus, where the settlers were interested only in hunting and trapping, good relations usually existed but "whenever the whites developed agriculture, conflicts developed quickly."[2] When fighting initially erupted, the tactics used by the Indians seemed to be incredibly cruel to the whites and they soon reciprocated in kind. Although colonial government officials often sought to protect the Indians from unfair treatment, the colonists typically feared the Indians and pressed for their removal.

Of those Indians who survived, most were relocated—sometimes voluntarily but often forcibly—away from the eastern lands. Initially, they moved to areas west of the Allegheny and Appalachian Mountains or north to Canada. Later, it was to areas west of the Mississippi River. The twin processes of population decline and physical displacement of the Indians began during the colonial era but they accelerated throughout most of the nineteenth century after the country became independent.

When the thirteen former colonies along the Atlantic seaboard ratified the Constitution to form the United States in 1788, it is estimated that there were only about 76,000 Indians living in the same geographical area east of the Appalachians.[3] Other Indian tribes, however, soon found themselves under the aegis of the United States after it became a nation and as it expanded and consolidated its political boundaries.

In the East, the United States purchased Florida from Spain under the terms of the Adams-Onis Treaty of 1819. Florida, while under Spanish rule, had been a haven for runaway slaves from southern plantations, and it had also been a base for hostile attacks by the Seminole Indians on southern plantations in Georgia. With the acquisition of this new land, of course, came the Seminoles. As white settlers flooded into Florida, a protracted war with the Seminoles broke out that lasted from 1835 to 1842. The upshot was that most of the surviving Seminoles were forcibly moved out of the area and resettled in the governmentally designated "Indian Territory" of the West (later to become Oklahoma). Those who escaped this fate fled into the vast swamp region of the Florida Everglades.

The treatment of the Seminoles was in concurrence with the federal government's general policy that was enunciated in the 1820s. Namely, the only solution to the Indian issue was to physically remove most of them to land west of the Mississippi and Missouri Rivers. The relocations were supposed to be voluntary with the federal government assuming the financial costs and giving the relocated Indians a year's supplies. In fact, force was used to accomplish this feat. The Indians in the Southeast (i.e., the Cherokees, Creeks, Chickasaws, Choctaws, and the Seminoles) resisted efforts to take their lands but, after President Andrew Jackson took office in 1829, they received no protection from the federal government as local authorities denied Indians legal rights and allowed their lands to be taken over by settlers and plantation owners. Thus, by 1840, almost all of the eastern tribes had been deprived of their lands and were confined to reservations or moved west. The treatment of the Indians remains a national blemish but it is not possible to blame particular individuals or groups for what transpired in this formative period of nation-building. As the historian Henry Bamford Parks has written, "it was the mass of the American people who insisted that the Indians had no right to keep their lands."[4]

The larger concentrations of Indians were west of the Mississippi River even before they were joined by the exiled Indians of the East. Those western Indians were involuntarily incorporated into the nation as the result of the series of land acquisitions that occurred during the first half of the nineteenth century: the Louisiana Purchase of 1803 from France; a negotiated border agreement in 1846 with Britain formally making the 49^0 parallel the northern boundary of the so-called "Oregon Territory" with Canada; and a war with Mexico from 1846 to 1848. Unfortunately for everyone involved, as the settlement process expanded into these regions, fighting with the Indians usually ensued. Treaties that supposedly had guaranteed certain western land areas to the Indians "for as long as they wished to occupy them" were often unilaterally abrogated.

By the 1880s, the Indian population of the entire United States had declined to about 200,000 persons. The vast majority were confined to desolate rural reservations—mostly in the West.[5] Thus, the surviving Indians were forcibly subsumed into the nation's population but largely left out of the development of its industrial labor force during these critical years of the nation's economic development. It was not until 1924 that Indians were finally granted citizenship rights.

The Mexican Heritage Population

Another group acquired under terms of duress was the portion of the Mexican population in 1848 who had lived in what is today the southwestern United States. This area, explored in the early sixteenth century had originally been claimed by Spain. But in 1821, Mexico revolted from almost three centuries of Spanish rule and became an independent nation. During the Spanish and Mexican eras of domination, efforts were made to subjugate the Indians and to establish missions and trading centers across the region.[6] The intention was to link these separate outposts over time. These plans, however, were frustrated by violent opposition from the two most intractable Indian tribes in all of the Americas, the Apaches and the Comanches. As the result of their unrelenting attacks, the remnants of the Spanish settlement efforts that were acquired by Mexico consisted mostly of isolated outposts. The largest of these surviving communities were located in what is today northeastern New Mexico (in the Taos–Santa Fe area). There were smaller settlements around where the cities of Los Angeles and San Francisco in California are presently situated and in scattered parts of what is now Texas.

Most of the Spanish-speaking people at that time is this region were *mestizos* (that is, they were descendants of a new race that was a mixture of the Indians of the region with the Caucasian Spanish explorers). Unlike the later colonists from England who mostly came to stay, most of the original Spanish *conquistadores* did not bring their families. They came for glory, to gain wealth, and to spread Christianity, after which time most returned to Spain. In the process, the *conquistadores* did transplant their language, religion, and many other institutional practices to the Americas—but they "did so largely through the instrumentality of other groups."[7] In the land area later to be taken over by the United States, the Spanish *conquistadores* mixed mostly with the women of the four branches of the sedentary Pueblo Indian tribe (i.e., the Pueblo, Zuni, Hopi, and Pima). It was their ancestors who primarily represented the portion of the Mexican population who were incorporated into the United States in 1848.

As a consequence of the war with Mexico (1846 to 1848) and the terms of the Treaty of Guadalupe Hidalgo signed in 1848, as well as the subsequent Gadsden Purchase in 1853, the United States acquired the vast land area that now constitutes its Southwest. The newly acquired territory represented a land mass about the size of present-day India. It extended from Texas west to California and set the southern border of the country. It also included area as far north as parts of Colorado and Wyoming. With the land came the Indians of the region and the remnants of the population of Mexican heritage who elected to remain in these territories. The war had been fought over land as a part of the "manifest destiny" philosophy of the Federal government of that time. It was not fought over people although they were included in the political settlement.[8] It is estimated that there were about 75,000 persons of Mexican or Spanish heritage in this entire region in 1848. About two-thirds of these people were concentrated in the Taos-Santa Fe area.[9] Those who chose to stay where they were (as opposed to moving to the area that remained Mexico) became U.S. citizens by the Treaty terms. As McWilliams has pointedly observed, "it should never be forgotten that, with the exception of the Indians, Mexicans are the only minority in the United States who were annexed by conquest; the only minority, Indians excepted, whose rights were specifically safeguarded by treaty provision."[10]

Due largely to the continuing resistance of the nomadic Indians of the region, there was relatively little new settlement or economic development of the region outside of California from 1848 to the mid-1880s.[11] In the late nineteenth century, economic activity commenced. Some people of Mexican ancestry became involved in railroad building and mining development in the Southwest. But for the most part, they continued to survive off the land as a small and geographically isolated segment of the U.S. labor market. It was not until the early twentieth century, when the region's economic development began in earnest, that immigration caused their numbers to become significant.[12] The vast preponderance of the nation's Mexican heritage population immigrated to the United States in the twentieth century.

The Blacks

The last group that represents an exception to the voluntary immigration phenomenon is, of course, the black slaves. Those who entered in bondage from Africa (as opposed to their descendants who were later born in the English colonies or in the United States) were involuntary immigrants. Blacks originally arrived in the Virginia colonies in 1619 aboard a Dutch slave ship. Because slavery did not exist at that time in the English colonies, they were initially treated the same as many white settlers. They became indentured servants who eventually earned their freedom. By the 1640s, for reasons that are still unknown, these practices ceased and the policy of treating blacks as permanent slaves began and continued for the next 225 years.

Slavery grew slowly in the South until the 1690s when the rise of the Southern plantation system caused the demand for slaves to increase sharply. In the early eighteenth century, the flow of slaves became enormous. By 1710, it had reduced the supply of white indentured servants in the South to negligible numbers.[13] The legacy of this regional labor supply policy was that the white indentured servants from Europe and their lineal successors—the European immigrants—became the backbone of the workforce of the North and the Midwest but not of the South.

It is ironic that the only provision in the U.S. Constitution that had anything to say at all about immigration pertained to the importation of slaves. It was the product of compromise language whose inclusion was essential to the effort to unify the former colonies into a single nation after the Revolutionary War. Both Georgia and South Carolina had threatened to withdraw from the union if the importation of slaves were banned. The compromise was that the Constitution would permit slaves to continue to be brought into the new nation for twenty years—or until 1808—after which time Congress would have to decide the issue. Subsequently, in 1807 legislation was adopted that prohibited the importation of slaves after January 1, 1808.

It should be noted, however, that this legislation did not actually end slave trading, nor did it have any immediate impact on the institution of slavery. In fact, the demand for slaves increased markedly in the years after 1808. During the 1820s, cotton became "king" and the modern cotton industry of the South began to develop.[14] The number of slaves in the labor force increased sharply during subsequent decades—growing from 893,602 slaves in 1800 to 3,953,760 slaves on the eve of Civil War in 1860. Much of the growth was the result of the natural biological increase of the slave population. Some of the growth—about 40,000 slaves—was the result of the slaves being included with the land in the Louisiana Purchase of 1803. Another 4,000 slaves were acquired by the annexation of Texas in 1845. But the continual import of slaves was also a factor in the continuing growth of the South's slave population. Obviously, no data exist on how many slaves were imported after the practice became illegal in 1808, but it is estimated that the number was about 279,000 slaves.

In short, slave trading flourished despite the ban on the practice. The agencies given responsibility for enforcing the importation ban (first the Department of the Treasury, then the U.S. Navy, and later the Department of the Interior) all had multiple duties to perform and the funds appropriated by Congress for patrol of the long sea border of the southeastern United States were grossly inadequate. Nationwide, there was general public apathy about the importance of addressing the slave trade issue since it was seen to be regional in nature.[15] As a consequence, slave trading did not end until slavery itself was abolished. This was finally accomplished by President Abraham Lincoln in 1862 when he issued the Proclamation of Emancipation, which freed all slaves as of January 1, 1863, and by the ratification in 1865 of the Thirteenth Amendment to the Constitution, which forbade the practice of slavery.

The immediate effect of slavery on the composition of the labor force was, of course, primarily felt in the South. In 1800, 28 percent of the nation's labor force was made up of slaves, but 96 percent of the slave population was in the South. By 1860, that slave population accounted for 21 percent of the nation's labor force with 97 percent of the slave population located in the South. Some of the slaves worked in towns and cities of the South, but most were tied to rural plantations. While these slaves worked in a variety of occupations (since most plantations sought to be self-sufficient) the slave population worked primarily in agriculture, which remained overwhelmingly the base of the entire Southern economy.[16]

As late as 1910, 90 percent of the black population still lived in the South. With the end of the Civil War, the resurgence of mass immigration from Europe and China to the North and West precluded any opportunity for the newly-freed black population of the South to leave the region even if they were inclined to do so.

It was not until mass immigration was reduced during—and restricted following—World War I that the black population was able to begin its exodus from the South in general and the rural South in particular. Thus, throughout the entire nineteenth century and the first decade or so of the twentieth century, the black population was essentially excluded from the rapid industrialization that was occurring in the North and West. This meant that American blacks were locked out of the new array of industrial occupations that were coming into existence. Throughout this critical era of the nation's economic development, the black population was bypassed. Blacks remained disproportionately concentrated in the poverty-stricken South and tied to its agriculturally dominated employment structure.

The Colonial Roots of Immigration

It was primarily a labor supply problem that launched the initial English settlements along the Atlantic Coast of what would later become the United States. Although there were other factors involved, it was the existence of a large surplus of labor and mounting fears of overpopulation in England in the sixteenth and early seventeenth centuries that sparked a political consensus favoring the creation of colonies in the New World.[17] It was with the full support of the English Crown and with the firm expectation that English society would financially benefit from the consequences that the settlement process commenced.   Grants of territories were given either to charter companies or to individual proprietors who agreed to find ways to defray the transportation and initial living costs of those individuals who came to settle.

As for the colonists themselves, they came to settle for myriad reasons. For some, it was the opportunity to escape religious persecution; others, especially in the Chesapeake colonies, came initially as servants to richer settler families; while still others came as free men who paid their own passage, enticed by the opportunity to own land and to develop it for themselves and their families. It was also the case that some came in lieu of being imprisoned in England for being in debt or having committed crimes.

Most of the colonists came from urban backgrounds. Most came as unskilled workers although some were skilled artisans as well. Most had nonagricultural work experience. Gradually the labor supply process became institutionalized by the creation of the indentured servant system.

These participants, before boarding ships, agreed to be contractually bound to work for a set period of time for someone in one of the colonies in return for payment of their transportation costs. When in the eighteenth century the Industrial Revolution began in England, the economic forces in its labor market changed. There was a need for workers to fill the jobs in the factories that industrialization had spawned. Hence, in England, political pressures developed to reduce the outflow. The only exception was for convicted felons who continued to be sent to the colonies. Convicts were not welcomed in the New England colonies but, in the Middle Atlantic and Southern colonies, settlers were generally glad to receive anyone they could. So a new source of labor supply for the colonies had to be found. It came in the form of redemptioners. These were, typically, poor peasants—usually from Scotland, Ireland, Germany, and Switzerland. Redemptioners signed repayment contracts after they arrived in the colonies. Hence, local demand and supply forces determined their actual length of subsequent servitude.

Throughout the colonial period from 1607 to 1776, the population grew rapidly. Most people lived close to the ocean or along navigable rivers. When the Revolutionary War began (1776), Philadelphia, with a population of 40,000, was the second largest city in the British Empire. The growth of cities led to an increased demand for a variety of workers in a range of trades—tailors, shoemakers, coach makers, shipbuilders, silversmiths, and glassmakers. Wages were much higher in the colonies (ranging from 30 to 200 percent higher) than in England and the other source countries for workers in similar occupations. This situation further encouraged free skilled workers to emigrate from their countries. But in all of the colonies, most workers had close ties to agriculture. The relative ease by which free workers could acquire land meant that many skilled workers as well as semiskilled and unskilled workers who completed their indentures (or those who simply wandered away before their bondage period was up) could become independent farmers. In every colony, therefore, agriculture was by far the dominant industry of the economy and the predominant occupation of the labor force up until the Revolutionary War.

Aside from immigration, the rapid population growth of the colonial era was also spawned by very high birth rates. With abundant land, there was strong inducement for raising large families. The first Census of the new nation in 1790 recorded a population of 3.9 million people—with 94.9 percent of the population living in rural areas. The first data on the nation's labor force (which measured persons "engaged in work, self-employment, or unpaid family work over the age of 10") set its size in 1800 at 1.9 million workers of whom 1.4 million were free workers and 500,000 were slaves. Of the free workers, 74 percent were employed in agriculture.[18] Indicative of the preindustrial stage of the economy was the fact that 90 percent of the free labor force in 1800 were not employees.[19] They were self-employed as farmers, tradesmen, and mechanics. It was from this base line that the free labor force of the United States was to be built.

The Onset of Mass Immigration

From the end of the Revolutionary War until 1820, relatively little immigration occurred. It is estimated that about 250,000 persons immigrated over this period but there are no data on immigrants prior to 1820. From the time of its independence until about 1850, the nation's economy continued to be dominated by agriculture. Aside from providing most of the jobs, the native-born farm population also provided most of the workers for both the farm and nonfarm sectors. In New England, the newly emerging textile industry initially relied upon children and women as a source of labor, many of whom came from farm families. The lure of available land often made it hard for employers to attract and retain many of the region's native-born young men for factory work.

Although the size of the workforce employed in farming increased slightly from 1800 to 1810, it declined thereafter from about 80 percent of the nation's labor force in 1810 to about 55 percent in 1850.[20] The seeds of industrial diversification and of urbanization were beginning to sprout. New jobs were created in manufacturing, trade, construction, and in various services. Initially, these developments were highly localized and largely restricted to the Northeast and the Midwest. In the South, the percentage of the labor force employed in agriculture actually increased over the first half of the nineteenth century (from 82 percent in 1800 to 84 percent in 1850).

It was against this economic backdrop that the phenomenon of mass immigration had its beginnings. The historian Marcus Hansen has written that the very word "immigrant" itself dates from 1817 Although the piecemeal process has be going on for over 200 years, during the seventeenth and eighteenth centuries, the new arrivals were known as "emigrants." The emphasis was on the fact that those who came to the colonies had "migrated *out* of something." By 1817, however, the newcomers were being called "immigrants" because they were "migrating *into* something"—the new nation which had come into being.[21] It is a subtle but significant shift in wording but it does provide support for Stanley Lebergott's contention that, in the nineteenth century, the "pull" force of the emerging U.S. economy overshadowed the "push" factors in workers' homelands and set the process of mass immigration in motion.[22]

In 1818 Congress made a crucial decision that would have lasting consequences on how the future immigrant experience would unravel. In that year Congress refused to respond to a petition from the New York Irish Emigrant Society for a sizable land grant of the public lands in Illinois to establish an Irish immigrant community.[23] Other Irish and German immigrant groups had been considering making similar requests to create culturally homogeneous communities. But Congress refused to permit such settlements when it accepted a special committee report that said "it would be undesirable to concentrate alien people geographically."[24] If permitted, the precedent would have been set for the creation of "a patchwork nation of foreign settlements." Hansen asserts that "no decision in the history of American immigration policy possesses more profound significance."[25] For unlike the fate that has befallen the late Soviet Union in contemporary times, the United States did not try to become a "nation of nations." Ethnic enclaves of immigrants would periodically develop but the land had to be purchased by individuals and open market competition would determine the results. Such enclaves could not be maintained over time by keeping others out. There would be no special privileges given to specific immigrant groups to encourage them to come or to stay.

Throughout the entire nineteenth and early twentieth centuries, immigration became the nation's major human resource development policy. The pace of this inflow was continual but the tide of the influx was punctuated by three distinct spurts of mass immigration. Each deserves separate mention.

The "First Wave" of Mass Immigration

The nation's initial experience with mass immigration began in the early 1830s. It lasted until the mid-1850s after which the domestic tension associated with the forthcoming Civil War led to its diminishment. The

British continued to be a prominent source of immigrants while the earlier trickle of immigrants from Ireland and Germany suddenly sustained a quantum increase in numbers. These groups, which were the largest sources of immigrants in the "first wave," were soon joined by a large influx of French Canadians. There were also the first signs of Italians and Scandinavians arriving in the East and of Chinese moving into the West—all of whom would increase dramatically in numbers after the Civil War. As shown in Table 3.1, five million immigrants entered the United States between 1830 and 1860.[26] In order to grasp the significance of the onset of the "first wave" of mass immigration from past experience, it is only necessary to reflect on three points. First, the cumulative number of immigrants—voluntary and involuntary—from 1607 to the early 1830s had been no more than one million people.

Secondly, over this entire timespan while the United States was a colony and then became an independent nation, it was seldom that more than 20,000 immigrants arrived in any one year. Thirdly, the vast preponderance of those who came prior to the early 1830s had come from two places: the British Isles and Africa. Suddenly, as a consequence of famine in Ireland and political unrest in Canada and in continental Europe, there was a flood of new immigrants to the United States. Their collective arrival was not viewed as a benign development. To the contrary, immigration became the subject of extensive domestic controversy.[27]

The "first wave" began a crescendo during the 1840s. It was the first decade in which the nation sustained an increase of over one million immigrants. In contrast to the experiences of the pre-1830s immigrants as well as to those of the new ethnic groups who came in the "first wave," most of the Irish immigrants were originally from rural farming backgrounds. Arriving without financial resources and usually as single males, most were forced to find jobs in the urban economy—usually as unskilled laborers and factory workers. Far fewer of the German and French Canadian immigrants were from agricultural backgrounds but they too came mostly from unskilled work backgrounds and most sought nonagricultural jobs. Thus, as Lebergott notes, "somewhat surprisingly, the greatest beneficiaries of the flow of immigrant labor was never agriculture though farming was our primary industry" in these early decades of the nineteenth century.[28]

Although the data are fragmentary and the job categories of that era are somewhat vague, Table 3.2 at least gives a general order of magnitude of

Table 3.1. Immigration to the United States: Fiscal Years 1820 - 1930

Year	Number	Year	Number	Year	Number	Year	Number	Year	Number	Year	Number	Year	Number
1820	8,385	1835	45,374	1851-60	2,598,214	1867	315,722	1882	788,992	1899	311,715	1914	1,218,480
1821-30	143,439	1836	76,242	1851	379,466	1868	138,840	1883	603,322	1900	448,572	1915	326,700
1821	9,127	1837	79,340	1852	371,603	1869	352,768	1884	518,592	1901-10	8,795,386	1916	298,826
1822	6,911	1838	38,914	1853	368,645	1870	387,203	1885	395,346	1901	487,918	1917	295,403
1823	6,354	1839	68,069	1854	427,833	1871-80	2,812,191	1886	334,203	1902	648,743	1918	110,618
1824	7,912	1840	84,066	1855	200,877	1871	321,350	1887	490,109	1903	857,046	1919	141,132
1825	10,199	1841-50	1,713,251	1856	200,436	1872	404,806	1888	546,889	1904	812,870	1920	430,001
1826	10,837	1841	80,289	1857	251,306	1873	459,803	1889	444,427	1905	1,026,499	1921-30	4,107,209
1827	18,875	1842	104,565	1858	123,126	1874	313,339	1890	455,302	1906	1,100,735	1921	805,228
1828	27,382	1843	52,496	1859	121,282	1875	227,498	1891-1900	3,687,564	1907	1,285,349	1922	309,556
1829	22,520	1844	78,615	1860	153,640	1876	169,986	1891	560,319	1908	782,870	1923	522,919
1830	23,322	1845	114,371	1861-70	2,314,824	1877	141,857	1892	579,663	1909	751,786	1924	706,896
1831-40	599,125	1846	154,416	1861	91,918	1878	138,469	1893	439,730	1910	1,041,570	1925	294,314
1831	22,633	1847	234,968	1862	91,985	1879	177,826	1894	285,631	1911-20	5,735,811	1926	304,488
1832	60,482	1848	226,527	1863	176,282	1880	457,257	1895	258,536	1911	878,587	1927	355,175
1833	58,640	1849	297,024	1864	193,418	1881-90	5,246,613	1896	343,267	1912	838,172	1928	307,255
1834	65,365	1850	369,980	1865	248,120	1881	669,431	1897	230,832	1913	1,197,892	1929	279,678
				1866	318,568			1898	229,299			1930	241,700

Note: The numbers shown are as follows: from 1820-67, figures represent alien passengers arrived at seaports; from 1868-91 and 1895-97, immigrant aliens arrived; from 1892-94 and 1898-1989, immigrant aliens admitted for permanent residence. From 1892-1903, aliens entering by cabin class were not counted as immigrants. Land arrivals were not completely enumerated until 1908.

Source: U.S. Immigration and Naturalization Service.

the occupational distribution of the immigrants of this period. It shows that, of those in the "first wave" who reported an occupation at the time of entry, the unskilled categories of "farmer" and "laborers" were dominant.

The cotton textile industry in southern New England was the first industry in the United States to become fully mechanized. As already noted, it initially recruited children and women, but Irish immigrants soon displaced them in the 1830s—only to be displaced themselves by French Canadians a few years later. Flour milling, meat packing, and other light manufacturing enterprises also began to develop. The growth in manufacturing enterprises necessitated a machine tool industry, which required iron foundries, which, in turn, required an expansion of mining activities. All of these growth sectors led to expanding demand for various local services. In each of these new employment sectors, immigrant labor played a prominent role.

Turning to the public sector of the pre-Civil War era, there were mounting demands for internal transportation improvements—mostly by Westerners who wanted roads and canals to transport their goods. Similar support was soon manifested for railroad construction. In most instances, the actual construction of these projects was done by private companies who relied heavily upon immigrant labor to do much of the physical work. There was, however, one way in which the public sector became directly involved in the employment of immigrants. It is estimated that one-third of the nation's regular army in the early 1840s was composed of foreign-born persons.[29] Moreover, the percentages of immigrants serving in the various state militias in the Northeast and Midwest at the time are estimated to be even higher.

It should be noted, for later comparison with present-day happenings, that the rise of these new industries with their sustained needs for additional workers was fostered by the presence of a system of tariffs on imports imposed by the Federal government. Tariffs were first enacted in 1789 against certain imported items as a means to provide revenue to support the governmental activities of the new nation. Alexander Hamilton had proposed the use of tariffs to protect infant industries as they tried to get started, but his advice was not initially heeded. After the War of 1812 with Britain, however, domestic business interests gained sufficient political influence to have protective legislation adopted. During that war, British imports had been cut off and U.S. manufacturers thrived. After the war, those commercial interest groups feared that the

Table 3.2. Percent Distribution of Immigrants, by Major Occupation Group at Time of Arrival, Selected Years, 1820-95

Year	Total[1]	Professional	Commercial	Skilled	Farmers	Servants	Laborers	Misc.	No Occupation[2]
1820	10,311	1.0	9.0	10.6	8.5	1.3	3.2	–	66.3
1825	12,858	1.6	14.3	11.0	12.8	.5	5.0	–	54.7
1830	24,837	.5	5.7	7.0	5.7	.1	2.9	–	78.0
1835	48,716	1.0	8.0	12.3	12.6	1.2	5.9	–	59.0
1840	92,207	.5	5.8	11.7	20.0	.2	10.5	–	51.3
1845	119,896	.5	4.2	9.1	16.1	2.1	13.8	–	54.3
1848	229,483	.2	1.5	10.8	13.8	1.9	20.1	–	51.7
1850	315,334	.3	2.0	8.4	13.6	1.0	14.8	–	59.9
1855	230,476	.3	6.4	7.6	15.1	1.1	18.5	–	51.0
1860	179,691	.4	6.2	10.8	12.1	.8	17.4	–	52.3
1865	287,399	.6	4.4	12.7	7.0	3.2	15.7	0.1	56.2
1870	387,203	.5	1.8	9.2	9.2	3.7	21.8	.2	53.5
1875	227,498	1.1	2.2	14.9	7.2	4.7	20.6	2.5	46.9
1880	457,257	.4	1.7	10.9	10.3	4.1	23.0	2.1	47.6
1885	395,346	.5	1.7	10.1	7.0	5.1	21.0	1.0	53.6
1890	455,302	.7	1.7	9.8	6.4	6.3	30.6	1.5	43.0
1895	258,536	.8	2.1	17.0	5.0	13.9	23.8	1.8	35.7

[1] For 1820-65 the data includes returning citizens.
[2] Includes dependent women and children and other aliens without an occupation or who did not report an occupation

Source: U.S. Department of Labor

renewal of British imports would wipe them out. They were joined by western farmers who wanted protection for certain agricultural products from foreign imports. Thus, the Tariff Act of 1816, the first protective tariff in the nation's history, was enacted. Coverage was expanded and the rates were raised by the Tariff Act of 1824. Similar steps were taken by the Tariff Act of 1832. Some downward revisions were made in 1833 only to have tariffs raised and coverage expanded once more by the Tariff Act of 1842. During this period, the tariff issue evolved into one of the key divisive forces in the nation. The tariffs stimulated economic development in the Northeast and Midwest (where immigration was occurring) but they caused prices of manufactured items to rise in the South (where immigration was not occurring). Eventually the political system became divided over the merits of protective tariffs. The Whig Party of the Northeast strongly favored tariffs while the Republican Party (which later would become the Democratic Party) was divided between Hamiltonians (who favored tariffs) and Jeffersonians (who opposed them). The outcome of this political debate was settled by the military outcome of the Civil War in the early 1860s. The victory of the North over the South gave support to those who favored the retention and expansion of protective tariffs—a policy that lasted for almost another one hundred years.

"The Second Wave" of Mass Immigration

From the early 1860s to the early 1880s, over five million immigrants entered the United States (see Table 3.1). During this time period, the proportion of the nation's labor force employed in agriculture remained essentially constant (at just over 50 percent). The major population and labor force growth of the nation occurred in the North Central states of the Midwest (essentially those states adjoining the Great Lakes). The growth in this region was more than twice the concurrent growth in the Northeast and almost twice that of the South.[30]

As with the "first wave," the "second wave" of immigrants came largely from Germany, the United Kingdom, Ireland, and Canada. But its ethnic composition is distinguished from the earlier wave by the addition of a significant flow of immigrants from Scandinavia and China.

The Scandinavians provided the exception to the immigrant work pattern of this period in that they tended to pursue agricultural work after entry. Many settled in rural areas of the upper Midwest. But the general pattern for most of the other "second wave" immigrants continued to be one in which they were employed disproportionately in nonagricultural work—especially in manufacturing, mining, and service work. Only 10 percent of the nation's agricultural workers in 1870 were foreign-born—despite the fact that this industry was still the nation's largest single employment sector.[31] As most of the immigrants of this period were unskilled, they could easily have become the mainstay of the agricultural labor force. But they did not. Instead, as Lebergott has noted, they became the backbone of the urban labor force of the new industries that rapidly developed during and after the Civil War.[32]

The Civil War, which lasted from 1861 to 1865, brought economic ruin to the agrarian economy of the South but it served to accelerate business development in the Northeast and Midwest. Government contracts for immense quantities of munitions, clothes, and food supplies to support the war effort were an immediate stimulus. As labor was scarce—due in part to military conscription of soldiers, the new high production levels could only be met through greatly increased use of machinery. Thus, the industrial boom accelerated the trend toward the use of mass production techniques which displaced reliance on the extensive use of hand labor. Under such circumstances, large corporations had significant advantages over small-scale enterprises. New factories were built in the Northeast and Midwest, and mining grew rapidly in the Midwest and West.

Agriculture in the West also received a similar boost as hundreds of thousands of pioneers moved westward and brought new land under cultivation. As was the case with industry, the general scarcity of labor also led to a rapid spurt in technological progress in the spread of labor-saving machinery in agriculture as well. The Homestead Act of 1862, which provided that a citizen or alien who had declared an intention to become a citizen could obtain the title to 160 acres of public land for a nominal fee after he had lived on it for five years, was a major prod to settlement. In addition, the Morrill Land Grant Act of 1862 set the stage for the promotion of agricultural development in the decades after the War through its support for the creation of public colleges that conducted training and research for scientific advancement in agricultural production.

It was also in 1862 that Congress passed the long-sought legislation for the construction of a transcontinental railroad. The earlier political controversy over the precise route to be taken that had held back this project was no longer an obstacle as the South had withdrawn from the Union. The alternative Southern route, for the time being, ceased to be an option. Hence, the Union Pacific Railroad was commissioned to build westward from Nebraska while the Central Pacific Railroad was contracted to build eastward from California. Each company was provided generous grants of public land and a loan from the federal government for each mile of track they laid. Most of the actual construction did not begin until after the war when the pace of work moved rapidly. The two lines met in Utah in 1869.

It should also be noted that in 1861 the Morrill Tariff Act raised the *ad valorem* duty on imports to 47 percent—the highest rate in U.S. history up until that time. The immediate impetus for the new schedule of tariffs was to raise revenue to support the war effort but the tariffs also served to protect expanding business enterprises from foreign competition. When the war ended, Northern industrialists, who now held power over Congress, kept the high tariffs in effect even though the government no longer needed the revenue they provided. Hence, the accommodation of the "second wave" of immigrants would also occur behind the shield of tariffs.

In response to the dramatic increase in the demand for unskilled workers during the Civil War to meet the job requirements of the expanding goods-producing industries, immigration again became important. There was no particular need for educated or trained workers or even any necessity to be literate in either English or one's native tongue. What was needed was large numbers of manual workers and this is what mass immigration again provided (see Table 3.2). In every decade through 1880 (indeed, this pattern continued to 1930), the largest group among the immigrants reporting an occupation on entry was that of an unskilled "laborer."[33]

The worker shortage in the North during the Civil War was so severe that it prompted the passage of the first immigration statute in the nation's history. Business interests sought to find a way to increase the supply of urban workers, but not of settlers who would bring their families and be tempted to move westward. In response, President Abraham Lincoln, in a message to Congress in December 1863, proposed a law to foster immigration. Early in 1864, the Act to Encourage Immigration was adopted. Due to its unique procedural aspects, it was more popularly called the Contract Labor Act. The law allowed private employers to recruit foreign workers and to pay their transportation expenses to the United States. The enlisted workers signed legally binding contracts whereby they agreed to pledge their wages for up to twelve months to the employer to repay their transportation costs. In addition, they were often induced to sign contracts for additional years of work to defray the costs of their maintenance during the initial year.

The law was designed primarily to attract unskilled workers. Under its terms, private firms—especially the American Emigrant Company—entered into very lucrative business ventures. In return for recruiting immigrants in foreign countries, these companies were paid fees by both the employers for whom they contracted workers and the steamship lines who transported the recruits from Europe.

Domestic opposition to the Contract Labor Act from existing worker organizations arose at once. In some instances, the new immigrants were used during the war in labor disputes as strikebreakers. When the war ended, the economy slipped into a serious recession that lasted from 1866 to 1868. Organized labor—especially the newly formed National Labor Union (NLU)—blamed the immigration law for the unemployment and depressed wages that existed in the postwar period.[34] The NLU sought repeal of the Contract Labor Act and was successful in doing so in 1868. Contract labor continued into the 1880s, however, because the practice itself was not banned. In 1885, the Alien Contract Law specifically prohibited further use of contract labor although there continued to be violations of its terms for many years afterward.

One of the new immigrant groups affected by the use of contract labor was the Chinese. Chinese immigration had begun in the late 1840s. Their entry had been spawned by the discovery of gold in 1848 in California—only one month after the territory had been acquired from Mexico. California, which became a state in 1850, was located far from the other states of the union. As such, it was immediately confronted with a chronic shortage of unskilled workers needed to meet the booming demand for workers. During the 1850s, 45,000 Chinese entered the state, over 20,000 of them employed in gold mining in 1861. Others were hired to work in myriad unskilled jobs in service enterprises, domestic service, and small factories. The Chinese immigrants were overwhelmingly males (approximately 9 males to 1 female). Despite the fact that most Chinese workers came from impoverished agricultural backgrounds, relatively few were employed in agriculture in California. They accounted for less than 10 percent of the state's agricultural labor force in 1870.

The major impetus for expanded Chinese immigration in the 1860s came from the use of contract labor to work as laborers on construction of the transcontinental railroad eastward from California. When this feat was completed, most of these workers had to look elsewhere for employment. The completion of the railroad also meant that it was now possible for workers from the East to come west to California—and they did so in droves. Nonetheless, in 1870 the Chinese were the largest ethnic component of the foreign-born workforce in California (numbering 14 percent of the total labor force).[35]

Throughout this period, the Chinese were viewed as workers who would work for meager wages and would accept any conditions of work no matter how minimal or oppressive they might be. Indeed, they were desparagingly referred to as "coolie labor" by other workers who felt deterred from competing with them. Under such circumstances and prodded by a recession in California after the completion of the transcontinental railroad, there was agitation for the restriction of further immigration from China. A number of laws were passed in California and later in other western states to restrict employment of Chinese workers in certain industries. There were anti-Chinese riots in several cities in the 1870s. As a consequence, and with strong support from the existing labor organizations, Chinese immigration became a national issue.[36] The culmination of these concerns came with the passage of the Chinese Exclusion Act of 1882 which forbade any additional Chinese immigrants for ten years. The law was regularly extended each decade until it was repealed in 1943 when China was given a small annual quota of 105 immigrants which continued in effect until 1965.

The total exclusion of the Chinese was part of an earlier movement in the mid-1870s to screen immigrants and to end the era of unrestricted immigration that had existed for almost a century. Federal laws were passed in the 1870s to exclude certain classes of immigrants regardless of their country of origin. The initial exclusions of this period applied to convicts, prostitutes, idiots, lunatics, and paupers.

The "Third Wave" of Mass Immigration

The 1880s witnessed the largest inflow of immigrants—over five million persons—in a single decade up to that time. It was followed by a small retrenchment to 3.6 million immigrants in the 1890s—a period in which the nation's economy sustained the worst depression it had yet known. But by the late 1890s, recovery had set in and immigration soared to new heights in the first decade of the twentieth century (see Table 3.1). Over

8.7 million immigrants entered between 1901 and 1910. Record annual levels of immigrants continued until 1914 when World War I broke out in Europe. During 1905, 1906, 1907, 1910, 1913, and 1914, over one million immigrants entered the United States each year. It would not be until 1989 that there would be another time when over one million immigrants were legally admitted in a single year. The pace of mass immigration revived briefly after World War I but, as will be discussed, the "third wave" of immigration came to an end in the mid-1920s as the result of legislation.

To be sure, not all of these immigrants stayed permanently. It is crudely estimated that throughout the late nineteenth and early twentieth centuries the emigration rate was about 30 percent.[37] This was due to the fact that some immigrants never intended to stay. As the number of male immigrants exceeded the number of females by more than a two to one ratio over this entire time span, some immigrants simply carried through with their original intentions to return home to their relatives and their families that they had left behind.[38] These immigrants were known as "birds of passage" who came for a while before migrating back to their homelands. Others, who had originally intended to stay, left because they could not adjust to the new society or they became disenchanted with the harshness of life—especially in the large cities of that time.[39] Some others were deported for criminal activities or other violations of existing laws and immigration restrictions imposed in the 1890s that were being seriously enforced for the first time.[40]

Aside from the escalation in the level of immigration, the "third wave" is also distinctly characterized by the shift in the lands of origin of the new immigrants. The emerging trend began slowly in the 1880s but it quickly became discernible. Prior to 1890, 85 percent of all the immigrants who came to the United States since 1820 had come from Western and Northern European countries. Beginning in the early 1890s, the numbers of immigrants from these countries began to decline while those from Eastern and Southern European nations increased dramatically. In 1896, for the first time, immigration from Eastern and Southern European nations exceeded that from Western and Northern Europe and the gap quickly widened over the ensuing years. By 1910, 70 percent and 20 percent, respectively, of all the immigrants to the United States came from these two separate regions of Europe.[41]

In the West, the major new source of immigrants were the Japanese. It was not until after 1884 that the Japanese government permitted its citizens to work in foreign lands. It was the same year that diplomatic relations between Japan and the United States were established and it was also the year that sugar planters in Hawaii (who were mostly U.S. citizens) initiated efforts to recruit Japanese workers.[42] It was not long before substantial numbers of Japanese workers were employed in Hawaii. Indeed, their numbers increased so rapidly that the United States—fearing Japan would take control of the islands—unilaterally annexed them in 1898 and made them a territory in 1900. Meanwhile, Japanese immigrants—mostly coming from Hawaii—began to arrive in the West Coast states of the U.S. mainland. With immigration from China prohibited, the Japanese workers moved to fill the labor supply void for unskilled workers. As their numbers increased, the identical fears that had been raised about the Chinese soon manifested themselves.

The Japanese were also viewed as workers who would work for low wages and who would seldom complain about working conditions no matter how bad they might be. They also were used as strikebreakers on occasion. After several ugly incidents, some of which had the potential to become international incidents, a diplomatic understanding—known as the Gentlemen's Agreement—was reached in 1908. In return for the United States agreeing not to pass formal legislation to exclude Japanese immigrants, the Japanese government agreed to cease issuing passports to its citizens who wished to go to the United States to work or to settle. This agreement remained in effect until 1924 when the United States abrogated its terms and legislatively banned all Japanese immigration. The ban remained in effect until 1952 when Japan was given a nominal quota.

Of those Japanese who did immigrate to the United States, their occupational backgrounds resembled that of the European immigrants of "the third wave": namely, both groups during this period disproportionately came from agricultural backgrounds.[43] This characteristic distinguishes the "third wave" immigrants from those of the "first" and "second" waves. As shown in Table 3.3, "farm laborers" became the largest occupation cited at time of entry up until 1914. The unskilled categories of "farm laborer" and "laborer" dominated by far the occupational pattern of those who listed an occupation. The Europeans of the "third wave," however, found employment largely in the nonagricultural sectors of the urban sector of the U.S. economy. The Japanese immigrants were the exception. They were disproportionately employed in the agriculture and food packing sectors of California and other Western States.

SCCCC - LIBRARY
4601 Mid Rivers Mall Drive
St. Peters, MO 63376

Table 3.3. Percent Distribution of Immigrants, by Major Occupation Group, at Time of Arrival, Selected Years, 1900-30.

Fiscal Year	Total	Professional, Technical, and Kindred Workers	Farmers and Farm Managers	Managers, Officials, and Proprietors (except Farm)	Clerical, Sales, and Kindred	Crafts, Operatives, and Kindred	Private Household Workers	Service Workers except Private Household	Farm Laborers and Supervisors	Laborers, except Farm and Mine	No Occupation[1]
1900	448,572	0.5	1.2	1.6	0.6	12.2	9.0	1.0	7.1	36.6	30.1
1905	1,026,499	1.2	1.8	2.7	1.2	15.5	12.2	.6	13.9	28.3	22.6
1910	1,041,570	.9	1.1	1.4	1.2	11.7	9.3	.9	27.7	20.8	25.0
1914	1,218,480	1.1	1.2	1.8	1.5	12.3	11.9	1.6	23.6	18.8	26.3
1915	326,700	3.5	2.0	3.3	2.9	14.0	12.2	3.7	7.6	15.2	35.8
1920	430,001	2.5	2.8	2.2	3.3	13.0	8.7	4.3	3.5	19.4	40.3
1925	294,314	3.0	4.7	1.9	5.2	12.5	9.1	5.2	5.4	12.4	40.3
1930	241,700	3.6	3.5	1.9	6.0	13.4	12.0	2.8	5.7	7.5	43.7

[1]Includes dependent women and children and other aliens without occupation or occupation not reported.

Source: U.S. Department of Labor.

Many Japanese immigrants entered the continental United States by way of Hawaii where they often had worked in the sugar industry. The Japanese immigrants of this era quickly displaced the remaining vestiges of Chinese workers who had previously been employed in California agriculture.[44] Some did laborer work on the railroads and in construction. Others worked in mining. But they generally did not work in the manufacturing sector as had the Chinese before them.[45]

Brief mention should also be made of the entry of immigrants from two other Asian countries whose numbers were small in this period but, in contemporary times, would become substantial. One of these new source countries was Korea. Although there had been a few Korean immigrants in the 1880s, it was not until the early 1900s that several thousand arrived. Like the Japanese, they mostly came by way of having first worked in Hawaiian agriculture and they mostly continued to work in agriculture when they migrated to California. But this flow ended when Japan made Korea a protectorate in 1905 and put a stop to such emigration for the next forty years.

The other Asian country that briefly supplied agricultural workers to West Coast growers was the Philippines. The Philippines had become a U.S. colony in 1898 (after being ceded by Spain to the United States following the Spanish-American War of that year). Given this special status, immigrants from the Philippines were briefly able to fill the vacuum after Japanese immigration was restricted. Tens of thousands of Philippine immigrants entered the mainland of the United States in the 1920s but this flow quickly dried up because of increasing competition from workers from Mexico in the 1920s and the advent of the economic depression in the 1930s that suddenly produced a surplus of agricultural job-seekers from the native-born white population. It was also in this context that the Filipino Exclusion Act of 1934 was enacted, which set an annual quota of fifty visas a year. In 1946, when the Philippines became an independent nation, the annual quota was raised to one hundred visas, which remained in effect until 1965.

Having noted the exceptions, the general rule was that most of the "third wave" immigrants did not seek work in agriculture despite the fact that most came from agricultural backgrounds and the fact that this industry remained the nation's largest employment sector until 1920. As noted earlier, agricultural employment had been virtually constant throughout the "second wave" of immigration at about 50 percent of total employment. But beginning in the 1880s, new employment patterns began to emerge that had long-term structural adjustment consequences. There was a rapid introduction of labor-saving agricultural technologies in the 1880s and the years that followed. The consequences were a surge in output and rapidly falling prices for most farm goods. In the wake of these developments, employment in agriculture began to decline—first in relative terms and later in absolute terms. The 1890 census showed that less than half of the nation's labor force (43 percent) were employed in agriculture for the first time. By 1920, the percentage had fallen to 26 percent. In absolute terms, agricultural employment gradually increased until it peaked in 1906 at 11.4 million agricultural workers. After this all-time high point, the absolute number of agricultural workers began to decline and has continued to do so ever since.

By 1920, the expanding manufacturing sector had displaced agriculture as the major employment sector of the nation's economy. During this critical period of industrial transition, the historic pattern continued: the vast majority of "third wave" immigrants did not work in agriculture. In 1900, only 13 percent of all agricultural workers were foreign-born; by 1930, when the "third wave" had ended, the percentage was 11 percent.[46] It was during this period that the other goods-producing industries —manufacturing and mining in particular—emerged to dominate the employment patterns of the U.S. economy. Between 1890 and 1920, manufacturing employment increased by 150 percent and mining employment by 168 percent. The corresponding occupations that increased the most in absolute terms were those of operatives and laborers. The need was for unskilled workers capable of doing manual work. Indeed, as late as 1917 when the United States entered World War I, less than 6 percent of the adult male workforce had graduated from high school.

In this economic environment, the paucity of the human capital endowments of the "third wave" of immigrants was of no great consequence. The fact that they came from largely impoverished peasant family backgrounds; that they had few skills and little, if any, education; and that most were illiterate in their own language to say nothing of their inability to speak or to understand English, was not a barrier to their finding employment in the growing goods-producing sector. In 1910, for example, immigrants accounted for: over half of all operatives in mining and apparel work; over half of all laborers in steel manufacturing, bituminous coal mining, meatpacking, and cotton textile milling; over half of all bakers; and about 80 percent of all tailors.[47] Likewise, their presence was disproportionately concentrated in the urban work-force—especially in the cities of the Northeast, the Great Lakes region of the Midwest, and the West Coast. In major cities such as Buffalo, Chicago, Detroit, Milwaukee, Minneapolis, New York, Portland, and San Francisco, foreign-born men constituted over half of the male labor force throughout most of this period.[48] Indeed, it was the influence of mass immigration into these industries and urban centers that was largely determining the prevailing wage levels and working conditions. For the most part, the effect was to depress real wages.[49] Indeed, organized labor as well as various socialist political organizations at the time were actively crusading for immigration restrictions for this very reason.[50]

The "third wave" of mass immigration was interrupted by the outbreak, in 1914, of World War I in Europe. It was no longer possible for most people to leave their countries even if they were disposed to do so. Following the end of the War in late 1918, mass immigration from Europe briefly resumed in 1919. But, in the meantime, a reaction against the adverse effects of mass immigration had set in. In 1917, the United States adopted a literacy test (in the immigrant's native language) of would-be immigrants and it created the "Asiatic Barred Zone" which banned most immigration from Asia. In 1921 temporary legislation was enacted that set an annual ceiling of 358,000 immigrants. This was the first time that a numerical ceiling on immigration had been imposed. When combined with the earlier legislation in 1917, this action signaled that the end of the era of essentially "open door" immigration.

In 1924, a more comprehensive statute was enacted that set an even lower quota of about 150,000 persons a year (plus their accompanying wives and minor children who were admitted as nonquota immigrants).[51] Each country covered by the law was eligible for a minimum quota of one hundred persons so the actual total number of available visas each year became 154,277. This ceiling, with only slight modifications over the years, remained in effect until 1965.

The Immigration Act of 1924 is also known as the National Origins Act because it went much further than simply limiting the level of Eastern Hemisphere immigration. It also sought to affect its composition by indicating which countries could send immigrants and which could not. Through a complex process to determine national origins that took five years to actually set up, 82 percent of the annually available quota slots were reserved for persons from Western and Northern European countries; 14 percent were reserved for Eastern and Southern Europeans;

and the remaining 4 percent were for the rest of the Eastern Hemisphere excluding Asia from where most immigration was already barred. Immigration from the Western Hemisphere, however, was not included in the new quota system and immigration from this large region remained unrestricted until 1968.

The momentum for this racially and ethnically restrictive legislation had been crystalized from the findings of an earlier presidentially established commission. Appointed by President Theodore Roosevelt in 1907, the Immigration Commission (also known as the Dillingham Commission) issued its final report in 1911. This famous report mixed its economic arguments about the adverse effects of the "third wave" of mass immigration on wages, employment, working conditions, and union organizational efforts with its sociological arguments about the difficulties the nation was having in assimilating such a racially, ethnically, and culturally diverse mix of immigrants. Because of the intertwining of these two arguments in this historic report, the topic of immigration policy ever since has been steeped in suspicion.[52]

Despite extensive criticism in later years, at the time of its enactment the Immigration Act of 1924 enjoyed widespread popular support from most business, labor, academic, religious, and social worker organizations and their leaders. True, it also received support from various fringe elements who were avowedly racist in their beliefs but their encouragement was largely incidental to its passage. The real issue was whether the nation was to have a formal immigration policy or was to continue to accommodate on an essentially unlimited basis those people from throughout most of the world who wished to live and to work in the United States. In choosing to limit immigration, the nation entered a new stage in which it would have to determine how this feat should be accomplished.

Summary Observations

Immigration policy prior to World War I was consistent with economic development trends and labor force requirements of the United States. Throughout its first century, the country had neither ceilings nor screening restrictions on the number and type of people permitted to enter for permanent settlement. In this preindustrial stage, the economy was dominated by agricultural production. Most jobs required little training or educational preparation. Policymakers did not concern themselves with human resource preparation issues. Because a vast amount of land was largely unpopulated, an unregulated immigration policy was consistent with the nation's basic labor market needs.

When the industrialization process began in earnest during the later decades of the nineteenth century, the newly introduced technology of mechanization (i.e., the substitution of machines for animal and human muscle power) required mainly unskilled workers to fill manufacturing jobs in the nation's expanding urban labor markets as well as in the other employment growth sectors of mining, construction, and transportation. Unskilled workers were what was needed and this is what prevailing immigration policy provided.[53] As one immigration scholar at that time wrote in 1913: "we may yearn for a more intelligent and better trained worker from the countries of Europe but it is questionable whether or not that type of man would have been so well fitted for the work America had to offer."[54] The supply of workers of that era may have been highly heterogeneous in their personal characteristics, but the demand for labor was essentially homogeneous in what it required of those who came.

There were surplus pools of native-born workers who were poorly skilled and barely educated who remained marginalized throughout the pre-World War I era. They could have filled some of these needs. Many were underemployed in the declining rural sectors of the economy. Of these, the most notable were the freed blacks of the former slave economy of the rural South. But mass immigration from Asia and Europe became the alternative of choice in the post-Civil War years. Before long, as noted, immigration from China and Japan was banned in response to negative social reactions, so various ethnic groups from Eastern and Southern Europe became the primary sources of unskilled workers around the turn of the twentieth century.

From purely an efficiency standpoint, the mass immigration of the late nineteenth century and the first quarter of the twentieth century was entirely consistent with the labor market needs of the nation. The jobs created during this expansive era typically required little in the way of skill, education, literacy, or fluency in English from the workforce. The enormous supply of immigrants who came during this time generally lacked these human capital attributes. Nonetheless, they reasonably matched the prevailing demand for labor. The technology of that period asked little in the way of human resource preparation. Available jobs required mainly blood, sweat, and tears, and most immigrants as well as most native-born workers of that era amply provided all three.

Notes

1. Henry Bamford Parkes, *The United States of America: A History* (New York: Alfred A. Knopf, 1953), p. 23.

2. Ibid.

3. Stanley Lebergott, *Manpower in Economic Growth* (New York: McGraw Hill Book Company, 1964), p. 8.

4. Parkes, op.cit., p. 189.

5. Dee Brown, *Bury My Heart at Wounded Knee: An Indian History of the American West* (New York: Holt, Rinehart and Winston, 1970), Chapter 1.

6. Paul Horgan, *Great River: The Rio Grande in North American History* (New York: Holt, Rinehart and Winston, 1954), Vols. 1 and 2.

7. Carey McWilliams, *North From Mexico* (New York: Greenwood Press, 1968), Chapters 3 and 4.

8. Ibid.,

9. Ibid., p. 52; see also Oscar J. Martinez, "On the Size of the Chicano Population: New Estimates, 1850–1900," *Atzlan* (Spring 1975), pp. 43-67.

10. McWilliams, op.cit., p. 98.

11. Ibid., p. 53.

12. Harry E. Cross and James A. Sandos, *Across the Border* (Berkeley: Institute of Governmental Studies, 1981).

13. Stanley M. Elkins, *Slavery* (New York: Gosset and Dunlap 1959), p. 49.

14. W.E.B. DuBois, *The Suppression of the African Slave Trade to the United States of America 1638-1870* (New York: Schocken Books, 1969), pp. 152-153.

15. Ibid., pp. 108-118.

16. Lebergott, ibid., p. 102.

17. Henry Pelling, *American Labor* (Chicago: The University of Chicago Press, 1960), pp. 1-2.

18. Lebergott, op. cit., p. 510.

19. Ibid., p. 139.

20. Ibid., p. 101.

21. Marcus L. Hansen, *The Immigrant in American History* (Cambridge: Harvard University Press, 1942), p. 11 [emphasis is in the original text].

22. Lebergott, op. cit., p. 40.

23. *Annals of the Congress of the United States* (15th Cong., 1st. Sess.) (1818) (Washington D.C.: Galen and Seaton, 1854), Vol. 31, pp. 1053-1054.

24. Hansen, op. cit., p. 132.

25. Ibid.

26. For a discussion of the forces prompting these movements, see Vernon M. Briggs, Jr., *Immigration Policy and the American Labor Force* (Baltimore: Johns Hopkins University Press, 1984), Chapter 2.

27. Ibid., pp. 19-22.

28. Lebergott, op. cit., p. 28.

29. Ibid., p. 27.

30. Ibid., p. 103.

31. Ibid., p. 28.

32. Ibid., p. 28-29.

33. A. Ross Eckler and Jack Zlotnick, "Immigration and the Labor Force," *Annals of the American Academy of Political and Social Sciences* (March 1949), pp. 96-97.

34. Joseph G. Rayback, *A History of American Labor* (New York: Free Press, 1966), pp. 119-20.

35. *Abstracts of the Reports of the U.S. Immigration Commission* (Washington, D.C.: U.S. Government Printing Office, 1911), Vol. 1, p. 656.

36. For more details, see Briggs, op cit., pp. 26-27.

37. Peter Roberts, *The New Immigration* (New York: The MacMillan Company, 1913), p. 363.

38. *Abstracts ... Immigration Commission*, Vol. 1, op cit., pp. 58-59.

39. The classic study of the harshness of urban life at the turn of the twentieth century is: Jacob Riis, *How the Other Half Lives* (New York: Sagamore Press, 1957).

40. Roberts, op. cit., pp. 363-364.

41. *Abstracts ... Immigration Commission*, Vol. 1, op. cit., p. 60.

42. For a more detailed discussion of how Japanese immigration began in the Hawaiian Islands and then spread to the U.S. Mainland, see Briggs, op. cit., pp. 33-35; See also *Abstracts ... Immigration Commission*, Vol. 1, op. cit., pp. 660-676.

43. *Abstracts ... Immigration Commission*, Vol. 1, op. cit., p. 663 and Roberts, op. cit., p 364.

44. *Abstracts ... Immigration Commission*, Vol. 1, ... op. cit., p. 658.

45. Ibid., p. 663.

46. Lebergott, op. cit., p. 28.

47. *Abstracts ... Immigration Commission*, Vol. 1, ..., op.cit., pp. 297-313.

48. Ibid., p. 151.

49. Lebergott, op. cit., p. 162.

50. Philip Taft, *Organized Labor in American History* (New York: Harper and Row, 1964), Chapter 23.

51. Children under the age of 18 and who were unmarried and wives of immigrants who were admitted were exempted from the quota, but husbands of admitted immigrants were not exempted until 1952.

52. For a more careful discussion of the Dillingham Commission and the other events leading to the enactment of the Immigration Act of 1924, see Briggs, op. cit., pp. 35-38.

53. Eckler and Zlotnick, op. cit., p. 97.

54. Roberts, op, cit., p. 61.

FOUR

Reprieve: The Cessation of Mass Immigration

The enactment in 1924 of an immigration policy with both numerical limits and restrictive screening put the labor force of the United States on a new developmental course. For the first time the nation had to depend essentially upon its native-born population for its future economic welfare and competitiveness. Over the next forty years, the percentage of the population that was foreign-born steadily declined (see Table 4.1). Before the reversal of this trend in the late 1960s, the lengthy reprieve from the mass immigration experience offered the nation an opportunity to see what the alternative effects of low immigration levels might be.

The Short Run Response to Immigration Limits

When legislation brought an end to the mass immigration from Europe, past experience would have suggested that the immediate concern would be to meet the demand for unskilled workers. However, this turned out to be a nonissue. The short-run effect of the new law was far less than would have been anticipated with respect to reducing the level of immigration (see Table 4.2). Over 4.1 million immigrants were legally admitted to the United States during the 1920s, 1.8 million of whom were admitted after 1924. Although the Immigration Act of 1924 dramatically reduced immigration from most of the countries that had dominated the flow of "third wave" immigrants, the law—as previously noted—did not apply to the entire Western Hemisphere. As a consequence, immigration from Canada and Mexico soared in the 1920s[1] Immigration from the Caribbean area also increased as did the migration of U.S. citizens from

Table 4.1 Foreign-Born Population of the United States, 1920-1989

Year	Number (Millions)	Percentage of Total Population
1920	14.0	13.2
1930	14.2	11.6
1940	11.6	8.8
1950	10.4	6.9
1960	9.7	5.4
1970	9.6	4.7
1980	13.9	6.2
1989*	17.8	7.3

*Note: As the 1990 Census data on the foreign-born were not yet available, the 1989 estimate is from sample data provided by November 1989 add-on question to the *Current Population Survey* as adjusted for estimated misreporting errors. It is taken from an article in preparation for publication by Karen A. Woodrow entitled "A Consideration of the Effect of Immigration Reform on the Number of Undocumented Residents in the United States," mss., p. 6.

Source: U.S. Bureau of the Census.

the Island of Puerto Rico (which had been acquired by the United States in 1898 from Spain as part of a treaty ending the Spanish-American War and whose residents were granted U.S. citizenship in 1917).[2]

Over 900,000 Canadians immigrated to the United States in the 1920s. Most settled in U.S. communities near the U.S.-Canadian Border.[3] The urban economies of the Great Lakes states were thriving during this decade.

Likewise, along the southern border, an old but hitherto minor immigrant stream began to gather momentum and to increase in scale. It was destined to become the major component of the future "fourth wave" of immigration. This flow consisted of immigrants from Mexico. Although there had been earlier periods when Mexicans had immigrated to the United States, it was not until after 1910 that the numbers became significant. During the period 1910 to 1917, Mexico sustained a convulsive civil war in which over one million people out of a total population of 15 million were killed. For ten years after the formal fighting subsided, internal chaos which verged on anarchy in many regions led to sporadic outbreaks of more violence. In this lengthy period of domestic turmoil, Mexicans moved north in significant numbers. Over a quarter million Mexicans immigrated to the United States between 1910 and 1920 and another 459,000 did so during the decade of the 1920s. The vast majority of these Mexican immigrants settled in the four border states of the Southwest—California, Texas, New Mexico, and Arizona. At the time most of this region was still in the early stages of economic development. Indeed, Arizona and New Mexico had just become states in 1912. The demand for unskilled workers—especially in the Southwest's agricultural sector—was assuming major proportions. The need for agricultural workers was spurred by the completion of a massive system of federally financed irrigation projects that stretched from the lower Rio Grande Valley in Texas to the Imperial Valley of California.[4] Millions of acres of previously arid land were brought into production after 1910 and over the following two decades. These new water projects had been the product of one of the nation's most ambitious examples of beneficial public works legislation—the Reclamation Act of 1902. As the noted historian of the Southwest, Carey McWilliams, has written, "irrigation had more to do with the economic growth of the Southwest than any other factor."[5] Likewise, the parallel expansion of railroads into previously remote sections of the border region during this period facilitated both the entry of Mexican workers and the exit of agricultural produce to markets across the country. Thus, "the economic development of the American Southwest coincided with the northward drift of Mexico's population."[6] The arrival of Mexicans in significant numbers followed immediately after the implementation of the Gentlemen's Agreement which had reduced the flow of immigrants from Japan into California as well as other western states, and which had paralled the total legislative ban on Japanese immigration that was imposed in 1924. As discussed in the previous chapter, the Japanese immigrants had been extensively employed in agriculture in this region.

The entry of Mexican workers into the agricultural labor force of the Southwest provided growers with yet another extremely cheap supply of labor. By Mexican standards, however, the U.S. wage rates were very high. As a result, many agricultural employers came to believe that Mexican workers could be hired for considerably less than non-Mexican workers. It is an industry perspective that has persisted ever since.

Agriculture in the Southwest did not suffer the severe contractive effects that other agricultural areas of the nation experienced during the 1920s.

Table 4.2 Legal Immigration to the United States 1921 to 1970

Year	Number	Year	Number	Year	Number	Year	Number	Year	Number
1921 - 30	4,107,209	1931 - 40	528,431	1941 - 50	1,035,039	1951 - 60	2,515,479	1961 - 70	3,321,677
1921	805,228	1931	97,139	1941	51,776	1951	205,717	1961	271,344
1922	309,556	1932	35,576	1942	28,781	1952	265,520	1962	283,763
1923	522,919	1933	23,068	1943	23,725	1953	170,434	1963	306,260
1924	706,896	1934	29,470	1944	28,551	1954	208,177	1964	292,248
1925	294,314	1935	34,956	1945	38,119	1955	237,790	1965	296,697
1926	304,488	1936	36,329	1946	108,721	1956	321,625	1966	323,040
1927	335,175	1937	50,244	1947	147,292	1957	326,867	1967	361,972
1927	307,255	1938	67,895	1948	170,570	1958	253,265	1968	454,448
1929	279,678	1939	82,998	1949	188,317	1959	260,686	1969	358,579
1930	241,700	1940	70,756	1950	249,187	1960	265,398	1970	373,326

Source: U.S. Immigration and Naturalization Service.

In part this was due to the lower costs made possible by the use of Mexican labor, but it also reflected the fact that the mix of agricultural products in the Southwest was (and still is) dominated by specialty produce. Such crops were less susceptible to the decline in general agricultural prices that occurred during the 1920s in other agricultural regions.

By no means, of course, did all Mexican immigrants of this period seek agricultural employment, nor did they all remain in the Southwest. The urban areas of the Southwest as well as some cities of the Midwest (especially the Chicago area) also attracted a significant number of Mexican immigrants.[7]

The Emergence of the Illegal Immigration Issue

Another reason there was no shortage of unskilled workers in the 1920s, despite the passage of the Immigration Act of 1924, was that many foreign-born nationals who were legally prohibited from entry simply came anyhow. It was during the 1920s that the issue of illegal immigration—which would become a paramount concern after the mid-1960s—first emerged on a noticeable scale. The roots of the illegal immigration issue, however, reached back to the initial attempts of the nation to improve any restrictions on entry.

As noted in the preceding chapter, there really was no effort by the federal government to create any semblance of barriers to immigration until 1875. It was then that prohibitions were enacted that banned the entry of prostitutes and convicts. This list of excludable groups was expanded in 1882 to include paupers, idiots, and lunatics. The Secretary of the Treasury was given the authority to enforce these restrictions. Then, also in 1882, the Chinese Exclusion Act was adopted and later, in 1885, the Alien Contract Act was passed which restricted employer recruitment of foreign labor. Those persons found to be in the country in violation of these various restrictions could be deported. The federal government, however, had no enforcement agency to carry out these mandates. Hence, it relied upon state law enforcement bodies.

In the late 1880s, several congressional committees reported that these exclusionary laws were being violated by significant numbers of persons each year and that stronger deterrent measures would be required. The result was the enactment of the Immigration Act of 1891 which ended the dual federal-state administration of immigration policy. Immigration policy and its enforcement became the sole responsibility of the federal government.   The Bureau of Immigration (BI) was set up in the Department of the Treasury to assume these duties and twenty-four border inspection stations were set up at various seaports as well as at land crossings on the Mexican and Canadian borders.   New exclusions for persons with contagious diseases and for persons who were practicing polygamists were added to the BI's workload.   It was not long after its establishment that the BI regularly reported to Congress that it was increasingly difficult to enforce the existing immigration laws due to illegal crossings across the Mexican border.[8]

In June 1906 Congress added the administrative responsibility for naturalization of aliens to the duties of this agency.   It was renamed the Bureau of Immigration and Naturalization (BIN).   In 1907 additional exclusionary laws were enacted to restrict entry of imbeciles, persons with mental defects that would limit their ability to work, persons with tuberculosis, and women coming to the country for immoral purposes. In 1910, legislation was also adopted to suppress white slave traffic (essentially of white women).   In 1914, in a very important step that recognized that there was a fundamental relationship between immigrants and the labor market, BIN was transferred to the newly created U.S. Department of Labor where it remained until 1940.

In the years prior to and following World War I, BIN reported continuing problems with illegal entry but it was not until the passage of the quota laws in 1921 and in 1924 that the issue of illegal entry grew to major proportions.[9]   BIN also brought to the attention of Congress that "a thriving smuggling industry" of illegal immigrants was developing along the Mexican border. This illegal flow involved not only "criminal" elements, "diseased persons," and "Chinese aliens"—all of whom had caused entry problems in the past—but also now included Europeans who were unable to get visas due to national origin quotas as well as Mexicans who were excluded on the grounds of being either illiterate or paupers. In response, Congress created the U.S. Border Patrol in 1924 to augment the enforcement of the immigration laws along the land borders with both Canada and Mexico. During the decade of the 1920s, the numbers of apprehended aliens, deportations, and arrests of smugglers of illegal aliens soared. Despite these efforts, it is widely acknowledged that many persons escaped detection and were successful in their illegal entry attempts.

It is highly probable that most of the illegal immigrants were unskilled workers.   Thus, the data on immigrants in Tables 4.2 and 3.3 should be interpreted as underestimates of both the overall size of the inflow as well as the number of unskilled workers who actually entered the United States in the 1920s.

The Changing Domestic Economy of the 1920s

Aside from the fact that immigration did not immediately come to a halt and that illegal immigration flourished, there was an even more consequential development underway that rendered moot any serious concern over the availability of a supply of unskilled workers. The earlier trend toward urbanization of the population not only continued but accelerated. During the decade of the 1920s, six million persons moved from the rural to the urban sector of the economy. It was the first decade in U.S. history in which the rural population sustained a net loss. The historian Arthur Link has called this internal movement "one of the most important changes in the American social fabric."[10] It was, of course, a harbinger of a trend that would continue over most of the remainder of the twentieth century. The out-migration was part of a long-term decline in the demand for agricultural workers due to the mechanization of much of the work. The reduction in the need for agricultural workers led to a diminished need for other rural workers in local support industries. The pace of rural employment contraction was hastened by the collapse of agricultural prices—especially for crops raised in the Prairie states, the Midwest, and in the South—throughout the 1920s. The depression that was to hit the nation in the 1930s had already begun in these agricultural regions.[11]

The pull factor that attracted the rural workers was the sharp increase in real wages that occurred in these urban industrial centers in the 1920s.[12] In what has been described as "the largest decennial increase up to that time," the annual gain in nonagricultural real wages tripled over the decade.[13] During World War I, the capacity of the nation to produce had been greatly expanded by the requirements of the military. The extensive investments in research and development that had been made by many corporations during World War I began to produce results in the 1920s and enhanced the nation's production expansion still further. Furthermore, much of the manufacturing sector of the economy was in the process of adopting assembly line production techniques—known also as continuous process technology. Although this major advancement in technology had been introduced in the automobile industry just prior to World War I, it was not until the 1920s that it was widely replicated in other mass production industries, such as home appliances, radios, and machinery manufacturing.[14]   As a consequence of these happenings, productivity in manufacturing increased by 40 percent in the 1920s.

Bearing these developments in mind, it is not surprising that for urban America the 1920s were known as "the prosperity decade." The significant increases in productivity and real wages generated an increase in the capacity to consume which, in turn, led to enhanced employment opportunities. The labor force increased by six million workers with all of the increase in employment sustained in the nonfarm sector of the economy. The rapid decline in agricultural employment elevated manufacturing to the position as the nation's largest employment sector. It would retain this status for the next fifty years. Manufacturing employment had expanded in absolute terms during the military buildup phase associated with World War I. But, ironically, during the 1920s the overall level of manufacturing employment remained virtually constant. The stability over this decade, however, masks the fact that the manufacturing sector was in the midst of considerable flux. Significant employment expansion occurred in the manufacturing of electrical appliances, electrical machinery, aviation equipment, and radios while employment contracted in other manufacturing enterprises associated with the production of nonmotorized transportation and nonelectrical appliances. The major growth sectors of the 1920s were construction, wholesale trade, retail trade, finance, and government. The nation's economy was continuing to diversify in terms of the types of jobs it was creating. It was a period when numerous openings were created for entry-level employment opportunities. It was also a time of extremely unbalanced geographic growth in employment. While the rural economy was floundering almost everywhere, large urban communities sustained significant growth and development.

As noted, the major source of new workers responding to the growing needs of the urban economy were people who migrated from the nation's declining rural sector. By far the majority of these workers were white but they also included a substantial number of blacks. As late as 1910, the percentage of the black population living in the South (about 90 percent) was the same as it had been on the eve of the Civil War in 1860. Moreover, in 1910 over two-thirds of the entire black population of 9.8 million people lived in rural areas (almost exclusively in the South). During the decade 1910–1920, there was a net out-migration from the South of 454,000 blacks; during the 1920s it jumped to 749,000 blacks.

One push factor was the collapse of the "cotton culture" of the rural South following the devastation of the cotton crop by the boll weevil.

Planters were forced to diversify their crops, but prices for these new crops generally remained depressed throughout the period. As a result, many blacks were forced to leave the South and seek jobs elsewhere. It was also the case that in the period 1890 to 1920, the South had imposed its comprehensive system of de jure racial segregation (i.e., "Jim Crow" laws) and it was the period when the Ku Klux Klan was reorganized.

But the powerful economic lure of rising real wages in the nonagricultural industries of the Northeast, Midwest, and the West Coast was also of consequence. Blacks joined in the general migration of rural workers to these urban sectors. The significance of the black exodus lay not in its size (which was small compared to the out-migration of rural whites) but rather in the fact that the departure of blacks from the South had finally begun. This trend would continue until the mid-1980s when, as will be discussed later, the return of mass immigration to urban labor markets contributed to the retreat of blacks to the South.[15]

The Actual Cessation of Mass Immigration

It was not just legislation, therefore, that finally brought a halt to the nation's mass immigration experience. It was the onset of the Great Depression in late 1929. With the collapse of employment, wages, and prices in all industrial sectors and geographic regions of the country, the urban attraction of opportunities for jobs and income vanished. As shown in Table 4.1, immigration fell in the 1930s to its lowest levels in over a hundred years. In 1933, only 23,068 persons immigrated to the United States; the number had not been that low since 1829. Even the minimal quotas assigned to the countries of Eastern and Southern Europe were not met during the early 1930s. It is believed that in 1933 more people emigrated than immigrated. Mass unemployment had replaced mass immigration as the labor market issue of the times. With a general labor surplus, there was no need for immigrant workers of any skill capability. Workers who formerly held skilled jobs took unskilled jobs, if they could be found, and unskilled workers were bumped into the ranks of the unemployed or out of the labor-force.[16]

The Emergence of the Refugee Issue

Despite the significant reductions in the scale of immigration throughout the 1930s, immigration policy itself lost none of its controversial aura.

It was in this decade that one of the most perplexing issues—then and now—to confront immigration policymakers emerged. It pertained to the subject of refugee admissions in the context of a ceiling on overall immigration flows.

Prior to the Immigration Act of 1924, there was no need for the United States to be concerned about how it might respond to the needs of persecuted people who wished to flee their homelands. They were generally admitted without question if they could physically get to the United States. But once an immigration ceiling was put into place with specific country quotas and, in some instances, specific bans on entry from certain countries, the era of automatic admission ended. Indeed, the Immigration Act of 1924 contained no provisions for any exceptions to its terms.

In the 1930s when the events in Asia and Europe that would culminate in World War II began, there were people in Japan, Germany, and Italy who feared the actions of their own governments as well as others in neighboring nations who either sensed imminent danger or were actually experiencing the effects of persecution. Many wished to immigrate to the United States—or to any country that would have them.

The United States, having just ended a century of mass immigration and being in the throes of the worst economic collapse in its history, was, understandably, preoccupied with domestic needs. Consequently, as one scholar wrote of this era, "the force of events are surging the pendulum of public opinion so far in the direction of anti-immigration that, unfortunately, we might say that for all practical purposes we have become opposed to immigration on a selective or any other basis."[17]

To be sure, there were many persons who fled their homelands in fear who were able to be admitted under the available quotas. About 250,000 such refugees from the Axis nations or Axis-occupied countries in Europe were admitted to the United States for permanent settlement from 1933 to the outbreak of the war in late 1941. This flow represented about one-half of all of the immigrants to the United States over this time span. About two-thirds of these refugees were Jews but, in all, the refugees came from twenty-one different nations.[18] More would have come but were prohibited from doing so by the restrictions of prevailing policy.

With regard to their characteristics, the European refugees who were admitted represented a sharp departure from the immigrants of the past. By and large, they were people who did not want to leave their countries under normal conditions but now felt they had no choice. They were not from the rural peasant classes as had been the case with most of the "third wave" European immigrants. Instead, they were from the "middle and upper economic classes and included disproportionately large numbers of white-collar workers, professionals, businessmen, and manufacturers. Among the professional groups, the most numerous were physicians, scholars, and scientists."[19] It is not surprising therefore, that the occupations cited by these immigrants of this period showed "professional, managers and administrators" to be the most dominant group—the highest percentage, in fact, in U.S. immigration history up until this time—while, those citing "laborers" as their occupation were the lowest (see Table 4.3 and compare with Table 3.3). Moreover, "most of the refugees were from the larger cities rather than rural villages and towns...and were comparatively well educated, many having attended or been graduated from universities, colleges, or professional or technical schools."[20]

In a real sense, the European refugees of this era were an aberration with respect to their human capital endowments, compared to either those of previous or subsequent immigrant flows. The refugees who were admitted in the 1930s and 1940s (and, as will be discussed, in the 1950s too) came at a time when total immigration was low. This further augments their incidence of consistently high levels of human capital characteristics. Consequently, econometric studies that neglect to note explicitly the unique historical circumstances of this period when they draw comparisons between these immigrant flows and subsequent immigrant flows are distorting the picture of what public policy sought to accomplish.[21]   One could mistakenly conclude that the prevailing "national origins" system of that era was responsible for the high human capital characteristics of the immigrant flow of these decades when, in fact, it had virtually nothing to do with these results in any causative sense. These refugees did not come to the United States because they planned to do so but because they were fleeing persecution. In every sense, most were "involuntary emigrants" from their homelands. Prevailing policy, if it did anything, served to restrict the number who came. It certainly did not seek to encourage them to come.

The War Years: Eliminating Labor Surplus and Creating New Opportunities

As the events in both Europe and Asia that eventually led the United States into World War II became increasingly ominous, the country began to take precautions. In mid-1940, President Franklin Roosevelt began the

Table 4.3 Percent Distribution of Immigrants, By Major Occupation Group At Time of Arrival, Selected Years 1930-1965

Fiscal year	Total	Professional technical, and kindred workers	Farmers and farm managers	Managers officials, and proprietors	Clerical sales, and kindred	Crafts operatives and Kindred	Private household workers	Service workers, exc. private household	Farm laborers and supervisors	Laborers exc. farm and mine	No occupation[1]
1930	241,700	3.6	3.5	1.9	6.0	13.4	12.0	2.8	5.7	7.5	43.7
1933	23,068	7.0	1.3	3.0	2.6	7.9	2.4	4.0	.6	3.8	67.4
1935	34,956	6.4	1.7	3.9	2.9	7.7	4.1	4.0	1.2	3.9	64.3
1940	70,756	9.6	1.2	10.5	6.2	8.1	4.1	1.3	.4	3.0	55.7
1945	38,119	7.5	1.3	3.8	9.7	11.8	3.9	2.7	.6	2.3	56.2
1946	108,721	5.7	.9	3.3	7.7	8.1	2.3	2.0	.2	1.4	68.5
1950	249,187	8.2	7.1	2.6	6.7	16.6	3.6	2.0	1.6	2.3	49.3
1955	237,790	5.9	1.9	2.2	7.6	14.4	5.0	2.7	2.3	7.4	50.7
1965	296,697	9.7	1.0	2.4	10.0	10.7	3.3	3.6	1.0	2.9	55.9

[1] Includes dependent women and children and other aliens without occupation or occupation not reported.

Source: U.S. Department of Labor.

process of rearming the nation. Various committees were established to plan for the possible conversion of domestic industries to military production and for the enlargement of the military services. In the latter months of 1940, funds were appropriated by Congress to accumulate strategic resources, and the military draft was reintroduced. Although most citizens sympathized with the victims of the aggression by Germany, Italy, and Japan, it was not until after Japan attacked Pearl Harbor, Hawaii on December 7, 1941, that the nation actually declared war and the full-scale war mobilization of the economy commenced.

It was fortunate, in a way, that the massive increase in the demand for labor associated with rearmament occurred at time when there was still a significant backlog of unemployed citizens from the lingering effects of the depression. In 1940, the official unemployment rate for the year was 14.6 percent (or 8.1 million unemployed workers). Even a year later, in 1941, the unemployment rate for the year was 9.9 percent, and on the eve of the Pearl Harbor attack there were 5.5 million unemployed workers in the nation. With this number of unemployed persons, the transition to all-out war production was accomplished with far less strain than would have been the case if every worker and soldier had to be taken from the ranks of the employed civilian workforce. Nonetheless, labor shortages quickly developed for particular kinds of jobs and in particular geographic areas.

On the military front, about eighteen million men between the ages of 18 and 35 years old were screened for the military draft and about 11.4 million were actually accepted during the course of the war years. About 700,000 draftees were rejected because they were illiterate; another 600,000 were taken into the military but put into special training programs to achieve literacy before they could actually be trained for combat. Still another 700,000 servicemen were inducted but classified as being on the borderline of
literacy (e.g., they could read the word "fire" but not "danger"; they could sign their names but they could not write a letter).[22]

Of those who were drafted or enlisted, about 60 percent were employed in industry at the time they were inducted or, under normal circumstance, would have been employed in the civilian sector.[23] Not only did they have to be replaced but, with the dramatic expansion of military production to support the war effort, additional sources of home front workers had to be found. President Roosevelt created the War Manpower Commission in April 1942 which, in conjunction with the U.S. Employment Service, was assigned the responsibility for recruiting workers in areas of labor surplus, to advise and aid them in relocating in areas of labor shortage, and to place workers in the most highly skilled jobs for which they were qualified.

Despite the massive withdrawal of millions of men and women from the civilian labor force to enter the armed forces, the civilian labor force still expanded by over five million workers over the course of the war years. This feat was accomplished by tapping existing domestic reserves that, in the past, had been ignored, underutilized, or arbitrarily prevented from developing their employment potential.

The farm sector, which during the 1930s had briefly reversed into downward slide in employment of the 1920s, was an obvious source of underutilized human resources. During the war years farm employment declined by over one million workers while nonfarm civilian employment grew by over six million workers. The percent of the population living in rural areas declined from 43.4 percent in 1940 to 40.4 percent in 1950. As one labor economist observed, "the vacuum created by the wartime demands was sufficient to reach into the most backward areas."[24] The rural South proved to be an especially prolific source and blacks were especially responsive to the new employment opportunities. Indeed, during the decade of the 1940s, there was a net out-migration of 1.6 million blacks from the South to urban areas of the North and the West Coast.

Special efforts were also made to encourage older workers to defer retirements or to entice them back to employment on a full or part-time basis. Likewise, national programs were initiated to assist handicapped workers to be prepared for jobs and to find jobs. Legal exceptions were also made to allow youth, under certain circumstances, to work in industries from which they had been barred during peacetime.

But the major new source of labor reserves to be brought into the paid labor force was women. Over six million women were employed during this period—about four million of whom were added during the war years. The major change in labor force behavior came with the entry of married women in general and white married women in particular into the civilian labor force. Black married women had already been in the labor force in disproportionate numbers relative to white married women. While many women were employed in entry-level occupations, it is also true that many old stereotypes about what types of jobs women could do or could not do were quickly put aside. Among these were notions that women should not work in factory occupations, or in occupations where men were the major proportion of the workers, or in jobs that required arduous physical exertion. "Rosy the Riveter" became a popular national symbol of the patriotic contribution of women to the war effort. It was not a phrase of derision. The roots of the social revolution involving women workers in the workplace that was to explode in the 1970s and 1980s can be traced directly to the precedents established in the 1940s.

It was also in this context that significant public policy steps were initiated to attack the issue of racial discrimination in employment. As Ray Marshall has written, "despite years of hostile racial discrimination by employers and unions, until the Second World War America's governments generally adopted very few measures to counteract discrimination in employment."[25] But when the prospect of war became a reality, tightening labor markets opened up opportunities for government to address this long-neglected aspect of American life. These pioneering governmental initiatives of the 1940s paved the way for the passage of the Civil Rights Act of 1964 with its historic Title VII (i.e., the equal employment provisions) that would come a generation later.

At the federal level, President Roosevelt in September 1940 publicly condemned employment discrimination. This public rebuke of prevailing attitudes and practices was not effective in changing practices. But the following year, on June 12, 1941, Roosevelt issued the President's Nondiscrimination Order in which he advised industry "to take the initiative in opening doors to all loyal and qualified workers regardless of race, national origin, religion, or color." This action is regarded as a milestone in the history of equal employment opportunity.[26]

Black leaders, however, who had been pressuring the President to act on this issue were not satisfied with this gesture. A. Philip Randolph, the president of the Brotherhood of Sleeping Car Porters union and a pioneer civil rights leader, stated that far stronger steps were required. He initiated plans for a protest march on Washington to force stronger action. As the leaders of the nation were openly criticizing the rise of Nazism, in part, for its avowal of racial superiority principles, it would have been a source of national embarrassment if the same charges were made of racial practices in the United States. Consequently, President Roosevelt issued Executive Order 8802 on July 25, 1941, which created a federal Committee on Fair Employment Practices (FEP). It was empowered to investigate employment discrimination in defense industries. Because there was a conservative coalition of Southern Democrats and Northern Republicans in Congress who were adamantly opposed to any legislative action in this policy area, there was no way at the time to pass any legislation at the federal level to address this issue. Consequently, the President's actions were steps as strong as were possible at the time.

This original FEP Committee met widespread resistance as it sought to engineer social change. Indeed, the entire membership of the committee resigned January 1943 in protest at the resistance it encountered. They were replaced in June 1943 by a new committee with a stronger mandate as the result of the issuance of another executive order on the subject. This second FEP committee also met defiance, especially by the companies and unions in the railroad industry, but it also had a number of important pioneering successes. There were also a number of changes in employment practices undertaken voluntarily by the private sector during this period of tight labor markets. When the war ended, congressional opponents succeeded in killing the federal FEP committee by cutting off its funding. In the immediate postwar years, however, twenty-four states passed FEP laws (all in Northern and Western states).

Thus, the era of labor shortages did have the positive effect of at least opening the door for wider job opportunities for racial minorities even though the issue itself was still far from resolved. It can be said, however, that the labor shortages of the World War II period provided the leverage needed to launch the economic plank (i.e., the equal employment opportunity goals) of the broader civil rights agenda that would later come to a head as a full-scale movement in the 1950s and 1960s.

Thus, on the domestic front, the World War II era was a period of full employment. Labor shortages forced the nation to reach out to segments both of the population that had not been previously encouraged to work and to members of the labor force who had been hitherto underutilized or denied opportunities to use and develop their latent human resource abilities. It is true that this task of providing labor market access and opportunities to these subgroups—most of whom were untrained and poorly educated—was greatly facilitated by the nature of most of the jobs that were created. Continuous process remained the basic technology of the era. The military needed vast amounts of standardized products. Steel and wheeled vehicles were the backbone of the military procurement requirements. The automobile industry was the dominant manufacturer of the metal products required by the war effort in almost limitless quantities. Thus, Detroit became "the greatest center of war production."[27] But there were other needs for mass produced items—such as uniforms, food, tents, armaments, and aviation products. Hence other established industrial centers in parts of the Northeast, Midwest, and West Coast also became deeply involved in war production. Normally, the factories previously used for civilian goods were converted to production of military goods but new factory construction also occurred on a huge scale.

Thus, it was the manufacturing industry that sustained the largest increase in employment during the war years. At its high point in 1944, manufacturing had added over six million jobs over its level in 1940. With over seventeen million workers in 1944, manufacturing accounted for 41 percent of the employed nonagricultural labor force of the nation. Prior to this period, the manufacturing sector had not experienced any net increase in employment since 1917–1918 (i.e., since World War I). The other goods-producing industries—mining and construction—sustained absolute decreases in employment during this war period.

Most of the occupations that sustained the greatest growth in the manufacturing industry during the period were in the unskilled and semiskilled categories. While it is true that there were significant advances made in public and private training initiatives and there were extensive efforts made by employers to redesign job requirements so less skilled workers could do them, it remained the case that the applicable technology in manufacturing did not require extensive education, training, or literacy from its workforce. Indeed, the motto of the job recruiters of the Detroit manufacturers who were sent into the rural South during these years for the first time has become legendary: "if he or she is warm and breathing, we hire them." Job credentials could not get any lower. Moreover, most of these manufacturing jobs were unionized and provided good wages, job protections, and fringe benefit packages. They were among the best available for blue-collar workers anywhere in the nation.

The tight labor markets of the war years forced employers and government to look inward to the nation's domestic population and labor force for workers. Market pressures, combined with creative employment policies by the private sector and assisted by a strong prod from the public sector to abandon artificial barriers to employment, proved that there was a viable alternative to mass immigration as a means to find workers in a growing economy.

A Fateful Wartime Shift in Federal Policy Administration

The advent of World War II also served as a pretext for a critical shift in the administrative responsibility for the nation's immigration policy. It has had lasting consequences. As discussed in the previous chapter, immigration policy was assigned to the U.S. Department of Labor (DOL) when this agency was created in 1914. The two immigration functions—administering the immigration laws and supervision of the naturalization of aliens—were performed by two separate bureaus within DOL. On June 10, 1933 President Roosevelt issued Executive Order 6166 that combined both functions into a single agency known ever since as the Immigration and Naturalization Service (INS). It remained within the U.S. Department of Labor.

By the late 1930s, the relationship of immigration to the welfare of U.S. society had come under close scrutiny for a new reason. The prospect of U.S. involvement in a war in Europe raised concern that immigration might be a way for enemy saboteurs and subversive elements to enter the country. Hence, a fateful short-run decision that has had lasting long-run consequences was initiated. On May 20, 1940, President Roosevelt recommended to Congress that INS be shifted from the Department of Labor to the Department of Justice as part of the President's Reorganization Plan No. V.[28] He urged that "quick action" be taken on his request.[29] On June 14, 1920, Congress approved the transfer.[30] In his message to Congress, President Roosevelt stated:

In normal times much can be said for the retention of the Bureau [sic] of Immigration and Naturalization in the Department of Labor where it has long resided... Today however, the nation is confronted with matters relating to aliens in our midst. It is more than necessary to exercise, for national safety, certain measures and controls over aliens, which are not demanded in normal days.[31]

In subsequently published background papers, the specific rationale was explained as follows:

The Immigration and Naturalization Service was originally placed within the Department of Labor because of the historical reason that it was, formerly, mostly concerned with problems pertinent to American labor.

In recent years, however, there has arisen a dangerous threat from abroad in the form of the fifth column and other activities. It seemed expedient, therefore, to transfer the Immigration and Naturalization Service to the Department of Justice in order to cope with this danger as a matter of national defense.[32]

It is of consequence to note that the original draft of this Presidential Message concluded with the following sentence which the President crossed out in his own writing before issuing the formal message:

After these days of emergencies have passed, the Congress can and should, of course, consider whether the Bureau [sic] of Immigration and Naturalization should remain in the Department of Justice or be returned to the jurisdiction of the Department of Labor.[33]

In the place of this sentence, a sentence is written in his own handwriting in which President Roosevelt simply urges "quick action" on his recommendation.   Why Roosevelt struck out the above sentence is unknown. It may have been that he just wished to shorten the message and not raise the issue of later reflection on the wisdom of the decision. It is known, however, that the Attorney General Robert H. Jackson opposed the idea of making this shift to his agency and that the Bureau of the Budget was not consulted about the actual change until after it was about to be made public.[34]   The Secretary of Labor, Frances Perkins, however, strongly favored the move. As she wrote in her autobiography:

I had been recommending for five years that the Immigration Service be taken out of the Department of Labor and put in some more appropriate place. During the war the opportunity came to do this. Because the main problems of immigration during the war period were the recognition and apprehension of spies and foreign agents, it seemed appropriate to move it to the Department of Justice near the FBI. The Immigration Service had for many years swamped the Labor Department. Immigration problems usually have to be decided in a few days. They involve human lives. There can be no delaying. In almost every administration the Secretary and his principal assistant had functioned chiefly in the immigration field. That is, I think, one of the reasons there had been, until the New Deal, so much neglect of the true function of the Labor Department.[35]

Apparently, it was the work burden placed on her agency that caused her to favor this critical administrative change. She suggests that these functions were overshadowing the chronic need for the Department of Labor to address the urgent employment, collective bargaining, and work standards issues confronting the nation's labor force. Thus, she felt the

Department of Justice was not the appropriate permanent home for this vital responsibility as indicated by the following retrospective thoughts:

> The President decided to transfer the Immigration Service to Justice for the duration of the war. Whether that is the appropriate place for it in years to come has not been decided. I doubt that it is. It deals with human affairs and, I should say, is more properly related to the Federal Security Agency or the Department of the Interior. It should not be a permanent function of the Labor Department or the Department of Justice, and certainly not of the FBI.[36]

When the war ended, however, there was no effort made to return INS to DOL or to shift it anywhere else. It has remained in the Department of Justice ever since.

There are multiple reasons why the Department of Justice is an inappropriate agency to oversee immigration policy. To begin with, the Department of Justice consists of a dozen or so major governmental divisions (e.g., criminal justice, civil rights, and antitrust), all pleading for attention from the U.S. Attorney General. In this context, immigration matters have tended to be neglected or relegated to a low order of priority. Moreover, the Department of Justice is the most politically sensitive of all federal agencies. When confronted with politically expedient solutions, it often makes decisions that overlook long-term consequences. With regard to immigration matters, this agency has seldom manifested interest in the economic effects of immigration policy, nor has it ever seen fit to establish any ongoing research program to monitor the influences of immigration on the labor market or the economy. Moreover, the statistical data on immigration that it generates are primarily designed to meet administrative purposes rather than to serve analytical needs.

An important ancillary administrative consequence of the shift of the INS to the Justice Department was that the Senate and House judiciary committees gained the responsibility for formulating immigration policy and for overseeing immigration affairs. Traditionally, membership on these committees has been reserved almost exclusively for lawyers. The result is that immigration law in the United States has become obsessively complex and procedurally protracted. It also has meant that immigration lawyers and consultants have found a flourishing business—a "honey pot"—in the intricacies of immigration law. In this legalistic atmosphere that typically focuses on individual situations, the broader economic considerations that affect the collective welfare of society have seldom become a concern.

The Wartime Exception: The Use of Foreign Workers in Agriculture and its Postwar Legacy

With the approach of World War II, growers in the Southwest anticipated that there would be a worker shortage in the region's labor intensive agricultural industry. Even before the Pearl Harbor attack, growers lobbied the federal government to meet their anticipated needs by allowing them to tap the supply of cheap farm labor available in Mexico.[37] A precedent had been set during World War I whereby the federal government had authorized such a temporary worker program. The growers were optimistic that a request for a similar program would be approved if they agitated for it.[38] Their initial petition, however, was denied in 1941 but the next year the government reversed its position in the wake of changing world events. In August 1942, following bilateral negotiations between the governments of the United States and Mexico, legislation was adopted that created the Mexican Labor Program. It is more popularly known as "the *bracero* program" (a term that literally means "one who works with his hands"; the word is a corruption of the Spanish word "brazos" which means "arms").

The growers argued that, with both the military draft and the expansion of the nation's manufacturing sector to fill war contracts, the southwestern agriculture industry could not retain or attract a sufficient number of unskilled workers to feed the nation. It is of consequence to note that the legislation that authorized the program, P.L. 45, was part of an omnibus appropriation bill. It was not an amendment to the nation's immigration statutes. Indeed, the recruited workers were not immigrants—they were workers who were legally allowed to be employed temporarily in the United States even though they were foreign nationals. After the growing and harvest season was over each year they were expected to return to Mexico. In the parlance of immigration policy, they were known as "nonimmigrant workers." In the case of the *braceros*, they could only work in agricultural jobs. The legislation specified that they were to be afforded specific protection with respect to transportation, housing, meals, medical care, and wage rates. P.L. 45 authorized the program's continuance until the war ended. It was subsequently extended by law for two more years until 1947 and was continued informally, without regulation, until 1951 when it was again formally reauthorized during the Korean Conflict by P.L. 78. This law, in turn, was extended after the war ended in 1953 on three separate occasions by Congress until it was finally terminated unilaterally by the United States at the end of 1964. Thus, what was supposed to be a temporary wartime measure ended by lasting twenty-two years. Indeed, the years in which it had the largest number of participants—when it averaged almost one-half million farm workers a year in the late 1950s—were years when peace prevailed.[39]

Without going into a prolonged discussion of the controversial program, it is important to note that the program was continually immersed in charges that U.S. employers did not honor their commitments. They did employ the Mexican workers but they often ignored or circumvented the labor protection and wage rate provisions.[40] There were also numerous charges of corruption—in the form of kickbacks and favoritism—in the selection process by government officials in Mexico.

The extension of the *bracero* program beyond the dates of its original mission as a temporary wartime measure resulted in its becoming a subject of extensive political controversy. The availability of *bracero* workers exerted a narcotic effect on the agricultural employers of the Southwest. They became addicted to cheap Mexican labor that entered under contractual terms that bound the *braceros* to work for them or be returned directly to their homeland. The effect of the program on citizen workers was to reduce agricultural worker wages levels in some localities; to moderate wage increases that would have occurred in the program's absence; and to shorten the duration of seasonal employment.[41] In essence, the program functioned as a public subsidy to the private agricultural sector. For this reason, it came under protracted criticism from the American Federation of Labor—Congress of Industrial Organization (AFL-CIO), various Mexican American citizen groups, and an array of other organizations who were empathetic with the plight of low-income citizen workers. It was not until the Kennedy Administration took office in 1961 that sufficient political support could be garnered to terminate the program. In response to a plea from the Mexican government, it was agreed to phase the program out gradually. On December 31, 1964 it ceased to exist. But, as will be discussed later, the program had served to expose a substantial number of rural Mexican workers to the U.S. labor market. Thus, when the program ended, its effects did not. Many former *braceros* simply kept coming—albeit as illegal immigrants after 1964.

Paralleling the Mexican Labor Program in the Southwest was a similar program known as the British West Indies Program (BWI) along the East Coast. Also initiated as a temporary wartime measure, it was the product of intergovernmental agreements negotiated between the United States and the governments of Jamaica, the Bahamas, St. Lucia, St. Vincent, Dominica, and Barbados that were signed in April 1943. The BWI program was also created in response to concerns voiced by employers in East Coast states that they too were experiencing labor shortages for unskilled workers—especially in agriculture. But as these employers were generally unfamiliar with Spanish, they needed English-speaking workers. The surplus of black workers on the islands of the British West Indies provided a convenient labor supply to tap.

Originally, the BWI program was authorized under the same legislation as the *bracero* program, namely, P.L. 45. But when P.L. 45 ended in 1947, the BWI program was converted into a temporary worker program as authorized under the Immigration Act of 1917 to meet emergency situations.[42] The BWI program, because its scale was much smaller than the bracero program, never attracted the same amount of scrutiny. It was however, criticized for its abuse by employers of its worker protection provisions.[43] There were also consistent charges of favoritism and corruption in the selection process by the officials on the Islands. At its height in 1945, it supplied 19,391 workers. Most were employed in agriculture—especially in Florida—but there were also instances during the war years when BWI workers were permitted to work in some nonagricultural occupations. In 1951, when the bracero program was reconstituted under P.L. 78, the East Coast employers requested not to be included in its *ad hoc* authorization because it functioned outside of the immigration statutes. They wanted a program that would be less subject to quick termination. The following year, they got what they sought. Congress passed the Immigration and Nationality Act of 1952. (This legislation will be discussed in greater detail in the next chapter). Among its multiple features was a new provision (Section H-2) that created a nonimmigrant category for the admission of temporary unskilled foreign workers (popularly called "H-2 workers"). The BWI program was subsumed under this section of the new immigration law where it has continued to function to this day (although since 1986, the agricultural workers from foreign countries have been separated from other nonimmigrant temporary workers into a new category and are now referred to as "H-2A workers"). In the process of authorizing such temporary worker programs within the immigration statutes, the Immigration and Nationality Act repealed the Alien Contract Act of 1885 which had banned such arrangements.

The Postwar Prosperity and Low Levels of Immigration

With the end of the World War II in 1945 there were dire predictions by some scholars and policymakers that the anticipated massive reductions in military spending would lead to a return of another era of mass unemployment. It did not happen. To the contrary, the nation entered into a period of unprecedented economic prosperity that, with the exception of a short recession in the late 1950s, extended over the next twenty-five years. The pent-up demand and the forced savings by consumers that occurred during the war years led to a veritable explosion in consumer spending when the war was over. In addition, fully one-third of the nation's population moved up into the middle class during the 1940s which brought additional demand for durable goods. The return of the troops also resulted in a "baby boom" that would last into the early 1960s, adding further fuel to the mounting tide of consumer spending. In the short run, the Servicemen's Readjustment Act of 1944 (the so-called "G.I. Bill") provided funds for veterans to enter training and education programs rather than to immediately seek to reenter the labor force. Over seven million veterans availed themselves of the opportunities provided by this historic human resource development program. Also, of course, the outbreak of the Cold War in Europe between the Soviet Union and the Western democracies in the late 1940s, as well as the three-year war in Korea in the early 1950s, meant that the anticipated major reductions in defense spending did not materialize. Indeed, the opposite occurred. Defense spending rose and the military draft of young men was continued in peacetime for the first time in U.S. history.

The complacency of the nation that was bred by this prolonged period of postwar prosperity was, however, severely shaken in 1957 when the Soviet Union successfully launched the world's first space orbiting satellite, Sputnik I. The adequacy of the nation's education system was immediately called into question. The preparation of students and the quality of teaching in mathematics and sciences were found to be seriously wanting. In the name of national defense, the federal government enacted pathbreaking legislation in 1958 to provide funds for higher education to prepare teachers and to assist students seeking careers in these fields. A new era of technology—based on the use of the computer and the principles of automatic control—was dawning. As will be discussed in Chapter 7, entirely new demands would be made on the preparation of the labor supply. There were other indications in the late 1950s that the structure of the economy was changing and that there might be difficult adjustments for workers in the future but the signals were not altogether clear at the time.[44]

It was also in 1957 that another social major event began to unfold that would have lasting consequences on U.S. society and its labor force. It began when Rosa Parks, a black woman in Montgomery, Alabama, refused any longer to sit in the back rows of a public bus as required by state law. This simple act of defiance, along with the ensuing consumer boycott led by Rev. Martin Luther King, ignited the civil rights movement in the heart of the Old Confederacy. Initially, it was focused on social and political treatment of blacks in the South. But in short order it moved to the national level, spread to include economic concerns, and was joined by other racial and ethnic groups as well as by women in a full-scale assault on inequality of opportunity throughout society and the workforce. This movement quickly revealed that the nation had huge reservoirs of human talent that remained marginalized or excluded from the development of their human resource abilities. It would not be until the mid-1960s, however, that this movement and its goals would finally make it to the top of the nation's domestic political agenda.

Against this postwar backdrop of unprecedented general prosperity along with the gradual revelation that the *status quo* was being undermined by major international, technological, and social changes, immigration slumbered in a state of relative dormancy. As shown in Table 4.2 the aggregate level of immigration from the mid-1940s to the late 1960s rose only to the low levels of the late 1920s. As discussed earlier, it had fallen well below the legally permissible levels in the 1930s and early 1940s.

The low levels of immigration in the postwar era, however, do not mean that controversy over immigration policy had abated. To the contrary, immigration policy was under virtually constant attack throughout this period. The criticisms, however, were not directed at the limits on the level of immigration. There were few who wished for a return to the unregulated days of pre-1924 mass immigration. Rather, the focus of attention was on the discriminatory screening restrictions and differing ethnic quotas that affected the composition of the immigrant flow.

By far the most immediate conflict in the postwar years between the prevailing immigration policy and the national interest dealt again with the quandary of refugees. As noted earlier in this chapter, the Immigration Act of 1924 made no provision for refugees or for any exceptions to its terms. When the war ended in 1945, the refugee issue, rather than abating, worsened. There were millions of Europeans who had been displaced from their native countries during the years of conflict. Since many had come from Eastern European nations that were now being taken over by communist governments, a large number of these refugees refused to return to their homelands. Moreover, the wartime refugees were soon joined by many others who were continuing to flee from these same Eastern European countries. The Western European nations, however, had themselves been devastated by the war. They were in no position to absorb or to support such an enormous and growing refugee population while they simultaneously sought to reconstruct their economies.

In this situation, it was imperative that the United States take some humanitarian action to relieve the human suffering. Its immigration laws, however, had not changed and there was no political expectation that they would be.[45] President Harry Truman felt compelled to act so he bent the letter of the law while adhering to its spirit. In December 1945, he ordered that 80,000 refugees mostly from Eastern and Southern European countries be admitted to the United States. He accomplished this feat by using the accumulation of unfilled quota slots that these countries had not used during the war years. Truman was then successful in having the Displaced Persons Act of 1948 passed, which admitted another 205,000 refugees originally from Eastern European nations. It was the first refugee legislation in the nation's history. This legislation also stretched the intentions of the existing immigration law by allowing these countries, which mostly had low annual immigration quotas, to mortgage one half of their future admission slots for various numbers of subsequent years for a large number of immediate admissions. In the long run, the ethnic composition of the nation that the national origins law sought to protect would not be altered. In 1950 and 1951 the Displaced Persons Act was amended again to admit another 188,542 European refugees under essentially the same entry arrangement.

There were, however, only so many such contortions of existing immigration policy that could be performed. The refugee problem was one of the reasons that President Truman pressed Congress to overhaul the nation's immigration system. Ultimately, when Congress did respond with the Immigration and Nationality Act of 1952, Truman was forced to veto it because it did not make any allowances for refugee admission and it did not repeal the national origins system that controlled the ethnic composition of admissions. Truman had supported a move for comprehensive reform but Congress, as will be discussed in the next chapter, had responded with only minor changes. All of the major policy problems remained unresolved.

As a consequence, the only other option for addressing the refugee issue would be to seek special legislation to admit refugees outside normal immigration channels. This, in fact, is what the Eisenhower Administration did in 1953. The Refugee Relief Act of 1953 authorized the admission of 215,000 refugees from Europe and China (the Nationalist Chinese government had been defeated in 1949 by communist forces which had formed the People's Republic of China). Likewise, in 1956 another flow of refugees poured out of Hungary after the Soviet Union sent troops into the country to suppress a civilian uprising. As urgent action was required, President Dwight Eisenhower introduced yet a new twist to refugee admission policy: the Immigration and Nationality Act of 1952 contained a provision that authorized the Attorney General to "parole" persons for admission to the United States for "emergent reasons" that were in the "public interest." The parole authority was never intended to be used for the admission of groups of persons and there was never any intentions that it be used to admit refugees. But in the continuing tradition of creative *ad hoc* responses to the refugee issue, Eisenhower used this loophole to admit 21,500 Hungarian refugees in 1956 and another 10,000 such persons in 1958. The use of the parole authority clearly stretched the intentions of the law and it greatly added to the discretionary powers of the presidency.

In early 1959, following the successful overthrow of the Cuban dictator Fulgencio Battista by revolutionary forces led by Fidel Castro, there was an immediate exodus of Battista supporters from the island—mostly to the United States. By the Spring of 1959, Castro had made known the fact that he was not only replacing the Battista regime but intended to create a Marxist socialist state. Private property was confiscated and political trials were initiated. As a direct consequence, there was a mass departure of middle and upper economic class members. Those Cubans who were able to make it to the United States were given paroles by the

Attorney General that allowed them to remain. Over 65,000 Cubans were given paroles by the Eisenhower and Kennedy Administrations before Cuba halted travel between the two countries in 1962.

In 1960, under the United Nation's banner of "World Refugee Year," a concerted effort was made to finally close the refugee camps in Europe that still contained refugees from World War II and that had been swelled by "refugee escapees" from the Iron Curtain countries of Eastern Europe since then. Under this legislation, Congress authorized the Attorney General to use the parole authority to admit another 19,700 persons to meet this particular situation. Similarly, in 1962, the same procedures were used to parole 15,000 Chinese refugees who had fled to Hong Kong for admission to the United States.

By the early 1960s, it was obvious that the refugee issue was not a temporary problem; that it was not confined to developments in Europe; and that the prevailing U.S. immigration policy had to come to grips with this issue in a legislative manner. *Ad hoc* remedies could not be applied indefinitely to what had become an ongoing occurrence.

In terms of their human capital characteristics the post–World War II refugees of the 1945–1962 period essentially replicated the characteristics of the refugees admitted to the United States prior to and during World War II. The postwar displaced persons from Europe were also disproportionately from the professional, technical, managerial, and business occupations. Such was generally the case for many of the Chinese and most of the Hungarians.[46] Likewise, the Cuban refugees of the 1959 to 1962 period have been called the "golden exiles" because of the high levels of education and skills they brought to the United States with them.[47]

The relatively high human capital endowments of the refugees in the 1945–1962 era and their large numbers (about one million people) exerted a disproportionate effect on the characteristics of the total immigrant flow of this period. This is because between 1945 and 1952 only about one-third of the available quota slots of the legal immigration system were actually used, as were only about 60 percent in the period from 1952 to 1965. When it is recalled that the legal system was distorted in favor of Western European immigrants, it can be seen that the combined effect of the legal immigrants and the refugee flows further skewed in an upward direction the human capital characteristics of the 1950, 1960, and, 1970 cohorts of immigrant admissions. The fact that the immigrants and especially the refugees of this period were generally skilled and well educated meant that the adjustment to the U.S. labor market was relatively easy. Learning the English language was often a problem that took time to overcome. Once English was acquired, however, most already had the skills, talents, and work experience that were commensurate with the needs of the labor market. It is also true, of course, that the unemployment levels in these postwar years were relatively low when compared to the higher rates of the 1970s, 1980s, and early 1990s, which no doubt facilitated their locating jobs. The occupational data for those admitted during these postwar years were similar to those of immigrants of the 1930s and 1940s but they too represented a very sharp departure from the occupational characteristics of the pre-1924 waves of immigration (see Table 4.3). The unique methods of admitting the postwar immigrants—mostly outside the provisions of the legal immigration system—also complicate the interpretations of econometric studies that purport to compare these decennial cohorts of immigrants with those who came before or after and relate the results to prevailing immigration policies.[48]

Summary Observations

The rapid decline in the level of immigration from the late 1920s through to the late 1960s provided the opportunity for the nation to look internally to unused and underused subgroups of the population to draw upon for its labor force needs. During this lengthy period, the economy was confronted with periods of mass unemployment (the 1930s), full employment (the 1940s), and unprecedented prosperity (most of the 1950s and early 1960s).

While the aggregate demand for labor fluctuated over these years, human capital requirements to secure available jobs did not appreciably change until the late 1950s. The goods-producing industries, with their extensive blue-collar occupational structure, dominated the labor market needs for most of this period. Only by the late 1950s were there signs that the requirements for labor were changing, but at the time there was no consensus yet as to whether the new patterns reflected long-term structural shifts or were merely short-term cyclical swings.

On the labor supply side of the equation, however, this forty-year period witnessed a major departure from the past. For the first time in over one hundred years, the nation had to rely on the domestic labor supply to respond to employer needs. As a consequence, subgroups of the population who had been previously underutilized, ignored, or purposely excluded from participation in the labor market became utilized, sought after, and included. It was not a utopian period in which the changes occurred without resistance, hostility, or hardship. But the combination of events and circumstances created a climate for change and it was seized. In later years, these changes would become institutionalized features of the nation's labor force characteristics and its related public policies. Perhaps these changes would have eventually occurred without the reduction in mass immigration that occurred over this timespan but that is a philosophic question for idle speculation. The reality is that, with immigration levels sharply reduced from all previous experience, women, minorities, disabled persons, older persons, youth, and rural migrants did enter occupations and industries as well as move to geographical areas where they had not been present before.

It was also in this context that conscientious efforts to develop the employability of the nation's actual and potential labor force were launched. Public and private investments in human resource development were initiated on a scale not previously experienced.

Although there were serious ethical and political problems with the nature of the nation's immigration laws in this era, the low levels of immigration were highly appropriate to the national interest. There was no need for immigrants in the depression economy of the 1930s and, even when labor markets tightened in the 1940s, it was time for the nation to turn its attention toward previously excluded and underutilized segments of the domestic population. Black Americans, in particular, but also other excluded or marginalized groups needed a chance to enter the workforce and to develop their latent human resource abilities. Likewise, it was also in the national interest that the lengthy period of a generally pauperized and unskilled labor force associated with the initial building phase of the nation came to an end. For on the horizon lay the era of postindustrialism when the quality rather than quantity of labor inputs would become the first requirements for a new stage of economic development.

Notes

1. Kingsley, Davis and Clarence Senior, "Immigration from the Western Hemisphere," *Annuals of the American Academy of Political and Social Science* (March,1949), pp. 70-81.
2. Ibid., pp. 77-79.
3. Ibid., p. 75.

4. Harry E. Cross and James A. Sandos, *Across the Border: Rural Development in Mexico and Recent Migration to the United States* (Berkeley, Cal.: Institute of Governmental Studies, 1981), p. 10.

5. Carey McWilliams, *North from Mexico* (New York: Greenwood Press, 1986), p. 175.

6. Arthur F. Corwin and Lawrence A. Cardoso, "Vamos al Norte: Causes of Mass Mexican Migration to the United States," in *Immigrants—and Immigrants: Perspectives on Mexican Labor Migration to the United States,* ed. Arthur F. Corwin (Westport, Conn.: Greenwood Press, 1978), p. 46.

7. Cross and Sandos, op. cit, p. 10.

8. U.S. Congress, Senate Committee on the Judiciary, "History of the Immigration and Naturalization Service," Report (96th Congress, 2nd Sess.) (Washington, D.C.: U.S. Government Printing Office, 1980), p. 13.

9. Ibid., p. 36 ff.

10. Arthur S. Link, *American Epoch* (New York: Alfred A. Knopf, 1956), p. 297.

11. Robert D. Patton, *The American Economy* (Chicago: Scott Foresman and Co., 1953), pp. 292-294.

12. Stanley Lebergott, *Manpower in Economic Growth,* (New York: McGraw-Hill, 1964), p. 163.

13. Link, op. cit, p. 302.

14. Walter Buckingham, *Automation: Its Impact on Business and People* (New York: Mentor Books, 1961), p. 18.

15. See Felicity Barringer, "Percentage of Blacks in South Rose in 1980s, *New York Times* (January 10, 1990), p. A-21; "Blacks on Move to South," *Syracuse Post-Standard* (January 10, 1990), p. A-1; and Vernon M. Briggs, Jr., "Immigration Policy Sends Blacks Back to South," *New York Times* (February 1, 1990), p. A-22.

16. See David Shannon, *The Great Depression* (Englewood Cliffs, N.J.: Prentice Hall, Inc., 1960) and Irving Bernstein, "Unemployment in the Great Depression," *The Social Welfare Forum* (New York: Columbia University Press, 1959), pp. 39-48.

17. Collis Stocking, "Adjusting Immigration Requirement to Manpower Requirements: *Annals of the American Academy of Political and Social Science* (March, 1949), p. 113.

18. Maurice Davie and Samual Kolnig, "Adjustment of Refugees to American Life," ibid., pp. 159-165.

19. Ibid., p. 160.

20. Ibid.

21. E.g., see George J. Borgas, "Immigrants in the U.S. Labor Market: 1940-80," *American Economic Review* (May 1991), pp. 287-291. For a more complete discussion of the evolution of U.S. refugee policy, see Vernon M. Briggs, Jr., *Immigration Policy and the American Labor Force* (Baltimore: Johns Hopkins University Press, 1984), Chapter 6.

22. Eli Ginzberg, *Manpower Agenda for America* (New York: McGraw-Hill Book Company, 1968), p. 12.

23. Joseph G. Rayback, *A History of American Labor* (New York: The Free Press, 1966), p. 375.

24. Garth L. Mangum, *The Emergence of Manpower Policy* (New York: Holt, Rinehart, and Winston, Inc., 1969).

25. Ray Marshall, *The Negro and Organized Labor* (New York, John Wiley and Sons, Inc. 1965), p. 211.

26. Philip Taft, *Organized Labor in American History* (New York: Harper Row, Publishers, 1964), p. 545.

27. Patton, op. cit, pp. 330.

28. Message to Congress from the President of the United States (May 20, 1940), The White House, p. 1. [Note: The President misidentifies the agency as the "Bureau of Immigration and Naturalization" in this message].

29. White House News Release, May 22, 1940, p. 2.

30. 54 Stat. 230.

31. Message..., op. cit., p. 1.

32. *Public Papers and Addresses of Franklin D. Roosevelt, 1940* (New York: McMillan Co., 1941), p. 229.

33. Message..., op. cit., p. 1. [Draft copy of the official message contained in the Franklin D. Roosevelt Library, Hyde Park, New York].

34. Letter from Attorney General Robert H. Jackson to the President (February 9, 1940). [Letter on file at the Franklin D. Roosevelt Library, Hyde Park, New York] and "Memorandum For The President" January 9, 1944 from James Rowe, Jr. asking for clarification for the reasons for the shift for the purpose of historical explanation for the *Public Papers* volume cited in footnote 32 [Memo on file in the Franklin D. Roosevelt Presidential Library, Hyde Park, New York].

35. Frances Perkins, *The Roosevelt I Knew* (New York: The Viking Press, 1946), pp. 360-361.

36. Ibid. p. 361 [Note: The Federal Security Agency to which she refers was created to administer domestic programs for the health and

welfare of the citizenry. It later achieved Cabinet status as the Department of Health, Education and Welfare during the Eisenhower Administration].

37. Ernesto Galarza, *Merchants Labor: The Mexican Bracero Story* (Charlotte, N.C.: McNally and Loftin 1964), and McWilliams, op. cit., *North from Mexico.*

38. George C. Kiser and Martha W. Kiser, *Mexican Workers in the United States: Historical and Political Perspectives* (Albuquerque: University of New Mexico Press, 1979).

39. See Briggs, *Immigration Policy...*, op. cit., pp. 98-102.

40. See Galarza, Chapters 12, 13, 15, 16 and 17.

41. U.S. Congress, Senate Committee on the Judiciary, *A Report on Temporary Worker Programs: Background and Issues* (Washington, D.C.: U.S. Government Printing Office 1980), pp. 47-51 and President's Commission on Migratory Labor, *Migratory Labor in American Agriculture: Report* (Washington, D.C.: U.S. Government Printing Office, 1951).

42. For details, see Briggs, Immigration Policy..., op. cit, pp. 97-98 and 102-103.

43. President's Commission,... op. cit, p. 58.

44. See U.S. Senate, Special Committee on Unemployment Problems, Report (86th Congress, 2nd Sess.), (Washington, D.C.: U.S. Government Printing Office, 1960).

45. For a more complete discussion of refugee policy evolution in this period, see Briggs, *Immigration Policy...*, op. cit, Chapter 6.

46. Julia V. Taft, David S. North, and David A. Ford, *Refugee Resettlement in the U.S.: Time for a New Focus* (Washington, D.C.: New TransCounty Foundation, 1979), p. 56.

47. Robert L. Bach, "The New Cuban Immigrants: Their Background and Prospects," *Monthly Labor Review,* October 1980, pp. 39-46.

48. E.g., see Borjas, op. cit.; and George J. Borjas, *Friends or Strangers: The Impact of Immigrants on the U.S. Economy* (New York: Basic Books, Inc. Publishers, 1990), Chapters 6 and 7.

FIVE

The Redesign of Immigration Policy in the 1960s: Replacing Social Goals with Political Goals

The protracted controversy over refugee admissions in the years preceding, during, and following World War II served to highlight the most onerous provisions of the Immigration Act of 1924: its inflexibility and its overly discriminatory provisions. Times were changing but immigration policy was not. Immigration policy in the early 1960s represented a classic example of how institutional practices, enacted in a bygone era, become completely out of step with the needs of a later period. As Thorstein Veblen has so aptly described this social phenomenon, "institutions are the products of the past process, are adapted to past circumstances, and are, therefore, never in full accord with the requirements of the present."[1]

The United States had emerged from World War II not only with its production capabilities unscathed while those of all other industrial powers had been devastated, but also with its production capacity enormously expanded. As the result of the extensive investment in research and development work that took place during the war, the nation's technology was in the vanguard of virtually every field of scientific inquiry. Given these advantageous circumstances as well as the power of its assembled military might, the United States found itself in the position of being the most politically, economically, and militarily influential nation in the world.

It was from this perspective of international leadership that President Harry Truman viewed immigration reform as a national imperative. Despite his best efforts, however, Congress refused to make major changes. Likewise, the Eisenhower and Kennedy Administrations were similarly stymied in their quests to overhaul the nation's immigration system. It remained for President Lyndon Johnson to accomplish this monumental feat with the enactment of the Immigration Act of 1965. The goal of this new legislation was to end the national origins admissions system; it was not to increase the level of immigration. But its passage triggered a series of events over the ensuing years that have served to revive the phenomenon of mass immigration. For this reason, it is critical to understand what was intended before turning attention to what actually occurred.

False Start: The McCarran-Walter Act

The Great Depression and World War II caused a greater reduction in the levels of annual immigration than even the advocates of the Immigration Act of 1924 had sought. From the time (1929) that the national origins quotas were formally put into place, until 1949, only 27 percent of the available quotas were actually used. Even with the inclusion of the nonquota immigrants from the Western Hemisphere who entered during this period, the total immigration for the period was only 75 percent of what the overall quota permitted. Given the considerable emigration that also occurred—especially in the 1930s, net immigration averaged only about 22,000 a year over this entire timespan. Immigration had ceased to be a prominent feature of the American economy. Indeed, its significance diminished with each passing year. But the low level of immigration was not the issue that bothered reformers. Rather, it was the fact that the ethnic and racial discrimination of the national origins admission system was distorting both the composition of the immigrant stream and the actual administration of the entire immigration system. Some countries, like Great Britain, which was entitled to 42 percent of all the visas that could be issued in any one year, had many unused quota slots each year. Other countries with very low quotas, like Italy and Greece, accumulated massive backlogs of applicants. Still other nations, like some of those in Asia, were precluded from sending any immigrants despite the significant interest of people from these countries in coming to the United States. Supporters of reform, both in the Truman Administration and in Congress, as well as those in the general populace, felt that it was time for the nation to move away from an admission system based on ethnic and racial selectivity. They favored a system based both on humanitarian principles, designed to assist those persons actually confronted with a threat of political persecution, and on the potential human resource contributions that immigrants could make to the nation's labor market. In other words, they wanted to see an immigration policy designed to meet defined national interests.

In response to President Truman's initiative, the Senate conducted a study of the immigration system in 1947 and, based on its findings, issued a report in April 1950.[2] Prepared by its Committee on the Judiciary, the Senate report dismissed most of the goals that were favored by the Truman Administration and other proponents of reform. Instead, the report argued essentially for the maintenance of the *status quo* with respect to the character of the admission system. It stated that "without giving credence to any theory of Nordic superiority, the Committee believes that the adoption of the national origins quota formula was a rational and logical method of numerically restricting immigration in such a manner as to best preserve the sociological and cultural balance of the United States."[3] Thus, the Committee dismissed the very issue that most reformers sought to make the core of legislative reform.

The subsequent legislation adopted by Congress was the Immigration and Nationality Act of 1952 (also known as the McCarran-Walter Act). It was enacted by Congress over a veto by President Truman. The new law perpetuated the national origins system and the prevailing ceiling on immigration from the Eastern Hemisphere. It did, however, make important modifications with respect to Asian immigration. All of the exclusions against Asian immigration were eliminated and the countries of that vast region were each given a small annual quota (plus permission for admission of immediate relatives).

To accommodate these additions, the Eastern Hemisphere ceiling was raised to 156,700 admissions a year. But several restrictive provisions for administering these new quotas were retained (e.g., Asian immigrants were charged against the quota of the country designated as the person's ancestral nation and not against the nation of birth as was the case with non-Asian immigrants from other Eastern Hemisphere nations). Thus, with respect to admission eligibility and the annual admission level, the Act was essentially a reaffirmation of the selective and restrictive policy principles that had been in effect since the 1920s.

But the Senate committee's report and the subsequent legislation also raised a new concern that communists might use the immigration system to infiltrate the country. It was, after all, a time when the Cold War was in its arctic-blast phase. The Iron Curtain had only recently fallen across Eastern Europe; the Soviet Union had blockaded Berlin for almost a year (from mid-1948 to mid-1949); the Nationalist government in China had fallen in 1949; and the United States was again at war, this time in Korea against the communist-led nations of North Korea and the People's Republic of China. It is not surprising, therefore, that the new legislation added membership in the Communist Party to the list of exclusionary categories that applied to all would-be immigrants and nonimmigrants. Thus, the hesitancy to make major changes was, in part, due to the political environment of the era. As Robert Devine has described the Act, it was "in essence, an act of conservatism rather than of intolerance."[4]

President Truman was infuriated by the unwillingness of Congress to enact a reform measure commensurate with the nation's emerging international leadership responsibilities. In his veto message, he stated:

The countries of Eastern Europe have fallen under the Communist yoke—they are silenced, fenced off by barbed wire and minefields—no one passes their borders but at the risk of his life. We do not need to be protected against immigrants from these countries—on the contrary we want to stretch out a helping hand, to save those who have managed to flee into Western Europe, to succor those who are brave enough to escape from barbarism, to welcome and restore them against the day when their countries will, as we hope, be free again....These are only a few examples of the of the absurdity, the cruelty of carrying over into this year of 1952 the isolationist limitations of our 1924 law.[5]

Nevertheless, Congress responded by overriding his veto by substantial margins in both the House of Representatives and the Senate.

Although the new law made only minor changes in the quotas, it made major changes in how priorities were assigned to those who were admitted. To be precise, it introduced a preference system to distribute visas within the quota allotments assigned to each country. Four categories were established and placed in order of significance. The first category, and highest preference, was for immigrants with levels of education, technical training, special experience, or exceptional abilities that were deemed by the Attorney General to be of benefit to the United States. By creating this category, Congress gave official recognition to the idea that immigration policy could be used as a human resource instrument to select immigrants on the basis of their training and in accordance with the needs of the nation's labor market. Half of all the visas were to be granted on this basis. The other three admission criteria assigned priorities to various categories of adult family relatives of citizens or permanent-resident aliens.

The McCarran-Walter Act also introduced the concept of labor certification as a prerequisite for the admission of immigrants admitted for work-related purposes. This certification, however, was to be administered in a purely passive manner. The Secretary of Labor was empowered to certify that the admission of nonfamily-related immigrants would not adversely affect the wages and working conditions of citizen workers who were similarly employed. The Department of Labor was obligated to refuse certification if it anticipated any adverse economic impact that might occur as a consequence of their admission. This agency of government, however, was not staffed in subsequent years to carry out that vital task. In practice, it acted only in response to formal complaints or when immigrants were used in a blatant manner such as to break a strike or to bring about a drastic alteration in prevailing work standards. As a consequence, this certification authority was rarely used.

The Immigration and Nationality Act of 1952 did not alter the status of immigrants from the Western Hemisphere. They remained immune from coverage by either the overall ceiling on immigration or the national-origin quotas and were still called "nonquota immigrants" who were subject only to the various exclusionary categories that applied to all immigrants.

Continuing Frustration with an Outdated Policy

As the McCarran-Walter Act had not addressed the most pressing immigration reform issues, the pressure for substantive changes continued to build. It was not until 1965 that there would be relief. It came in the form of the Immigration Act of 1965. It is of vital significance to understand how this legislation came into being because this legislation contributed to the launching of the "fourth wave" of mass immigration. This was not its goal, but it became its consequence.

Between 1952 and 1965 the immigration system found itself in a paradoxical situation. During this thirteen-year period, only 61 percent of the system's quota visas were issued. Yet tens of thousands of persons sought to immigrate to the United States who were ineligible to do so only because they were from the "wrong" country. During this interval, as previously discussed, Congress was forced to enact a series of temporary special admission programs for various refugee groups to circumvent the barriers imposed by the immigration laws. Most of those admitted under these arrangements were refugees from Western Europe and mainland China or escapees from various Communist-dominated nations of Eastern Europe. In sum, almost one-half million persons were admitted through channels other than through the immigration system in this thirteen-year period. Moreover, nonquota immigration from the Western Hemisphere was rapidly approaching the scale of total immigration from the Eastern Hemisphere. Expressed differently, only about one of every three immigrants legally admitted to the United States between 1952 and 1965 was admitted under the terms of the national origins system. Clearly, public policy was out of step with the events it sought to regulate.

The continuation of the national origins system was also crippling the operation of the new preference system created in 1952 that sought to regulate Eastern Hemisphere admissions. As already noted, the first preference and half of all the available visas were reserved for immigrants who had skills, talents, work experience, or educational backgrounds that were in short supply in the labor market. But over the thirteen-year period in which this priority was in effect, only about one percent of those admitted came as first preference immigrants.[6] The reasons were, first, that neither the preference system nor the ceiling on immigration applied to Western Hemisphere immigrants or their immediate family members. Second, those immigrants from Eastern Hemisphere countries that had large quotas (e.g., Great Britain) often had large numbers of unfilled quota slots so there was no need to apply the preference system to order the applicants. Thus, the only nations to use the first-preference slots were those Eastern Hemisphere nations that had skilled workers who wished to emigrate and that also had a backlog of applications for visas. But most of these nations had very low overall quotas available to them. Thus, the national origin system was seriously distorting the immigrant admission system. The vast majority of immigrants were admitted on grounds other than that they specifically possessed needed labor market abilities. Hence, the whole notion that the major purpose of the legal immigration system should be to meet labor market needs was being undermined. Most of those being admitted were granted entry on grounds that were incidental to what was supposed to be the highest priority and the primary source of legal immigrants to the nation. If they possessed needed skills or abilities, it was purely accidental to the conditions of their entry.

From this experience, the lesson to be learned is not that the goal of using immigration policy as a conscientious element of national human resource development failed. Rather, it is that the attempt to impose such a goal while retaining the restraints of the national origins admissions system was a monumental mistake.

The Spillover Effect of the Civil Rights Movement to Immigration Reform

By the early 1960s, the major domestic issue was the drive for a national civil rights policy. The movement had evolved into an activist stage that used demonstrations, marches, and boycotts to protest, in a nonviolent manner, the perpetuation of overt segregation against blacks in the South. The primary focus at the time was on the abuses of social dignity (e.g., segregated public facilities) as well as on the denial of political rights (e.g., restrictions on the right to vote).

The culmination of this phase of the movement came with the passage of the Civil Rights Act of 1964. In the wake of the Kennedy assassination in November 1963, the political logjam that had stymied his attempts to address a multitude of domestic policy concerns was finally broken. The new president, Lyndon Johnson, was one of the most politically astute men ever to hold the office. Shortly after taking office, he announced his intention to enact a broad social program under the rubric of building "The Great Society." Between 1964 and 1966 the most ambitious domestic reform agenda in the nation's history was proposed and enacted. Pathbreaking legislation spanning such diverse topics as poverty prevention; federal aid to elementary, secondary and higher education; environmental quality; food stamps; consumer protection; job training; tax cuts; regional economic development; public broadcasting; urban renewal; voting rights; medicare for the elderly; medicaid health coverage for the poor; civil rights; and immigration reform were passed in rapid-fire succession. Appointments of dedicated people were made to head the various government agencies to implement this social agenda. It was a brief period when serious governmental efforts were made to confront an accumulation of national issues that, for too long, had been ignored.

With regard to the subject of immigration reform, there was a direct link to the success of the civil rights legislation. For to invoke in legislation the explicit principle that overt racism could no longer be tolerated in citizens' treatment of each other implicitly meant that there could no longer be overt discrimination in the nation's laws that governed the way future citizens would be considered for immigrant admission. As Secretary of State Dean Rusk testified before Congress in support of immigration reform in August 1964: "The action we urge is not to make a drastic departure from long-established immigration policy, but rather to reconcile our immigration policy as it had developed in recent years with the letter of the general law."[7] It was the passage of the Civil Rights Act, therefore, that created the political climate needed to legislatively end the national origins system. Thus, as it had been observed, "the 1965 immigration legislation was as much a product of the mid-sixties and the heavily Democratic 89th Congress which produced major civil rights legislation as the 1952 Act [i.e., the Immigration and Nationality Act] was a product of the Cold War period of the early 1950s."[8]

There was, however, an ironic twist to the linkage of civil rights legislation to immigration reform. While it is true that both issues came to the forefront of the national agenda because of political and social concerns, it is also the case that both had significant economic effects with regard to their labor market impacts. The economic aspects of both issues, however, were not foreseen nor was the possibility that they could conflict.

In the case of civil rights, the Civil Rights Act of 1964 contained Title VII, which prohibited discrimination in employment on the basis of race, color, gender, religious belief, or national origin. When it actually went into effect on July 1, 1965, its terms applied to employers, labor unions, and private employment services. As opposed to the other sections of the Act that focused on social and political practices primarily occurring in the South, equal employment opportunity was an economic issue and it had significant national implications.

Literally within months after its enactment, a rash of civil disturbances broke out in urban areas across the nation.[9] They continued over ensuing years, reaching a level of nearly 150 such civil disorders in the summer of 1967. To identify the causes of these riots, a presidential commission, composed of eleven distinguished members from both the public and private sector, was established in July 1967. A year later, the National Advisory Commission on Civil Disorders issued its historic report. If found, among other things, that the issue of employment discrimination was a far more complex issue than the drafters of the Civil Rights Act had envisioned.[10] The manifestations of such discrimination were more likely to be covert (i.e., built into the way labor market institutions function) than overt in nature; the social and political forms of segregation were far easier to overcome by legislation than were the economic factors; and that the issue of employment discrimination was national and not just regional in scope. Accordingly, the public policies needed to overcome the past denial of job opportunities and employment preparation would entail far more programmatic action and public funds than the mere issuance of a ban on future discriminatory behavior.

If past patterns of employment for black Americans were not to be replicated in the future, affirmative action policies would be needed to reach out and to include *already qualified* blacks for jobs. But too many blacks were unqualified for the high-skilled, high-income jobs that were expanding in number and they were disproportionately concentrated in the low-skilled, low-income occupations and industries where jobs were declining. To change these patterns, it would be necessary to address the extensive human capital deficiencies of blacks that were the accumulated legacy of centuries of stifled aspirations, unequal educations, and inadequate training opportunities. The civil disorders, after all, had occurred at a time when full employment prevailed (i.e., the national unemployment rate was in the middle of the 3 percent range). But, because the black population had become highly urbanized and disproportionately concentrated in central cities, unemployment in these areas was found to be much higher than the overall national unemployment rate. Moreover, the black labor force was beset with inordinately high incidences of working poor, discouraged workers, underemployed workers, and involuntary part-time workers. Finding jobs and preparing blacks, through extensive human resource development programs, for jobs in growth sectors of the economy were the only ways to keep the past employment patterns of inequality from being perpetuated.

There was no thought at the time that many of these same urban labor markets where blacks were concentrated were about to receive a mass infusion of new immigrants—most of whom would themselves be from minority groups. The Advisory Commission on Civil Disorders boldly stated that the nation had unfinished business to address if it was serious about fulfilling the domestic goals of the Civil Rights Act. There was an economic imperative that it was in the national interest to upgrade the capabilities and expand the utilization of the available pool of black workers. Otherwise, many blacks would be condemned to lives in a permanent underclass—with all of the attendant hardships of welfare dependency, crime, alcholism, and irregular work habits that scar the victimized individuals and burden society as a whole. But with respect to blacks, there was also a clear moral imperative that recognized that their collective fate had been greatly influenced by external institutional forces over which they had only marginal control. As the Advisory Commission of Civil Disorders pointedly stated, "white racism is essentially responsible for the explosive mixture" that led to these riotous outbursts.[11] The moral imperative was for policymakers of the nation to initiate and carry through a programmatic agenda aimed at bridging the past period of denial of opportunities and a future period of equal opportunity. No one expected immediate correction of existing economic inequalities. What was anticipated, however, was that there would be a concerted effort made over the ensuing decade to give priority to the urgent needs of black Americans. Given the general economic prosperity of the era, it was clear beyond question that addressing the human resource development needs of blacks was the nation's most pressing domestic issue.

Who could have seen that immigration reform would once more become but another example of the institutional policies adversely affecting blacks that the Advisory Commission had condemned? In earlier times, immigration policy had kept blacks in the rural South after slavery ended by providing an alternative source of workers to meet the industrial expansion needs of the North and West in the late nineteenth and early twentieth centuries. In the late twentieth century, immigration policy would once more provide an alternative to providing the massive human resource development programs necessary to actually alter the economic status of blacks in U.S. society. Immigration reform was not designed to have this impact but the consequences have been no less damaging than if it had been purposely planned to inflict harm.

The Immigration Act of 1965: The Intentions of its Proponents

The intent of the supporters of immigration changes in the mid-1960s was the same as that of reformers for the previous several decades. Accordingly, when the Kennedy Administration formally sent its legislative proposals to Congress on July 23, 1963, it sought to change the character of immigration policy—that is, to abolish the national origins system. The goal was *not* to increase the level of immigration.[12] Indeed, there were widespread fears in Congress at this time that increasing the number of immigrants in general would lead to adverse employment and wage effects in the labor market. Indicative of these concerns was the fact that the Johnson Administration had followed through with an earlier decision made by the Kennedy Administration that terminated the Mexican Labor Program (i.e., the *"bracero* program") in 1964 after twenty-two years of existence largely because both the Administration and Congress believed that program was depressing wages, retarding improvements in working conditions, and causing unemployment for low-income citizen workers in the agriculture industry. Furthermore, the Republican Party had raised the specter of massive job displacement consequences from the pending immigration reform in its unsuccessful quest to unseat President Johnson in the election campaign of 1964.[13] It is also worth noting that the massive labor market effects of the postwar "baby boom" were just beginning to manifest themselves in 1965. One million more people turned eighteen years of age in 1965 than did so in 1964. The age of eighteen years is the primary labor force entry age in the United States. Thus, the tidal wave of young labor force entrants—which would continue at this high level of annual entries until 1980—meant that there would be a substantial growth of new labor force entrants even if there were no additional increase in the level of immigration. Thus, not only was there no intention by reform advocates to increase the level of immigration but there was absolutely no need to do so. As Dean Rusk aptly stated to Congress in 1965, "the significance of immigration for the United States now depends less on numbers than on the quality of the immigrants."[14] Indeed, the United States Department of Labor estimated that the labor force would only increase by about 23,000 persons a year if proposed legislation were enacted.[15]

It was not until early 1965 that Congress responded in a serious manner to the immigration reform proposals that had been first proposed by the Kennedy Administration and were now pressed by the Johnson Administration. The original bill had called for a five-year phase-out of the national origins admission system and immediate termination of the last traces of discrimination against Asian immigration. Instead of national origin being used as the primary admission criteria, the bill proposed retaining the preference system created by the McCarran–Walter Act to govern admissions. This would have meant that 50 percent of admission would be based on preferences given to immigrants who had skills and work experience that were currently in need by the U.S. economy. The other half would be granted on the basis of various adult family relationships of would-be immigrants to U.S citizens or permanent resident aliens. As before, the preferences would apply only to Eastern Hemisphere immigrants. But, as usual, it would be Congress that would have the final say concerning the actual content of the legislation.

Given the times, political agreement to end the overt racism of the national origins system was relatively easy. Finding common ground for a new political consensus over its replacement was much more difficult. It was the Judiciary Committees of Congress—which had remained under the control of politically conservative influences—that would set the legislative framework. In particular, members of the Judiciary Committee in the House of Representatives had the greatest influence on the final product—especially Representative Michael Feighan (D-Ohio) who was chairman of the subcommittee with original jurisdiction on immigration matters. From the onset, Congress made it known to the Johnson Administration that any new legislation in this area must contain two new components.

First, there must be a ceiling on Western Hemisphere immigration. Congress feared that the absence of such a limit, combined with the extraordinarily high population-growth rates in Latin America, would lead to an uncontrolled influx of immigrants in the near future. Hence, "the final inclusion of the ceiling in the enacted bill was a necessary *quid pro quo* in exchange for abolishment of the national origins quota system."[16] The Johnson Administration opposed this change on the grounds that it would adversely affect U.S. relations with Latin America but soon realized that without it the bill would not pass. Thus, an annual ceiling of 120,000 immigrants from the Western Hemisphere was included in the final version of the legislation. It took effect on July 1, 1968.[17] It was the first restriction ever to be placed on Western Hemisphere immigration.

Second, congressional leaders felt that the labor certification requirements for nonfamily-related immigrants had to strengthened. Prior to 1965, as noted earlier, the ability of the United States to protect citizens from any adverse effects on the wages and working conditions of nonrelative immigrants was restricted to purely a negative role. The Secretary of Labor could deny labor certification only if such immigrants would have an adverse labor market impact. The Immigration Act of 1965 reversed this logic. Under its terms, immigrants who were admitted on any basis other than family reunification or refugee status must receive certification from the U.S. Department of Labor that their presence would not adversely affect employment opportunities or the prevailing wage and working conditions of citizen workers. This change also reinforces the conclusion that Congress had no intention in 1965 of causing any significant increase in the level of immigration as the result of its actions.

Under other provisions of the Immigration Act of 1965, an annual ceiling of 170,000 visas was imposed on immigration from all the nations of the Eastern Hemisphere. This figure was slightly higher than the limit in effect since the 1920s that had been slightly modified in 1952 (i.e., the 156,700 ceiling figure). The rationale for the slight increase was recognition that refugees from Europe and Asia were likely to be a continuing reality and not just a temporary post–World War II phenomenon. It was hoped that the increase of about 14,000 visa slots a year in the Eastern Hemisphere ceiling would absorb such persons. Combined with the new Western Hemisphere ceiling of 1£0,000, the total number of visas to be issued in any year was 290,000. The 1965 legislation also set a ceiling of 20,000 visas for any single country in the Eastern Hemisphere. No such country limit was applied to any Western Hemisphere nation but, of course, the total for the entire region each year could not exceed the overall hemispheric ceiling. Under the new law, the country of origin of immigrants remained a basic policy component, but preference could not be given on the basis of race, sex, place of birth, or place of residence. This legislation also eliminated the last elements of the discriminatory treatment against Asians.

To determine which individuals were to be admitted within the framework of the numerical ceiling set for the Eastern Hemisphere, a seven-category preference system was created (see Appendix A). Within each category, visas were available on a "first come, first served" basis. The preference categories and the labor certification provisions of the law did not apply at the time to Western Hemisphere nations. Subject to the various general exclusions that apply to all immigrants, persons from nations in this region had only to comply with the total hemisphere ceiling.

The adoption of the new preference system represented a dramatic shift in policy emphasis away from the human resource development considerations (that had been in place since 1952) toward one that relied largely on family reunification as its priority concern. The new system did not alter the admission status of "immediate family" relatives (i.e., persons defined under the Act as being spouses and minor children although it did add parents of U.S. citizens over the age of twenty-one to this category). Immediate family members were not to be counted as part of the hemispheric or the individual country ceilings. But the new legislation stated that 74 percent of the available immigrant visas each year would go to immigrants who were related by family ties to someone who was already a U.S. citizen or a permanent resident alien of the United States (see Appendix A). Thus, family reunification became the "cornerstone" of U.S. immigration policy in 1965 and it has remained such ever since.[18]

It is of vital consequence to recall that the Johnson Administration had strongly supported the termination of the national origins system but it favored the retention of labor market need as the highest preference and held the position that most of the available visa slots should be reserved for such admissions. During the legislative process, however, Congress reduced the occupational preferences share of the available visas to no more than 20 percent. Moreover, the previous single occupational preference grouping for work-related immigrants was split into two separate categories that were downgraded from being the first priority to the third and sixth levels of priority: the third preference was reserved for professionals and persons of exceptional ability while the sixth was for skilled and unskilled workers. Ostensibly, the rationale for these changes was that between 1952 and 1965 the occupational preference category—for reasons cited earlier in this chapter—had been under-utilized, while the family preference groupings were chronically backlogged. The most significant shift in priorities, however, occurred as a result of the addition of a new fifth preference group for adult brothers and sisters of U.S. citizens and the assignment of 24 percent of the available visas to this new family grouping. Under the earlier Immigration and Nationality Act of 1952, would-be immigrants in this new category had only been eligible to compete for the system's limited number of unused visas (i.e., nonpreference visas, if any were available).

These drastic changes in the priorities of the admissions system were made in response to the lobbying of various groups (e.g., the American Legion and the Daughters of the American Revolution) that were strongly opposed to abolition of the national origins system. Recognizing that they could not block the reform drive on this fundamental issue, they sought to make the changes in the admissions criteria more symbolic than real. These groups and their congressional sympathizers on the House Judiciary

Committee believed that by stressing family reunification it would be possible to retain essentially the same racial and ethnic priorities that the national origins system had fostered even if this mechanism itself was abolished. It seemed unlikely, for instance, that many persons from Asia or from southern or eastern Europe would be admitted under the new system because the prohibitions imposed during the national origins era had prevented the entry of many of their relatives for the past forty years. Conversely, those favored in the past would most likely have the most family relatives who could use their citizenship status to admit others like them. Representatives of various Asian-American organizations, indeed, vigorously testified against the shift to family reunification as the primary entry criterion.[19] The Department of Justice, which was also opposed to this inordinate shift to family reunification, estimated that under this legislation Asian immigration might hit a high of about 5,000 immigrants a year before subsiding to an even lower level.[20]

Bearing these thoughts in mind, the House Judiciary Committee succeeded in its efforts to make family reunification the primary factor for determining eligibility for legal immigration to the United States. As the price for ending the national origins system, the Johnson Administration ultimately conceded to Congress the admissions priority system. Satisfying the private interests of some citizens rather than serving the national interest would become the distinguishing feature of the new immigration system. Thus, the principle of family reunification, which political supporters have strongly defended in subsequent years, does not rest on a strong moral foundation. It should not be overlooked that, aside from making nepotism the dominant attribute of the legal immigration system, family reunification was based on the nefarious belief that it would perpetuate past discrimination into the future but under a more politically acceptable mantle. As Congressman Emanuel Celler (D-N.Y.) stated on the floor of Congress during the final debate on the bill in which he urged its passage, "There will not be, comparatively, many Asians or Africans entering the country since the people of Africa and Asia have very few relatives here, comparatively few could immigrate from those countries because they have no family ties to the United States."[21]

In addition to seeking compromises that would make the new law politically palatable, Congress also sought to address issues about which the old law had been silent. Most prominent among these concerns was the troublesome issue of refugee accommodation. The addition of a seventh preference category—specifically for refugees—in the Immigration Act of 1965 marked the first time an explicit provision dealing with this issue had been included in the nation's immigration law. It represented an acknowledgment that refugee accommodation will continue to confront the nation. The 6 percent of the available visas (or 17,400 slots) set aside for refugees was far below the annual average of refugees admitted during the preceding thirteen years. As discussed in the previous chapter, those refugees—largely from Eastern Europe and Cuba—had been admitted under *ad hoc* arrangements involving both temporary admission legislation and the use of administrative powers assigned to the Attorney General. Continuation of both of these practices, however, was seen to be an unsatisfactory method of dealing with what had proved up until this time to be an ongoing issue. Thus, the Immigration Act of 1965 was the first effort by the nation to address this critical issue in a consistent manner. The new statutory definition of refugees, however, reflected prevailing foreign policy goals of the United States rather than an objective assessment of the actual dimensions of the refugee issue itself. That is to say, refugees were defined in the law as being persecuted persons who had escaped from a Communist country, or a Communist-dominated area, or persons fleeing from countries in the Middle East. Political ideology and political influence, rather than persecution *per se,* was the dominant feature of this new venture in public policymaking.

Thus, under the new law, 74 percent of the immigrant visas were reserved for family reunification (plus their immediate family members), 20 percent for meeting labor market needs (which required a labor certification); and 6 percent were for refugee admissions. Only if any of these visas were unused could someone who did not fit into one of these three categories be legally admitted as a nonpreference immigrant.

On October 3, 1965, President Lyndon Johnson signed the Immigration Act of 1965 into law. Technically speaking, this statute was an extensive series of amendments to the Immigration and Nationality Act of 1952, which remained as the basic immigration law of the nation. In fact, however, it was "the most far-reaching revision of immigration policy" since the imposition of the first numerical quotas in 1921.[22] Its focus was on changing the character of the immigration flow by eliminating its overtly discriminatory features. While it is true that it raised the annual immigration ceiling from 156,700 visas (plus immediate relatives) to 290,000 visas (plus immediate relatives), it was not intended to dramatically increase total immigration. Indeed, part of the increase in numbers was simply due to the fact that this legislation sought to have all refugees admitted to the United States included within the overall legal immigration ceiling of 290,000 a year. As the Senate floor manager for the legislation, Senator Edward M. Kennedy (D-Mass.) reiterated during the final debate on the pending legislation: "this bill is not concerned with increasing immigration to this country, nor will it lower any of the high standards we apply in selection of immigrants."[23] But, as will be seen, the new law did, in fact, set into motion processes whereby neither of his assumptions proved valid. Thus, the reemergence of immigration as a significant labor market influence virtually dates from the implementation of this historic legislation.

The Achievement of a Unified Immigration System

In the 1970s, two important amendments were added to the Immigration Act of 1965 that also have had long-term implications for the evolution of U.S. immigration policy. They both were also logical policy progressions.

Following the imposition of the ceiling on Western Hemisphere immigration in mid-1968, a massive backlog of applications for immigrant visas quickly developed from persons living in nations (especially from Mexico) in this region. The backlog gave credence to earlier arguments that population pressures in Latin America were so strong that, if restrictions were not imposed, a massive migration from these nations to the United States would eventually take place. By 1976, there was a waiting period of more than two-and-one-half years for eligible new applicants from this region.

There was little congressional support for removing the ceiling itself. Nonetheless, because of the size of the backlog, the speed with which it developed, and the fact that it was causing hardship to some families that were separated because of it, efforts were initiated to implement some sort of mechanism to regulate admissions under the new ceiling requirement. Accordingly, in 1976 an amendment was adopted that extended the seven-category preference system and the labor certification requirements to would-be applicants from Western Hemisphere nations as well. The effect of this extension was that, for the first time, it would be very difficult for any person from the Western Hemisphere who did not fit into one of the seven preference categories to enter legally. Indeed, there were no residual nonpreference admissions to the United States from 1978 until

1987 when Congress added a special provision to the Immigration Reform and Control Act of 1986 that specifically permitted a lottery to be used to choose 5,000 immigrants a year for two years to enter as nonpreference admissions. The 1976 amendments also imposed, for the first time, the annual ceiling of 20,000 immigrants from any single nation in the Western Hemisphere, a ceiling that already applied to nations in the Eastern Hemisphere. The extension of annual visa ceilings to all countries of the world marked the legal manifestation of an important ideal: that people of all nations should be treated equally in terms of their opportunity to immigrate to the United States. On the other hand, it further exacerbated the backlog problem for countries in the Western Hemisphere like Mexico that had previously been sending an annual number of immigrants far in excess of the new ceiling figure for each country.

In 1978 another amendment was added to the Immigration Act of 1965 which finally gave the United States the unified immigration system that reformers had sought for over three decades. The two separate hemispheric ceilings were added together to give a single worldwide quota of 290,000 visas a year.

With the amendments of 1976 and 1978, all preferences based on the place of birth of a prospective immigrant were eliminated. All applicants, regardless of nationality, would be subject to the same admission requirements.

Concluding Observations

The Immigration Act of 1965 was a turning point in the history of U.S. immigration policy. On the one hand, the Act and its amendments in 1976 and 1978 represented the achievement of a goal. All remnants of past overt discrimination on the basis of race and ethnicity were eliminated from the admission process. On the other hand, immigration policy had been converted into a political policy designed largely to service narrow special interests. Congress "created a policy aimed primarily at fulfilling the private interests of its legal residents and their alien relatives and it simultaneously delegated to these individuals (and to a limited number of its employers) much of the power to select future citizens and workers in the nation."[24] The opportunity to redesign the nation's immigration system to serve the public interest was lost. In the place of a system that was premised largely on racial and ethnic discrimination, a new form of discrimination—nepotism—became the driving force of the legal admission system. Moreover, whatever human capital characteristics the vast majority of legal immigrants possess at the time of their entry is purely incidental to the reason they are admitted. Only minimal concern was manifested about any possible broad economic effects that might be the product of the new law's provisions and which might have national implications. If the scale of immigration had remained small, as its supporters had promised, the consequences of such an ill-designed law would have been of little consequence. But, as will subsequently be explained, such was not to be the case.

Likewise, the humanitarian provisions of the Immigration Act of 1965, which gave the nation its first statutory recognition that refugees are going to be a continuing part of the nation's immigration experience, were clearly intended to further prevailing foreign policy objectives. With such a built-in bias, refugee policy also lacked a positive definition of national purpose. The mitigation of human suffering due to persecution was clearly a distant and secondary objective to the satisfaction of domestic political interests.

Unfortunately, the focus on placating political interests served to divert attention away from the fact that none of the assumptions made by supporters of the Act about its potential to have insignificant economic implications proved to be valid. As will subsequently be discussed, the size, the human capital endowments, and the personal characteristics of post-1965 immigrants have all differed significantly from what was anticipated. Moreover, the "fourth wave" of mass immigration which has been the result, has occurred at a time when domestic sources of labor force growth were more than able to provide an ample supply of new workers and precisely when it was imperative that the nation turn its attention to the correction of internal inequalities in economic opportunities among segments of its citizen population. Under these circumstances, it should be no surprise that the post-1965 immigration policy was destined to collide with the national interest.

Notes

1. Thorstein Veblen, *The Theory of the Leisure Class* (New York: Mentor Books, 1959), p. 133.

2. U.S. Congress, Senate Committee on the Judiciary, *The Immigration and Naturalization System of the United States* (Washington, D.C.: U.S. Government Printing Office, 1950).

3. Ibid., p. 455.

4. Robert Divine, *American Immigration Policy 1924-1952* (New Haven: Yale University Press, 1957), p. 190.

5. U.S. Congress, *House Document 520*, 82nd Congress, 2nd Session (June 25, 1952), p. 5.

6. David S. North and Allen LeBel, *Manpower and Immigration Policies in the United States* (Washington, D.C.: National Commission for Manpower Policy, 1978), p. 32-33.

7. "Statement by Secretary of State Dean Rusk before the Subcommittee on Immigration of the U.S. Senate Committee on the Judiciary," as reprinted in the *Department of State Bulletin*, "Department Urges Congress to Revise Immigration Laws" (August 24, 1965), p. 276.

8. U.S. Congress, House of Representatives, Committee on the Judiciary. *Immigration and Nationality Act*, 8th Edition (Washington, D.C.: U.S. Government Printing Office, 1989), p. 423.

9. For a brief historical review, see *Report of the National Advisory Commission on Civil Disorders* (New York: Bantam Books, 1968), Chapter 1.

10. For a comprehensive review of the Commission's findings and recommendations, see Vernon M. Briggs, Jr., "A Review Article: The Report of the Commission on Civil Disorders," *Journal of Economic Issues* (June 1968), pp. 200-210.

11. *Report of the Advisory Commission...*, op. cit., p. 203.

12. Ira Mehlman, "John F. Kennedy and Immigration Reform," *The Social Contract* (Summer 1991), pp. 201-206.

13. "Should the Gates be Opened Wider?" *Business Week* (October 17, 1964), p. 114.

14. "Statement of Dean Rusk...," op. cit.

15. Mehlman, op. cit., p. 205.

16. U.S. Congress, Senate Committee on the Judiciary, *U.S. Immigration Law and Policy: 1952-79* (Washington, D.C.: U.S. Government Printing Office, 1979), pp. 234-42.

17. Technically speaking, the Immigration Act of 1965 provided that the Western Hemisphere ceiling would take effect on July 1, 1968, unless other legislation was enacted prior to that date to change it. A special commission—the Select Commission on Western Hemisphere Immigration—was appointed to study the issue, but it was unable to agree upon a firm recommendation to Congress. As a result, the ceiling went into effect on the specified date.

18. U.S. Congress, U.S. House Select Committee on Population, *Legal and Illegal Immigration to the United States* (Washington, D.C.: Government Printing Office, 1978), p. 10.

19. E.g., see "Japanese-American Citizens League to Senator Thomas H. Kuchel," in U.S. Congress, Senate, *Congressional Record* 89th Cong., 1st Session (September 17, 1965), (Washington, D.C.: U.S. Government Printing Office, 1965), p. 24,503.

20. "Testimony of Robert F. Kennedy, U.S. Attorney General," U.S. Congress House of Representatives before Subcommittee No. 1 of the Committee on the Judiciary Hearing 88th Congress, 2nd Session (Washington, D.C.: U.S. Government Printing Office 1964), p. 418.

21. U.S. Congress, House of Representatives, *Congressional Record*, 89th Congress, 1st Session (August 25, 1965), (Washington D.C.: U.S. Government Printing Office, 1965), p. 21,758.

22. Elizabeth J. Harper, *Immigration Laws of the United States* (Indianapolis: Bobbs-Merrill, 1975), p. 38.

23. U.S. Congress, Senate *Congressional Record* (September 17, 1965), op. cit., p. 24,225.

24. David S. North and Marion F. Houstoun, *The Characteristics and Role of Illegal Aliens in the U.S. Labor Market: An Exploratory Study* (Washington, D.C.: Linton and Company 1976), p. 8.

SIX

Unexpected Consequences:
The Revival of Mass Immigration

Nothing in the reform movement that culminated in the passage of the Immigration Act of 1965 was intended to cause a significant increase in the scale of immigration. The primary goal had been to change the means of legal entry. When over the ensuing years the unanticipated consequence of rising immigration began to reveal itself, no attempt was made to restrain it. The launching of the "fourth wave" of mass immigration, therefore, was more the product of omission by policymakers than of commission.

Table 6.1 shows the dimensions of the resurgence of immigration since the Immigration Act of 1965 went into full effect in mid-1968 (compare Table 6.1 with Table 4.2). The data show those who, as immigrants, have been granted permanent resident status in each fiscal year. It includes: (1) those who entered through the legal immigration system; (2) those who entered as refugees and, after one year of residence, applied to adjust their status; (3) those who entered illegally but who have been made legally eligible to adjust their status under amnesty programs authorized in 1986 and who, after a waiting period, actually filed their applications to adjust their status; and (4) those who entered as nonimmigrant aliens and have subsequently been allowed to adjust their status to become immigrants. It is worthy of note that the number of immigrants admitted in 1990 is the highest annual figure in all of U.S. history.

Table 6.1 Immigration to the United States, Fiscal Years 1969-1990			
Year	Number	Year	Number
1969	358,579	1980	530,639
1970	373,326		
1971 - 80	4,493,314	1981 - 90	7,388,062
1971	370,478	1981	596,600
1972	384,685	1982	594,131
1973	400,063	1983	559,763
1974	394,861	1984	543,903
1975	386,194	1985	570,009
1976	398,613	1986	601,708
1976 TQ	103,676	1987	601,516
1977	482,315	1988	643,025
1978	601,442	1989	1,090,924
1979	460,348	1990	1,536,483

TQ= Transitional fiscal year quarter when the Federal government altered its fiscal year from ending on June 30 to ending on September 30.

Source: U.S. Immigration and Naturalization Service.

It is equally important to note that the data in Table 6.1 do *not* indicate the "true" annual flow of foreign-born persons into the U.S. population and labor force. The data exclude: (1) persons admitted as refugees who have been in the country for less than a year and those who have been in the country for more than a year but who have yet to file for permanent resident status; (2) illegal immigrants who were eligible but did not apply for the amnesty authorized in 1986; (3) illegal immigrants who were ineligible for the 1986 amnesty; (4) illegal immigrants who have entered after the various amnesty cutoff-dates prescribed by legislation; (5) the more than 435,000 non-immigrant aliens who, in an average recent year, availed themselves of the legal opportunity to work in the country for temporary periods of time. Hence, the data in 6.1 significantly understate the actual presence of foreign-born persons in the population and labor force of the United States.

Indeed, when allowances are made for these additional categories of foreign-born entrants into the nation, the "real" inflow of foreign-born persons into the United States for permanent settlement during the 1980s was certainly well in excess of ten million immigrants. Regardless of what the precise number may have been, it was the decade that experienced the largest inflow of immigrants for permanent settlement in the nation's history.[1]

If the intention of the reform legislation of 1965 had been to significantly increase the level of immigration (with its derivative effects on the size and composition of both the population and the labor force), the legislation would be deemed a smashing success. There would be no need for an analysis of a policy intervention that accomplished what it promised.

But the reality is just the reverse. The outcome was not expected—even by the legislation's strongest advocates. Hence, the experience requires careful scrutiny. It would be unfair to say that the revival of mass immigration was the product of purposeful deception. But this does not mean that its consequences should simply be rationalized in retrospect. How it happened is vital to understand—not only because of the unanticipated changes it has wrought upon U.S. society—but also because the "fourth wave" unlike its predecessors shows "no evidence of imminent decline."[2]

The Politicalization of Refugee Policy and the Advent of Mass Asylum

Hardly had the Immigration Act of 1965 been signed before events once more swamped its new refugee provisions. Developments in Cuba initiated the process by which the attempt by Congress to limit the use of the parole authority as a means to achieve mass immigration for refugees was literally nullified. Because of economic stagnation and political turmoil in Cuba, Premier Fidel Castro unilaterally announced on September 28, 1965, that any Cubans wishing to leave—except young men of military age—could do so. On October 3, 1965 (the same day that the Immigration Act of 1965 was signed into law), President Lyndon Johnson announced that any of those Cubans who desired to come to the United States could do so. His invitation was humanely generous but it was also strongly motivated by political considerations. President Johnson was willing to sacrifice adherence to a coherent immigration policy for the opportunity to embarrass the communist dictator of Cuba before the world community.

Cuba, in the meantime, announced that the port of Camarioca would be open for Cuban exiles to come by boat to pick up their relatives. A flotilla of boats brought about 5,000 persons to the United States over the next month. As this procedure was deemed to be unsafe, it was announced in November 1965 that the two governments had reached a mutual accord. An "air bridge," involving daily chartered flights, was established to transport Cuban refugees directly to the United States. From the time these "freedom flights" began until they were unilaterally stopped by Cuba in 1973, about 270,000 Cuban refugees were admitted to the United States under this arrangement. Many were relatives of Cubans who had sought refuge in the early 1960s.

Like the characteristics of the earlier era, those who came via the "air bridge" were members of "the upper socioeconomic class of prerevolutionary Cuba." Because they were "the able, the educated, and the successful," their migration has been described as being "the biggest brain drain the Western Hemisphere has ever known."[3] These persons have also been referred to as the "golden exiles" because of their extensive human capital endowments.

The legal authority used to admit the Cuban airlift refugees was, once again, the parole authority of the U.S. Attorney General. In 1966 a special law, the Cuban Refugee Adjustment Act, was passed to enable these refugees to become permanent-resident aliens without first leaving the country and applying for the appropriate visa.[4] Cuban refugees who entered the United States were allowed to adjust their status to become permanent-resident aliens after they had been in the United States for two years. These Cubans were originally counted as part of the new annual ceiling of 120,000 quota immigrants from the entire Western Hemisphere but this practice was subsequently declared illegal.[5] As a result of a court order, 145,000 additional visas above the established ceiling were issued to other persons from the Western Hemisphere who had sought entry to the United States but had been denied entry because these visas had been diverted for use by Cuban refugees.

By the time the Cuban airlift ended in 1973, a total of 677,158 Cuban refugees had entered the United States since 1959. Despite initial efforts to disperse the refugees around the country, a disproportionately high number of these persons returned or remained in the Miami-Dade County area of South Florida. While there is no question that the mass influx of Cubans into this area brought a new vibrancy to a local economy that had long been stagnant, it has also caused tension and conflict between and among the various native and foreign-born segments already residing in that community.[6] During the 1980s, for instance, there were four significant civil disorders in Miami—each with clear racial overtones.

The Southeast Asia Refugee Issue

No sooner had the Cuban "air bridge" ceased than the ending of the war in Vietnam set in motion a new refugee stream. In April 1975, the govern-ment of South Vietnam, which the United States supported, collapsed. With the withdrawal of U.S. military forces, "the largest emerging mass immigration of refugees to the United States" yet known com-menced.[7] Many of the initial refugees had been closely associated with the war effort. Between April and December 1975, 130,000 Indochinese refugees were admitted to the United States under the parole provisions as authorized by the Administration of President Gerald Ford. Most of these persons were either related to U.S. citizens or had been closely allied with the war effort itself. These Vietnamese refugees were soon outnumbered, however, by the outflow of refugees from other parts of Indochina who also sought to be admitted to the United States. In 1976, another parole program was undertaken to admit 11,000 refugees who had escaped from South Vietnam, Kampuchea, or Laos and who had relatives living in the United States. Included in this grouping were some of the first "boat people" (many of whom were ethnic Chinese) who had been forcibly expelled from Vietnam by the new communist government and who were having difficulty finding any country that would allow them to debark.

With events clearly spinning out of control, President Ford, decided that "relying upon the parole provision was not a desirable means of formulating U.S. refugee policy."[8] He announced in 1976 that he would no longer use this authority and called for new legislation to establish a systematic admission procedure. His administration, however, was voted out of office in November of that year. When President Jimmy Carter assumed office in January 1977, he made it known that he did not feel compelled to refrain from using the parole authority but he did express a preference for new refugee legislation.[9]

As economic conditions continued to deteriorate and as factional fighting broke out in Vietnam, Laos, and Kampuchea, the outpouring of refugees accelerated. Against this backdrop, President Carter announced that he would use the parole authority to accommodate a substantial portion of the human outflow in excess of those permitted to enter under the existing immigration law. On April 13, 1979, the Attorney General authorized the parole admission of 40,000 Indochinese refugees over the next six months. In July 1979, it was announced that an additional 14,000 Indochinese refugees a month—or a total of 210,000 such refugees—would be admitted under the parole authority between July 1, 1979, and September 30, 1980. As these mass admissions were taking place outside the preference limits of the prevailing immigration law, special legislation (similar to that given to Cubans) was temporarily enacted that permitted them subsequently to adjust their status to become permanent-resident aliens. A disproportionate number of the refugees from Southeast Asia (about 40 percent) settled in the urban areas of California, especially in the Los Angeles-Long Beach area.

The Refugee Act of 1980

By this time, it was clear that the prevailing refugee provisions of the Immigration Act of 1965 "were totally inadequate as the basis for a fair and coherent refugee policy."[10] Both President Carter and Congress agreed that a new refugee policy had to be formulated. In 1979, a bill was drafted in the Senate. It embodied many of the recommendations for reform that were under discussion by the Select Commission on Immigration and Refugee Policy during this same time period and that were contained in its subsequent final report. This bill became the Refugee Act of 1980. It was signed by President Carter on March 17, 1980 and went into effect on April 1, 1980.

The new legislation had the effect of removing refugee admissions from the legal immigration system. It did this by abolishing the seventh preference admission category for refugees that had been created by the Immigration Act of 1965 (with its 17,400 visas reserved for refugees). To compensate for its removal, the annual number of immigrant visas under the legal immigration system was then reduced from 290,000 to 270,000, which were allocated among the remaining six preferences categories that were left in place (see Appendix B).

The Act created a separate admission system for refugees. Under the new law, a refugee is defined as "any person who is outside any country of such person's nationality...and who is unable or unwilling to avail himself or herself of the protection of that country because of persecution or a well-founded fear of persecution due to race, religion, nationality, membership in a particular group, or political opinion." The intention was to remove the overt ideological bias of the 1965 legislation and to make the actual threat of persecution to an individual the determining eligibility factor. This definition meant that the United States had now accepted the same wording as an earlier protocol on refugees adopted by the United Nations (U.N.) in 1967. The language of the Refugee Act of 1980, however, went further than the U.N. protocol by stating that the term "refugee" also includes persons who are within their country of nationality and who are also subject to persecution. This grouping—those who were "within their country of nationality"—was restricted, however, to persons who were specifically designated as "refugees" by the President and could not be self-proclaimed. Otherwise, it was felt, endless numbers of persons in many nations could lay claim to refugee status. Persons who had contributed to the persecution of others were declared to be ineligible to later become refugees themselves.

Thus, having broadened the definition of the term "refugee," the critical question for policymakers was how many persons to admit each year under these new terms. There was disagreement between Congress and the Carter Administration as to whether a certain number should be specified in the law by Congress or whether the President should have the discretion to decide the number that he felt was in the national interest to admit each year. Ultimately, a compromise was reached. From 1980 to 1982, up to 50,000 refugees could be admitted each year by the President. This ceiling was considered to be "the normal flow" for those years. The number was arbitrarily selected on the basis that between 1956 and 1979 the average annual number of refugees admitted to the United States under the parole provision was 44,670 persons. With the exception of the Indochinese refugees, the ceiling of 50,000 refugees a year would have accommodated all of the yearly refugee admissions between 1956 and 1979. The President could admit additional refugees above the 50,000 figure in an "emergency situation" after consulting with Congress.

After October 1, 1982, the law specified that a new procedure would take effect. Prior to the beginning of each fiscal year, the President is required to state in advance the total number of refugees he wishes to admit in the coming year, and to consult with Congress through "personal contact" with specifically designated representatives as to the appropriateness of the requested number. Congress, in turn, is required to hold a hearing on the number. In addition, the law requires that the President assign geographic allocations to refugees from different parts of the world to prevent any single group or region from using all the available refugee slots. It is important to note that these assigned figures are ceilings. They are not goals. Although it is widely misunderstood, there is no implied obligation to reach the annually authorized refugee figure or the specific geographic allocations. The refugee program was created in such a way as to be deemed satisfactory if the ceilings are not achieved, for "the underlying principle is that refugee admission is an exceptional *ex gratia* act provided by the United States in furthering its foreign and humanitarian policies."[11]

For present purposes, it is of significance to note that there was no intention by Congress at the time of the passage of the Refugee Act of 1980 to increase the total number legal immigrants and refugees to be admitted over what had been the actual level prior to its passage. Elimination of the seventh preference category and the simultaneous reduction of the worldwide immigrant ceiling to 270,000 visas, with the addition of up to 50,000 refugees a year, created a new total of up to 320,000 legal immigrants and refugees admitted each year. This new total, however, was approximately the same as the previous aggregate total of immigrants (i.e., the old 290,000 quota of immigrants a year, 17,400 of whom were refugees) plus the remainder of the prior average annual number of refugees admitted as parolees between 1956 and 1979 (i.e., 44,670 refugees a year). Hence, supporters of the 50,000-refugees-a-year figure in the Refugee Act of 1980 argued that in fact "there would be no actual increase in the immigration flow as a result of the Refugee Act."[12] Having enacted what it believed was a more flexible admissions procedure for accommodating refugees, Congress sought assurances that the parole authority of the Attorney General would be used only as it had originally been intended—for individual emergency cases. Thus, an amendment was added. After May 15, 1980, the Attorney General would be forbidden to use the parole authority to admit refugees unless a "compelling reason" that was in "the public interest" with respect to a particular individual dictated that this person be admitted as a parolee rather than as a refugee.[13]

As for what has actually happened, Table 6.2 indicates the authorized admissions from 1980 to 1992. The first complete year in which the Refugee Act of 1980 was in effect was fiscal 1981. The range of authorized admissions has been from a high of 217,000 (in 1981) to a low of 67,000 (in 1986).

Table 6.2 Refugee Approvals and Admissions by Geographic Area of Chargeability Fiscal Years 1980 - 1992

Geographic area of chargeability	1980	1981	1982	1983	1984	1985	1986	1987	1988	1989	1990	1991	1992
Authorized admissions	231,700	217,000	140,000	90,000	72,000	70,000	67,000	70,000	87,500	104,500	110,000	131,000	144,000
Africa	1,500	3,000	3,500	3,000	2,750	3,000	3,000	2,000	3,000	2,000	3,500	4,900	6,000
East Asia	169,200	165,600	96,000	64,000	52,000	50,000	45,500	40,500	38,000	38,000	36,800	52,000	52,000
Eastern Europe & Soviet Union	38,000	39,900	31,000	15,000	11,000	10,000	9,500	12,300	30,000	50,000	58,300	55,000	66,000
Latin America & Caribbean	20,500	4,000	3,000	2,000	1,000	1,000	3,000	1,000	3,500	3,500	2,400	3,100	3,000
Near East & South Asia	2,500	4,500	6,500	6,000	5,250	6,000	6,000	10,200	9,000	7,000	5,000	6,000	6,000
Unallocated Reserve	X	X	X	X	X	X	X	4,000	4,000	4,000	4,000	10,000	11,000
Approvals	206,912	155,291	61,527	73,645	77,932	59,436	52,081	61,529	80,282	95,505	99,687	NA	NA
Africa	1,174	3,784	4,198	2,642	2,743	1,943	1,329	1,974	1,304	1,825	3,318	NA	NA
East Asia	161,132	124,719	37,481	51,476	58,697	39,628	35,193	37,082	41,450	35,196	30,513	NA	NA
Eastern Europe & Soviet Union	33,960	18,845	13,778	13,382	10,917	9,999	9,515	12,290	26,645	48,620	58,951	NA	NA
Latin American & Caribbean	7,692	1,210	580	710	156	1,868	47	99	2,452	2,848	1,863	NA	NA
Near East & South Asia	2,954	6,733	5,490	5,435	5,419	5,998	5,997	10,084	8,431	7,016	4,952	NA	NA
Admissions¹	NA	NA	93,252	57,064	67,750	62,477	58,329	66,803	80,382	101,072	110,197	NA	NA
Africa	NA	NA	3,259	2,382	2,704	1,952	1,279	2,068	1,708	1,998	3,585	NA	NA
East Asia	NA	NA	69,712	35,861	49,154	44,972	41,673	40,046	35,160	36,989	37,192	NA	NA
Eastern Europe & Soviet Union	NA	NA	13,438	12,986	10,497	9,720	9,270	12,450	28,906	48,416	57,081	NA	NA
Latin America & Caribbean	NA	NA	453	724	152	159	48	902	4,319	5,033	5,786	NA	NA
Near East & South Asia	NA	NA	6,350	5,110	5,242	5,674	6,059	10,619	9,486	7,699	5,636	NA	NA
Unknown	NA	NA	40	1	1	-	-	718	803	937	917	NA	NA

¹ Admissions may be higher than approvals because of the arrival of persons approved in previous years. - Represents zero. X Not applicable. NA Not Available.

Source: U.S. Immigration and Naturalization Service.

Since the consultation process began in 1982, the authorization level has become the annual subject of immense political pressure. As the Presdient sets the number, special interest groups try to influence his Administration to enlarge the number of persons for whom they advocate—usually an ethnic or religious group but sometimes a racial group.

The Achilles Heel: Asylee Policy

Prior to the Refugee Act of 1980, the immigration statutes contained no provisions for granting asylum to individuals who were already in the United States and who feared they would be persecuted if they were required to return to their homeland. Assistance to refugees was restricted to persons who were temporarily residing in some other nation of "first instance" after fleeing their homeland. In such instances, refugees could be screened with respect to their eligibility for admission before being physically allowed to enter the United States. Prior to 1980, the only existing authority that came close to being an asylum policy was a section in the Immigration and Nationality Act of 1952. It allowed the Attorney General to voluntarily block for an extended period of time the deportation of an alien who was already in the United States if it was believed that the alien would be subject to persecution on the basis of race, religion, or political opinion if forced to return home. Under the Refugee Act of 1980, however, the Attorney General was authorized to grant asylum protection to an alien who was already in the United States if the individual applied for such status and if the Attorney General determined that the individual could be otherwise classified as a refugee. The asylee status could be revoked at a later time if it was determined that the conditions in the alien's homeland had changed such that the status was no longer warranted. As the policy was intended to address the needs of individuals, the Refugee Act of 1980 specified that only 5,000 asylees each year could adjust their status, after one year, to apply for permanent resident status. Asylee admissions do not count as part of the annual ceiling on worldwide immigration or the individual country ceiling as specified under the legal immigration statutes.

Within weeks after passage of the Refugee Act of 1980, events quickly demonstrated that the asylum section was the weakest aspect of the new legislation. Its implications had not been thought through. As usual, the legislation had been formulated on the basis of past circumstances and experiences. The possibility that the United States itself might become a country of "first instance" for massive numbers of persons—all arriving within a very short period of time and all claiming asylum—had never been contemplated. This, however, was precisely what happened.

The Mariel-Haitian "Boatlift" Experience

Once more, it was events in Cuba that caused U.S. refugee policy to fall into disarray. In the early months of 1980, declining economic conditions in Cuba culminated in "a rising tide of dissatisfaction, particularly among those Cubans with relatives in the United States."[14] A number of violent outbursts occurred as increasing numbers of Cubans sought asylum in various foreign embassies located in Havana. Suddenly, in a moment of peevishness, Fidel Castro, announced on April 4, 1980 that anyone who wished to leave Cuba could do so. In response, thousands accepted his offer and they descended upon various embassies to apply. Initially, some were allowed to fly on chartered flights to Costa Rica where they were given temporary safe haven. But as the planes landed in Costa Rica, they became the center of worldwide publicity, which created a disparaging image of contemporary life in Cuba. In reaction, on April 18, 1980, the Cuban government suspended the refugee flights. Two days later, Castro unilaterally announced on radio that all Cubans who wished to emigrate to the United States were free to board boats at the port city of Mariel and go.[15]

Within hours of the broadcast, which was received in southern Florida, a flotilla of boats streamed toward Mariel from Florida, and on April 21, the first boat returned to Key West. Many of the persons who left Cuba were relatives of persons already in the United States, but it was also the case that "a deliberate policy of forcing acceptance of several nonrelatives for every relative on board" was also in effect.[16] Many of the nonrelatives were persons who had been committed to various state medical and penal institutions. Reflecting both the declining educational and training opportunities in Cuba over the preceding decade as well as the certain types of non-relatives included in the outflow, the human capital attributes of the Mariel people were considerably below those of the Cuban refugees of the 1960s. Indeed, in contrasting the two human outflows, one account has referred to the Cubans of the 1960s as "the promising ones" and those of the early 1980s as the "frightening ones."[17]

The number of Cuban refugees quickly soared, from several hundred a day in late April to over a thousand a day by early May. In a speech on

May 5, 1980, President Carter stated: "Ours is a nation of refugees. We will continue to provide an open heart and open arms to refugees seeking freedom from Communist domination brought by Cuba."[18] The next day, however, responding to an urgent request by the governor of Florida, the President declared that "a state of emergency" existed in South Florida. By May 9, 1980, 30,127 persons had arrived in South Florida and the massive scale of the movement was finally recognized. Moreover, the dangers of overcrowding, as well as the lack of sufficient safeguards on what were essentially pleasure boats designed for families, became apparent. Thus, on May 14, 1980, President Carter moved to halt the sealift. Ostensibly, his reason was that he wanted to find a safer way of conducting the transfer. No doubt the request was also an effort to reduce the size of the flow and to allow the government more time to develop an appropriate policy of accommodation and to seek international assistance in distributing the people to other nations as well. An international conference was hastily convened in San Jose, Costa Rica. At that meeting, eighteen nations agreed to accept some of the Cubans, but none agreed to take more than a few hundred persons.[19] Thus, the burden of trying to stop the flow of refugees as well as to accommodate the Cubans who were already ashore fell squarely upon the United States.

Technically speaking, the Cubans who were boatlifted to South Florida were illegal immigrants and the citizens who conveyed them were "smugglers." The Carter Administration did not treat them as illegal aliens and, initially, no action was taken against those who transported them. Indeed, the INS immediately accepted their applications for a status classification, granted them visas, and authorized them to seek work. Deciding what status to assign to the Cubans, however, proved difficult. The Administration declined to classify them all as refugees. They were already in the United States and the Administration wanted to avoid setting a precedent that might lead persons from other countries to think they could simply enter the United States without documents and claim to be refugees.[20] Thus, the 3,500 Cuban who entered the United States by way of Costa Rica, which was the number the U.S. agreed to accept as its share of the initial Cuban outflow, were classified as a group as refugees. This was because they were actually screened for eligibility in Costa Rica before being allowed to enter the United States. But those who had come directly to Florida from Cuba by boat were classified as "applicants for asylum". The Refugee Act of 1980 had provided for the assignment of asylee status to persons who were already in the United States, but the use of that classification had been intended for individuals, not for massive groups of persons. Declaring the flotilla Cubans to be "applicants for asylum" meant that each would have to be interviewed individually to determine his or her eligibility for asylee status. The situation in May 1980 was deemed by the Administration to be "a very special emergency situation."[21]

Meanwhile the Carter Administration continued to be unsuccessful in its efforts to arrange for U.S. officials to interview persons in Cuba to determine their eligibility for refugee status or to arrange for an orderly process that might regularize the flow. Thus, the "freedom flotilla" continued despite efforts that began in mid-May to crack down on those who were providing the transportation. The U.S. government's efforts included impounding the private boats that were being used as well as levying fines against the captains of the boats. By mid-June the deterrents imposed by the U.S. government as well as a change in the attitude of the Cuban government toward the exodus resulted in a sharp reduction in the number of Cubans who reached the United States, although the process continued at a reduced level through early October 1980.

As if the flow of persons from Cuba was not enough for policymakers to worry about, the entire situation was further inflamed when a number of boats crowded with people from Haiti also began to arrive. Such boats, with their human cargoes, were not new—they had been arriving in south Florida on a sporadic basis since December, 1972. But their arrival in the midst of the massive Mariel exodus ignited a long simmering dispute that has remained unresolved. Since Cuba and Haiti were neighboring islands and both had long been ruled by dictators, it was unavoidable that comparisons of the treatment of persons fleeing from each would be made. Successive U.S. Administrations had consistently contended that most Haitians are illegal immigrants while virtually all Cubans are refugees and asylees.[22] This difference in treatment has caused countless legal and political difficulties. It also evoked charges of racism because the Cubans tended to be white while the Haitians were exclusively black.

Over the years following 1972, several hundred Haitians had been returned to their homeland by the INS. The position of the U.S. government consistently had been that, with relatively few exceptions, most Haitians were fleeing from the general economic conditions of poverty and unemployment on the island rather than from specific political persecution. Those able to prove political persecution on an individual level were granted refugee status. But the vast majority of the Haitians were treated as illegal immigrants, a status that some began to challenge in protracted legal proceedings. When the number or Haitians increased during the Mariel era, the Carter Administration initially refused to exercise its parole authority for Haitians as a group. Instead, they were given the same entry status as the Cubans who entered in this period. Thus, on June 20, 1980, the U.S. Attorney General established a new temporary status— "Cuban-Haitian Entrant (Status Pending) "for the boatlift people from both countries who had arrived by that date and issued them a temporary six-month parole into the United States. Eligibility for this status was later extended to all persons who had arrived as of October 10, 1980. During this interval, the administration sought to have Congress give a statutory basis to this emergency classification, but Congress declined to do so. In total, about 123,000 Cubans and over 6,000 Haitians had arrived in the United States during this six-month period and were now in a legal limbo as to their immigration status.

In November 1980 President Carter was unseated by Ronald Reagan. In part the large influx of Cubans and Haitians had contributed to the charge by the Republican Party during the campaign that the Carter Administration was ineffectual in its ability to govern. The Reagan Administration did not want to fall victim to the same accusation in the future. Hence, in 1981 it initiated a controversial two-pronged policy of deterrence to prevent more Haitians from arriving *en masse* by sea. The U.S. Coast Guard was ordered to begin interdicting refugee boats on the high seas and to turn them back before the Haitians could actually touch U.S. soil and lay claim to being asylees. The government of Haiti formally agreed to accept back all such persons and to do so without reprisals. The Department of Justice also adopted a policy of placing all subsequent mass arrivals of people in detention centers rather than, as had been the practice up until this time, releasing them to private sponsors while their status was determined or while subsequent appeals were pending. There was a protracted legal challenge to the detention policy, partly on the basis of a claim that it was racially discriminatory against Haitians. Ultimately, after a series of conflicting decisions by lower courts, the U.S. Supreme Court upheld the legality of the policy on June 25, 1985 and ruled that the action was not discriminatory.[23]

As for those classified as "Cuban-Haitian Entrants," the Reagan Administration announced in 1984 that all of the Cubans whose status was pending could adjust their status to become permanent-resident aliens because they were covered by the Cuban Adjustment Act of 1966 which essentially gives blanket refugee status to all Cubans who reach U.S. soil (the exceptions would be for those who fall into any of the specific exclusionary categories that apply to all would-be immigrants and refugees). Many people believed that the Refugee Act of 1980 had superseded this specific legislation but this was held not to be so. There was a congressional effort in 1984 to repeal the Cuban Adjustment Act, but it failed so the preferential treatment for Cubans remained in effect. There were also unsuccessful efforts to introduce special legislation in 1984 to allow the Haitians of the Mariel era to adjust their status, but these too failed. Ultimately, however, the controversy over the status of the "Cuban-Haitian Entrants" ended with the passage of the Immigration Reform and Control Act (IRCA) of 1986. Among its multiple provisions were four amnesty provisions for various groups of people already in the United States who had entered outside the terms of existing policy. One of these amnesties permitted all of the 129,000 persons classified as "Cuban-Haitian Entrants" (and not excludable) to immediately apply to adjust their status to become permanent-resident aliens. About 3,000 Cubans were found excludable due to criminal histories. They were placed in prisons until such time as Cuba would agree to their return.

The Ongoing Dispute Over Disparate Treatment

The issue of the differential treatment afforded to Cubans has remained a topic of controversy—especially in the Miami area where Cubans and Haitians have continued over the years to arrive by various means. Cubans, unless excludable, are automatically given refugee status while Haitians and others must prove they would be specifically subject to persecution for their homelands. In the ten-year period from 1981 to early 1991, over 23,000 Haitians were intercepted by the Coast Guard and immigration officials as they attempted to enter the United States without proper documents. Only eight Haitians were granted political asylum over this period.[24] Most of the remainder were put in detention camps or returned to Haiti. In contrast, between 1988 and 1991, over 8,000 Cuban *balseros* (a name given to Cubans who arrive in South Florida on anything that will float) have been given official refugee status. As a consequence, the bitterness over the differential treatment has remained. It was expressed by the Director of the Haitian Refugee Center in Miami, Rolande L. Dorancy, in 1991 when he asked rhetorically, "If this is a country of immigrants, then why are some immigrants treated like dogs?"[25] The particular instance that prompted this bitter remark was that in mid-July 1991 a boatload of 161 Haitians had picked up two Cubans floating on a raft off the Florida coast before the boat was intercepted by the U.S. Coast Guard. The two Cubans were brought to shore and immediately given refugee status and allowed to remain in the U.S.; only nine Haitians were brought to shore (six of them because they were seriously ill; the other three, after being interviewed at sea, were allowed to file for asylum) while the boat and the other 152 people were returned to Haiti under escort of the Coast Guard. INS officials, speaking of this particular incident, stated "there is nothing perverse or discriminatory about it; it is the law."[26]

Efforts to establish a regularized procedure for the admission of Cubans has passed through numerous iterations throughout the 1980s and has remained unsettled as of the early 1990s. On December 14, 1984, the U.S. Cuban Migration Agreement was signed permitting a number of former Cuban political prisoners (and their immediate family members) to enter the United States in return for Cuban willingness to accept the excludable aliens from the Mariel era.[27] The accord also provided for "the normalization of immigration procedures" between the two countries. This meant that persons in Cuba could apply to immigrate and, if they fell into one of the established preference categories of the legal immigration system, they could do so up to the 20,000 annual visa ceiling that applies to all countries. It also meant that Cubans could once more enter the United States as nonimmigrant visitors, as can persons from other countries. Hardly had this agreement become operational before it was unilaterally suspended on May 20, 1985 by Castro. His action was a form of protest when a radio station (i.e., Radio Marti) that was authorized and funded by the United States government to broadcast from Florida to Cuba went on the air. The agreement was reinstated on November 20, 1987.

On May 20, 1988, as a result of an unprecedented agreement between a private political organization (the Cuban American National Foundation) and the Reagan Administration, 4,000 Cuban refugees who had been settled in Panama and Costa Rica during the Mariel era were permitted to resettle in the United States. The cost of the resettlement of these "third country" Cuban refugees was borne by the Foundation rather than by the Federal government. During that same year, the U.S. Catholic Conference also worked out an accord with the Cuban government to admit another 3,000 political prisoners and their family members. By mid-1991, in the wake of the disintegration of communism in the Soviet

Union, Cuba also showed signs of mounting economic weakness and political unrest. As a result, the number of persons fleeing Cuba on rafts or small boats began to rise. In addition, applications for nonimmigrant visas from Cubans in 1991 to visit the United States began to soar (i.e., they were approaching an annualized rate of 100,000 persons) and over one-third of those who came as of mid-1991 elected not to return. As Cuba continued to relax its travel restrictions, there was worry among immigration officials that a "slow-motion Mariel" was developing.[28] Fearing that Castro might again be using immigration as a means to reduce the domestic pressure that was opposed to his rule, the Bush Administration in August 1991 froze for six months the issuance of any new nonimmigrant visas to Cubans.

Before the freeze went into effect, however, thousands of Cubans who had entered as nonimmigrants had once more been given blanket refugee status just by asking for it. Against this backdrop, the differential treatment of Haitians again resurfaced in a major way. Namely, on September 30, 1991 the President of Haiti, Jean-Bertrand Aristide, was overthrown by a military coup and sent into exile. Aristide, who took office in February 1991 after winning a landslide victory, was the first duly elected president in Haiti's 187-year history as an independent nation. The United States declared a trade embargo and Venezuela immediately imposed an oil embargo on Haiti. About a month later, the U.S. Coast Guard intercepted the first, of what would soon be many, boats packed solid with Haitians seeking to flee the worsening economy and civil unrest on the island. In accordance with prevailing policy, the Haitians were taken aboard and interviewed to determine if any of those picked up wished to apply for asylee status and, if so, were they eligible. Some did not ask for asylum. The majority, however, were found to be ineligible because they were deemed to be fleeing economic deprivation, not political persecution.[29] Only 200 of the 6,000 Haitians picked up as of December 1, 1991 were found to actually be eligible to apply for asylum. But instead of taking those who were denied asylum to Florida, they were initially held on board the Coast Guard cutters until there was no room left on any of the thirteen vessels initially involved. The Bush Administration did not want to do anything to encourage a mass exodus from the island on overcrowded boats that were only marginally seaworthy. Then on November 18, 1991 the Bush Administration ordered that those denied asylum be returned to Haiti. The Administration contended that repatriation would save lives by deterring others from attempting such dangerous voyages. A total of 538 Haitians were, in fact, returned before officials at the Haitian Refugee Center secured a temporary court order from a federal district judge in Miami on November 19, 1991 that stopped the practice.[30] On December 4, the court order was extended pending an appeal to the 11th Circuit Court of Appeals.[31] In issuing this second ruling, the district judge dismissed a claim by the Federal government that he lacked jurisdiction because the actions were being taken hundreds of miles beyond U.S. territorial waters but he also made no provision for those in custody to be brought to the United States. In the meantime, the several thousand Haitians who had been held on ships were taken to the U.S. naval station located at Guantanamo Bay, Cuba. A tent city was set up with provisions made to accommodate 10,000 persons while the court drama was played out. Several hundred others were taken to camps in regional countries (Honduras, Venezuela, Belize, Trinidad, and Tobago) that agreed to provide temporary safe haven.

The Bush Administration made it clear during this period that it felt that most of the Haitians were ineligible for asylum status. If the Haitians were taken to the mainland of the United States while their status was unclear, the Administration felt it could trigger a massive exodus from Haiti of other impoverished persons. As experience has also shown, it has proven very difficult to make people leave once they are actually in this country. For these reasons, the Administration declined to offer "temporary protected status" for these Haitians, who were not eligible for asylee status as authorized under the new Immigration Act of 1990.

While this was happening, of course, any Cubans picked up at sea were taken immediately to Florida and, as usual, most were granted automatic refugee status. The difference in treatment once more aroused the bitter charge of racism.[32] Congressman Charles Rangel (D-N.Y.) charged that "this would not have happened if the refugees were Europeans" and Senator Connie Mack (R-Fla.) said "returning Vietnamese, Russian Jews, Cubans, Nicaraguans, and others back to the countries they were fleeing would be unthinkable; how can we justify it for Haitians?"[33] The INS acknowledged the differential treatment but rejected the implications of racism by simply pointing out once more that it is Congress that has required the special mandated treatment for Cubans. As INS Commissioner Gene NcNary stated, "the simple fact is that because of the Cuban Adjustment Act, Cuban nationals are treated differently under the law."[34]

On December 17, 1991 the 11th Circuit Court of Appeals struck down the District Court injunction. The majority opinion dismissed the lower court's injunction and held that Congress and the Executive Branch have the authority to set foreign policy.[35] In this case the events had entirely taken place beyond the boundaries of U.S. territorial waters so the district court lacked jurisdiction. On December 20, 1991, however, the same district court issued another injunction saying that lawyers have a right to speak to the Haitians before they can be returned to Haiti. No immediate action was taken by the administration to return the Haitians but negotiations did proceed to attempt to restore the Aristide government while the ruling was appealed to the U.S. Supreme Court. On January 31, 1992, the Supreme Court ordered that the stay issued by the district court be lifted. Two days later, the process of returning those Haitians deemed to be ineligible for asylum began. By this time there were about 12,000 Haitians in custody of whom only about 1,400 had been found to have plausible asylum claims.

The politicalization of refugee policy and its mass asylum consequences has been one contributing factor to the return of the immigration. The differential treatment of Cuban and Haitians indicates that refugee policy has continued to be plagued by foreign policy considerations. Along with the ever-present threat of another human hemorrhage, it also means that refugee admissions in general continue to be captive of a political process that has little regard for economic adjustment consequences.

The "Politicalization" of Human Rights: The Case of Central America

Throughout the 1980s, there were numerous other examples of the distortion of refugee policy to conform to foreign policy goals. The most striking of these instances was in the differential treatment of persons from certain countries in Central America. Beginning in 1981, the Reagan Administration concluded that "human rights"—which the preceding Carter Administration had championed—was a threat to its foreign policy goals in Central America. Hence, the U.S. Department of State decided that "human rights" should be defined as "political rights" in order to convey "what is ultimately at issue in our contest with the Soviet Bloc."[36] Thus, U.S. foreign policy in this region shifted from a focus on the sanctity of human life to a concern for political freedoms and civil liberties. As Charles Maechling of the Carnegie Endowment for International Peace observed, the Reagan Administration's policy sought "to divert public attention from the atrocities and abuses of 'friendly' governments to the constitutional imperfections and civil liberty infractions of adversaries."[37] Little attention was to be given to cruelties committed by constitutional governments against the native Indian populations and political dissidents by right-wing governments that had been elected into power in Guatemala and El Salvador. Conversely, major opposition was mounted against the Marxist Sandinista government that had seized power in Nicaragua. The implementation of this policy created grotesque problems for the administration of the nation's refugee policy in Central America. It is often said the origins of the instability in Central America are as much social as they are political. The rapid rate of population growth is a persistent negative influence on efforts to stimulate economic development.[38] Rapid population growth is the fundamental source of the region's political turmoil and violence because it is linked to the problems of health, housing, education, nutrition, and land use. Thus, it is not surprising that many people in this region would want to leave. For most Central Americans, the legal immigration system of the United States—with its visas restricted only to those with family ties or who possess specific job skills—offered no opportunities. But when civil war broke out in El Salvador and in Nicaragua and when "death squads" and guerrilla fighting flared-up in Guatemala, U.S. refugee policy offered a possible way out for many people in this region—if they qualified.

It should be pointed out, however, that under the prevailing policy of the 1980s, refugee status could not be given to individuals simply because they were caught in the midst of fighting or because civil authorities could not maintain domestic order. Refugee status could only be given to those individuals confronted with persecution for one of the five grounds specified in the Refugee Act of 1980. Otherwise, those who entered the U.S. without a visa, or overstayed a visa were considered to be illegal immigrants, subject to deportation if apprehended. It was in this context that several hundred thousand people from these three countries entered the United States during the 1980s by whatever means they could. The issue was whether they were asylees who should be permitted to stay, or illegal immigrants who, if caught, should be returned to their homelands.

To the Reagan Administration, most of those fleeing from El Salvador and Guatemala were perceived as being persons who were fleeing from poverty and related economic adversities and, therefore, they did not qualify for asylee status. On the other hand, a more lenient position was taken with regard to persons fleeing from Nicaragua. Indeed, on July 8, 1987 Attorney General Edwin Meese went so far as to issue an order that no Nicaraguan in the United States who had "a well-founded fear" of persecution would be deported and that they were to immediately be issued work authorizations if they requested them. He directed INS officials "to encourage and to expedite" such Nicaraguans to file such requests and also to "encourage Nicaraguans whose claims for asylum...have been denied to reapply for a reopening or rehearing."[39] It was essentially a declaration of "safe haven" for Nicaraguans for as long as the fighting between the Contras (the guerrilla forces supported by U.S. foreign policy) and the Sandinistas (the unelected Marxist government) continued.

In making this policy declaration, Meese indicated that the Department of Justice was simply implementing a U.S. Supreme Court decision rendered earlier in 1987. In that decision, the Court held that the Refugee Act of 1980 required only that an asylee applicant have "a well-founded fear of persecution" rather than "a clear probability of persecution," which had been the previous stricter standard.[40] Meese's statement, however, said nothing about the status of persons from El Salvador who were entering the United States in droves. Nor did he indicate that the Court's decision applied to all asylee requests regardless of the nation involved —which, of course, it did. Indeed, in May 1987 the Reagan Administration had denied a specific request from the President of El Salvador, Napoleon Duarte, that Salvadoreans apprehended from his country without proper documents not be deported because of the rapidly declining economic conditions and the reign of violence within the country. The number of such Salvadoreans in the United States at the time who had entered without inspection was estimated to be about 450,000 persons.[41]

When asylum requests were filed during the 1980s, the approval rate was over 80 percent for Nicaraguans while being only about 2 to 3 percent for requests from Salvadoreans and Guatemalans. It was in this context of seeming unfairness that a grassroots protest movement, known as the "Sanctuary Movement," was spawned in the Southwest and briefly flourished across the country.[42] Without going into detail, the supporters of this movement argued that refugee policy was being twisted by the Reagan Administration from a politically impartial policy to one designed to further its foreign policy agenda. They argued that asylee protections were readily available to refugees from "left wing" dictatorships (Nicaragua and other countries like Afghanistan, Poland, the Soviet Union, Vietnam, and Cuba) but seldom available for those fleeing "right wing" governments (like Guatemala, El Salvador, or Haiti). The Sanctuary Movement involved political and religious activists who had created an "underground railroad" that physically transported people from El Salvador and Guatemala from the U.S. border region through a series of loosely associated churches and "safe-houses" into the interior of the nation. Leaders of this movement in Texas and Arizona were subsequently arrested, tried, and convicted of smuggling illegal immigrants into the United States. Following their trials (in which they usually received suspended sentences), these leaders vowed to continue their activities, but in a less publicized way.[43]

As for Nicaraguans, the "Meese directive" of 1987 was widely interpreted as a green light to enter the United States *en masse* since there seemed to be little chance of being deported if apprehended. In April 1988, the Administration added support to this perception when the INS announced it would allow aliens crossing the U.S.-Mexico border to obtain asylum applications in Harlingen, Texas (the nearest U.S. land entry point to Nicaragua) but they would not have to file them until they reached their final destination (usually Miami but also, in significant numbers, Los Angeles and New York) in the interior. Many other Nicaraguans simply entered illegally and made a claim for asylum only if they were apprehended. As one might expect, asylum applications soared as thousands of Nicaraguans, mostly impoverished persons and families who were fleeing the declining economic opportunities and falling standards of living in their homeland, crossed through Mexico and into the United States. Unlike the original outflow of the Nicaraguan business class that had fled to Miami after the Sandinistas took control of the government in Nicaragua in the early 1980s, those who came in the late 1980s were from the countryside and were typically poor, unskilled, and illiterate.[44] As it occurred before with the Cubans and then the Haitians, it was the native-born American black population that bore most of the ill effects of the flood of Nicaraguans into the Miami-Dade Country labor market.[45] As one black resident of Overtown, a black ghetto in central Miami where riots erupted in early 1989, rhetorically asked: "I've been here all my life and I don't have a regular job. How long did it take to get funds for the Nicaraguans?"[46] Another black citizen in Overtown area described the issue in its broader racial context when he said: "You can see what is happening in Miami now; you have all these Nicaraguan people coming in while they're sending Haitians back."[47]

By late 1988, the folly of the Administration's political policy had become apparent. More than 27,000 Nicaraguans had requested asylum petitions at Harlingen over the preceding ten months. Hence, following the Presidential elections in November, the INS, on December 16, 1988, revoked its April 1988 order and reverted to its earlier policy that asylum requests had to be actually filed at the first port of entry in the United States. But the word that the "open door policy" was no longer in effect could not stop those already in transit. Hence, several thousand Central Americans (mostly Nicaraguans) quickly found themselves trapped in South Texas while still others continued to arrive. They were required to remain there until their claims for political asylum were acted upon. Detention camps were set up by the INS to hold those whose requests were denied while others, whose applications were pending, set up a "tent city" or moved into various abandoned buildings in the area to await decisions. Local social services were quickly overwhelmed by the associated food and medical costs. At its height, there were about 3,600 people living under such dire conditions. On January 9, 1989 a federal district judge issued a temporary restraining order that directed the INS to desist from its policy of keeping the applicants in South Texas while their claims were reviewed. The immediate effect was that most of the asylee applicants moved inland to cities like Miami and Los Angeles as had their fellow countrymen before them. Another 5,200 asylum applicants crossed into South Texas (including some Mexican nationals who felt they too had found a loophole in U.S. immigration policy) over the next five weeks before the judge lifted his restraining order. Thus, the INS policy of receiving and processing applicants at the point of entry was reinstated. Plans to establish detention camps in South Texas were announced where applicants would be placed while their applications were processed.[48] As a consequence, the flow of asylum-seekers declined sharply. A year later, in February 1990 the Sandinista government was voted out of office and replaced by a government more sympathetic to U.S. interests. Nonetheless, the economy of Nicaragua has not improved and thus the exodus of Nicaraguans has continued. However, there is no longer a political advantage to be gained from granting refugee status to those who flee to the United States. They are now considered to be illegal immigrants; had it not been for Attorney General Meese's interference, most of those who entered earlier would also have been so classified. Indeed, the majority of those Nicaraguans who requested asylum applications during this episode did not show up for subsequent hearings on their applications. They simply "disappeared" into the large Hispanic communities in their destination cities. Even many of those who did show up for hearings and, after adjudication, were denied asylum protection simply stayed in the United States, albeit as illegal immigrants. Only some of those who became involved in criminal activities sometimes found themselves physically deported out of the country.

As for those who fled from El Salvador and Guatemala during the 1980s, the fact that virtually none of their applications for political asylum were granted during this period became the subject of a class action suit that was filed in May 1985 by a number of church groups —many of which had been associated with the aforementioned Sanctuary Movement. The suit alleged that during the Reagan years the federal government had not acted in a neutral, nonpolitical manner as required by the Refugee Act of 1980. As a consequence, it was alleged that many persons from these two countries concluded it was futile even to apply for asylee status through administrative channels and that many of those apprehended were falsely classified as being illegal immigrants.

On December 19, 1990 the U.S. Department of Justice reached an out-of-court settlement with these churches whereby the government agreed to stop detaining and deporting aliens from El Salvador and Guatemala until it grants a hearing to 150,000 persons from these countries who had been declared to be illegal aliens because their asylum requests were denied over these years or whose final decisions on such requests were pending.[49] Moreover, the settlement also requires the INS to offer hearings to another estimated 350,000 persons from these countries who are be-lieved to have entered illegally during these years and who did not file for asylum because of possible beliefs that the procedures were weighted against them. Thus, almost one-half million persons from these countries can apply over the following eighteen months for political asylum and, while their cases are pending, they are to be given authorization to work in the United States.

The settlement also includes those aliens from El Salvador who were specifically given "temporary protected status" by the Immigration Act of 1990, which became effective October 1, 1991. Under this new addition to U.S. immigration policy (which will be discussed in Chapter 9), persons who enter illegally from countries where civil wars are in progress, but who do not qualify for refugee status because they were not specifically subject to persecution on any of the five grounds specified in the Refugee Act of 1980, will be allowed to remain in the United States for eighteen months and to seek work temporarily if they come forth and register with the INS.

The Continuing Weakness of Asylee Policy

As the preceding discussion suggests and the data in Table 6.3 confirm, asylee policy had taken on a life of its own. It has become a separate immigration admission system. Table 6.3 indicates the number of persons prior to 1980 who benefited from the exercise of the discretionary policy

Table 6.3 Asylum Cases Filed with INS District Directors Fiscal Years 1973-90

Year	Cases Received	Cases Completed	Cases Approved	Cases Denied	Cases Adjudicated	Percent Approved
1973	1,913	1,510	380	1,130	1,510	25.2
1974	2,716	2,769	294	2,475	2,769	10.6
1975	2,432	1,664	562	1,102	1,664	33.8
1976	2,733	1,914	590	1,324	1,914	30.8
1976,TQ*	896	370	97	273	370	26.2
1977	2,529	1,939	754	1,185	1,939	38.9
1978	3,702	2,312	1,218	1,094	2,312	52.7
1979	5,801	2,312	1,227	1,085	2,312	53.1
1980	26,512	2,000	1,104	896	2,000	55.2
1981	61,568	4,512	1,175	3,346	4,512	26.0
1982	33,296	11,326	3,909	7,255	11,164	35.0
1983	26,091	25,447	7,215	16,811	24,026	30.0
1984	24,295	54,320	8,278	32,344	40,622	20.4
1985	16,662	28,528	4,585	14,172	18,757	24.4
1986	18,889	45,792	3,359	7,882	11,241	29.9
1987	26,107	44,785	4,062	3,454	7,516	54.0
1988	60,736	68,357	5,531	8,582	14,113	39.2
1989	101,679	102,795	6,942	31,547	38,489	18.0
1990	73,637	48,342	4,173	24,156	28,329	14.7

Note: The Refugee Act of 1980 went into effect on April 1, 1980. Data for fiscal years 1982 and 1983 have been estimated due to changes in the reporting procedures during those two periods. Cases completed cover approvals, denials, and cases otherwise closed. Cases otherwise closed are those in which the applicant withdrew the case from consideration, never acknowledged a request for an interview with the INS, or died. Cases adjudicated cover approvals and denials.

TQ = Transitional fiscal year quarter when the Federal government altered its fiscal year from ending on June 30 to ending on September 30.

Source: U.S. Immigration and Naturalization Service.

of extended voluntary departure by various Attorneys General. In the middle of fiscal year 1980, the United States enacted its first formal asylum policy and the annual number of asylee applicants increased by several multiples. By the late 1980s and early 1990s, asylum applications soared for reasons already discussed. Thus, what was originally perceived as being ancillary to the nation's overall immigration system has become, itself, a major contributor to the overall influx of immigrants.

At first glance, the data in Table 6.3 would seem to indicate that, while the number of cases received each year is high, the number of approvals is not, and therefore the issue is insignificant. Nothing could be further from the truth. The preponderance of individuals who file asylee applications never show up for the scheduled interviews with INS officials. They simply fade into the local communities and become illegal immigrants. The likely reason for this behavior is that many, if not most, of the applicants who do not pursue their cases are economic migrants, not political migrants. They flee their homelands not out of fear of individual persecution, but in search of a better life in economic terms. Some may expect that there may be another amnesty given to illegal immigrants in the future if they just bide their time.

Furthermore, even those cases that are fully adjudicated give a false picture as to the consequences. The data in Table 6.3 show that in most years the majority of the applications are not approved. But just because the applicant loses does not mean that he or she leaves the country. Most, it seems, stay, albeit as illegal immigrants. One reason for not immediately escorting those who lose their cases directly back to their homelands is, in part, the lack of funds to do so. But another reason is that throughout the 1980s many of the asylee requests have been denied to people fleeing from countries that were dominated by communist governments (e.g., Cuba, Nicaragua, Poland) or where tyrannical regimes are in power (e.g., Iran) or areas where civil unrest is widespread (e.g., El Salvador and Guatemala). Under these circumstances, there was little disposition by the federal government to force people to leave even though they have no right to be in the United States.

On July 18, 1990 the Bush Administration initiated administrative steps whose purpose was to further liberalize the asylee review procedures. The action was, in part, a response to the legitimate criticisms of the biased application of asylum policy during the years of the Reagan Administration. It was announced that the INS would establish a corps of ninety asylum officers who would be specially trained to judge whether an applicant actually had "a well founded fear" of persecution in his or her homeland. New rules were also promulgated whereby asylum officers are directed to give the benefit of the doubt to asylum requests by aliens, and the officers are empowered to make independent decisions about the merits of such claims without necessarily following recommendations made by the U.S. Department of State on their validity. Moreover, an alien may qualify for asylum on the basis of the applicant's own statements without corroboration if the testimony appears "credible in light of general conditions" in the alien's home country. Furthermore, the applicant does not need to prove that he or she was being singled out individually for persecution if "there is a pattern or practice of persecuting the group of persons similarly situated." A new documentation center has been created to hold information about political conditions in various countries for use by the asylum officers. In praising this action, Senator Edward Kennedy stated that "too often in recent years we have tolerated a double standard, under which asylum has been unfairly denied to legitimate refugees for fear of embarrassing friendly but repressive governments."[50] He added that the new rules "are fairer and more generous."

There is no doubt that the policy changes in 1990 provide an "even playing field" for all asylum applicants. But, when these procedural changes are added to the existing disarray of asylee policy, they constitute an enormous loophole to any quest to establish a comprehensive national immigration policy. If one can reach the United States, all that is necessary, if apprehended or detained at a border, is to make a request for political asylum. While the case is pending, one can legally work in the United States. If the request is approved, one is on the road to becoming a legal immigrant. If denied or if one does not show up for an adjudication hearing, one can remain as an illegal immigrant and hope for a future amnesty. This is not the way asylum policy was intended to work. Its real mission—to serve as a humanitarian outlet for individuals who are threatened with death or torture due to the exercise of their human rights—is seriously endangered by the perpetuation of the prevailing state of affairs which invites mass abuse by economic migrants.

The Complex Case of Soviet Emigres

Still another, highly contentious refugee issue of the 1980s centered on the status of emigres from the Soviet Union. In the wake of the breakup of the Soviet Union in 1991, it is probable that this issue will test the ability of policymakers to alter refugee eligibility policies in light of rapidly changing political conditions.

From the time that the Universal Declaration of Human Rights was promulgated by the United Nations in 1948, the Soviet Union throughout the Cold War era was criticized for its restrictions on the emigration rights of its people. Throughout this period there were individual cases of Soviet citizens who sought asylum (or extended voluntary departure) after they were already in the United States. Usually they were musicians, athletes, dancers, students, or scientists, but sometimes they were former government officials or secret agents, who were already in the U.S. or who defected in another free nation but sought to resettle in the United States. But always there was the larger issue of the plight of individuals and groups within the Soviet Union who were not free in this era to leave. Among these were leaders of various dissident groups but also there were the larger general groupings, usually religious in nature, who were unable to pursue the practice of their faiths (e.g., Jews, Ukrainian Catholics, and various Evangelical Protestants). There were also members of various ethnic groups who felt they too were singled out for persecution.

Prior to the passage of the Refugee Act of 1980, there was a period of liberalization in Soviet emigration policy during the 1970s that was associated with the era of political "detente" in U.S.-Soviet relations. In 1979, for instance, over 70,000 persons were permitted to leave the Soviet Union. Some went to other Western European nations, some to Israel, but most were admitted to the United States through the dubious use of the parole authority. In December 1979, however, Soviet troops entered Afghanistan in an ill-fated attempt to suppress a coup against its puppet government. The era of "detente" ended and emigration was an immediate casualty of this renewal of the Cold War. The number of Soviet emigres fell to about 20,000 in 1980 and it continued to decline until 1985 when it fell to just over 1,000 persons. Most who were allowed to leave were Jews, Armenians, and ethnic Germans.

Throughout the 1970s and the first half of the 1980s, the very act of applying to emigrate had the effect of turning applicants and their families into refugees. "The applicant was identified as someone disloyal to the Soviet system who lost his or her employment, apartment, and, frequently, suffered social and political ostracism."[51]

But, beginning in 1987, another reversal in Soviet attitudes occurred as the policy of *glasnost* began to take hold. A significant number of Jews (8,000 persons) and Armenians (3,000 persons) were permitted to leave that year. Most entered the United States. Another 14,500 ethnic Germans were allowed to move to West Germany. Discriminatory actions against those who applied for exit visas rapidly diminished. In 1988, the liberalization trend continued in the Soviet Union and it was accompanied by similar actions in many Eastern European nations. Over 108,000 persons from the Soviet Union were permitted to leave, which made 1988 a record year. Most of the successful Soviet applicants in 1987 and 1988 who applied to the U.S. Embassy were required to be persons who had some family ties to U.S. citizens. The majority did, in fact, enter the United States. Other Soviet Jews without such family ties were allowed to apply to the Dutch Embassy for visas to immigrate to Israel or to West Germany. When these emigres arrived in Vienna, Austria (the usual railroad exit point from the U.S.S.R.) the majority then changed their travel plans, tore up their Israeli visas, and proceeded to Rome and applied directly to the U.S. Embassy to enter the United States as refugees. Their requests were usually granted with the Attorney General using his parole authority to accomplish the feat and with little attention given to whether or not the applicants were actually experiencing any persecution that would qualify them for refugee status.

This policy quickly led to a strange international confrontation over the application of U.S. refugee policy. Namely, the government of Israel requested that the United States cease giving refugee status to the Soviet Jews.[52] The Israeli government actually proposed that all Soviet Jews be required to go to Bucharest, Rumania to pick up their Israeli visas rather than to exit in Vienna. They would then have to travel directly to Israel and could not get to Rome to file for refugee admission to the United States. This Israeli action, in turn, was bitterly critized by Jewish groups in the U.S. (who felt Soviet Jews ought to be free to choose where they wish to resettle) and by various Arab groups (who did not want more Jews to settle in Israel). U.S. refugee policy had once more become a subject of external political manipulation. Pushed to the background was the more fundamental issue. Were these persons actually qualified to be political refugees because they were the target of individual persecution or were they economic migrants who were looking for a way to improve their economic conditions as the Soviet economy was collapsing?

As 1988 was again a presidential election year, the Reagan Administration chose to maintain the *status quo* with respect to the status of Soviet Jews and to leave a solution to its successor.[53] In the first nine months of 1989, 46,000 Soviet emigres were admitted to the United

States and the international tension over the issue continued to mount. Groping for a resolution, the Bush Administration announced that, as of October 1, 1989, all Soviet applicants who intended to apply for admission as refugees while still in the Soviet Union would have to apply at the U.S. embassy in Moscow. The "Vienna-Rome pipeline" was closed as of that date. In the following months, over 600,000 applications were distributed of which over 300,000 were completed and returned. In fiscal year 1990, about 50,800 Soviet refugees were admitted to the U.S. (of whom 8,000 were "third country refugees" whose expenses were privately funded by Jewish organizations under the same arrangement with the U.S. government that had been reached with private Cuban organizations in 1988). In May 1991, the Soviet Union adopted a new emigration law that eased the ability of persons to leave the country to resettle elsewhere.

Thus, there occurred a complete reversal of the emigration situation in Eastern Europe. Whereas in the early 1980s the policy concern of many of the nations of the free world had been directed to persons who wished to leave the Soviet Union and its Eastern European satellites but could not, the concern had switched in the early 1990s in Western Europe to a fear that far too many will actually elect to do so.[54] It is also a vital concern for policymakers in the United States. With restrictions falling on emigration and in the wake of faltering economies in the new republics of the former Soviet Union and Eastern Europe, it is more difficult to make the case that such emigres qualify as political refugees. It seems more likely that most who wish to leave are economic refugees who are not much different in their quest for better living standards and economic opportunities from persons from the myriad Third World nations who annually seek to enter the United States and Western Europe. Just because the United States and other free nations support the right of people to be able to leave their homelands does not mean that they must be automatically admitted to the United States or these other nations. As Senator Alan Simpson aptly observed, "we ought to stop this gimmickry of the use of the word 'refugee.' We must distinguish between the right to leave the Soviet Union and the right to enter the United States. They are not the same thing."[55]

China: Politics Cause Policy Chaos

On his last day as Attorney General before resigning from that office, Edwin Meese sought to add a new wrinkle to the "politicalization" of refugee policy. On August 5, 1988 he issued policy guidelines for asylum requests that instructed the INS to consider requests from individuals from China who cited the possibility of persecution on the grounds that they violated that country's "one couple, one child" family planning policy if they were forced to return home. Meese requested that, on a case by case basis, the INS consider whether such a refusal to follow government population policy constitutes political dissent and would, therefore, be a proper grounds for granting asylum.

There was immediate opposition to this arbitrary action. Critics pointed out that if the population policy of the China applies uniformly to everyone, it cannot be a form of individual persecution. After all, the purpose of the policy is to reduce the nation's population growth rate for equally compelling humanitarian reasons. The social goal is to provide a higher standard of living for the future generations of Chinese citizens.

In the first test case of this decision, the INS rejected an asylum request in May 1989 by a married couple from China who entered the United States illegally.[56] The policy itself, however, has yet to be revoked.

On November 30, 1989, President George Bush issued a related directive that permits asylum to be granted to people fleeing pressure in their native lands to have abortions or to be sterilized. The following May, the U.S. Department of State ruled that a Chinese couple who fled China ostensibly for these reasons qualified for refugee status.[57] The Department of State, however, refused to elaborate on the basis for its decision. Yet the precedent for creating an administrative category of "reproductive refugees" has been established. What its limits are will only be proven by subsequent events. The issue of abortion, however, is a major domestic political issue. As matters now stand, the subject has the potential to have major ramifications on the conduct of immigration policy.

On the other hand, when the Bush Administration was confronted with another situation in China in which refugee status seemed logical, it refused to grant it. Namely, after the failed student-led democracy movement in China in June 1989 that culminated in the Tiananmen Square massacre, there were as many as 40,000 Chinese students studying at U.S. universities. And many of them had openly supported the protests. The Bush Administration, however, refused to grant asylee requests and it vetoed a bill passed by Congress that would have allowed these Chinese students to remain in the country after their visas expired. President Bush, however, did issue on November 30, 1989 an executive order permitting all such students to remain in the country until June

1994. It was his view that this action, at least for the time being, accomplished the same result but without offending the Chinese government to the same degree as grants of asylum would have. Subsequently, the House of Representatives voted to override the President's veto but it was narrowly sustained when the U.S. Senate failed to vote for an override.[58]

The Explosion of Illegal Immigration

Although the problem of illegal immigration dates back to the 1870s and 1880s when the first restrictions on immigration were imposed, it was not considered a serious problem until after the Immigration Act of 1924 went into effect. Even then, the coming of the depression decade followed by the outbreak of World War II quickly dampened such tendencies. During the war years of the 1940s, apprehensions averaged only about 12,000 persons a year. There was a significant spurt of illegal immigration from Mexico following the war but illegal immigration then receded from the mid-1950s to the mid-1960s.[59] The sharp decline was largely the result of a "border sweep" of Mexican nationals conducted by the INS (called "Operation Wetback") in 1954 along the southwestern border and the residual publicity of that infamous endeavor.[60] But, following the passage of the Immigration Act of 1965, illegal immigration quickly soared.

Table 6.4 shows the rapidity of the escalation in illegal immigration as measured by actual apprehensions by the INS. It shows a tenfold increase in the number of illegal immigrants who were apprehended between 1965 and the early 1990s. To be sure, there are serious problems associated with the use of apprehension data. They contain multiple counts of repeat captures of the same individuals. But there is no reason to believe that this statistical problem is proportionately more serious in recent years than it was in 1965. Hence, apprehension data can serve as a general indicator of gross changes in illegal immigration trends. Conversely, apprehension data do not include what is believed to be a larger number of persons who enter illegally but who avoid apprehension. It is also the case that about 90 to 95 percent of those who are apprehended every year are Mexicans who are physically caught crossing or who are found within close proximity to the border. Thus, nonMexicans who are more likely to be visa "overstayers" are significantly undercounted in this data. But debates over the adequacy of the illegal immigration statistics are endless and usually fruitless.[61] Because it is an illegal activity, precise data will never be available. Thus, apprehension data are the best indicator that is presently available of the broad trends

Table 6.4 Aliens Apprehended, Fiscal Years 1961-1991			
1961-70	1,608,356	1976 TQ	221,824
1961	88,823	1977	1,042,215
1962	92,758	1978	1,057,977
1963	88,712	1979	1,076,418
1964	86,597	1980	910,361
1965	110,371	1981-90	11,883,328
1966	138,520	1981	975,780
1967	161,608	1982	970,246
1968	212,057	1983	1,251,357
1969	283,557	1984	1,246,981
1970	345,353	1985	1,348,749
1971-80	8,321,498	1986	1,767,400
1971	420,126	1987	1,190,488
1972	505,949	1988	1,008,145
1973	655,968	1989	954,243
1974	788,145	1990	1,169,939
1975	766,600	1991	----
1976	875,915	1991	1,197,875 (preliminary)

Source: U.S. Immigration and Naturalization Service.

in illegal immigration. No one contests the fact that the number is large and few disagree that the trend is generally toward annual increase.An immediate explanation for the increase in illegal immigration in 1965 was the fact that the Mexican Labor Program (i.e., the *bracero* program discussed in Chapter 4) was unilaterally terminated on December 31, 1964 by the United States. In 1965 (and for several years thereafter), many of these same agricultural workers from Mexico simply returned to the United States to seek work as they had done for the preceding two decades. This time, however, they were illegal immigrants and those apprehended were so treated. But it was also the aforementioned provisions of the Immigration Act of 1965 that contributed to the ongoing nature and the acceleration of illegal immigration. The Act, it is to be recalled, placed a ceiling on immigration from the Western Hemisphere that went into effect in 1968. This action legally capped the fastest growing component of the overall legal immigration stream. In the same vein, when the annual limit of 20,000 immigrants a year was extended to individual Western Hemisphere nations in 1976, it meant that Mexico in particular, which was supplying over three times that number of legal immigrants a year to the United States, quickly accumulated a massive backlog of would-be emigrants who could not legally leave. The application of the preference system for admission to all Western Hemisphere nations in 1976 also meant that, for the first time, the only way one could qualify for legal immigration was if one had a relative who was already a U.S. citizen; or if one had the specific skills, education or work experience needed by U.S. employers and could, therefore, qualify for the limited number of work-related visas; or if one was a refugee. Once the single worldwide ceiling on immigration went into effect in 1978, there were no nonpreference visas available to anyone for the next ten years. Hence, the only channel available for people determined to immigrate but who did not meet the preference requirements was to enter illegally. Hundreds of thousands of persons from the Western Hemisphere—especially from Mexico but also from the British West Indies (since Britain, after 1962, had made it almost impossible for people from these Islands to immigrate any longer to the former motherland of the Commonwealth) did just this. They were joined by other persons from other Caribbean Islands, as well as from Central and South American countries. Meanwhile, illegal immigration (especially of visa "overstayers") began to increase from other nations of the Eastern Hemi-sphere with which the United States had close commercial and/or military relations (e.g., Korea, Taiwan, Iran, the Philippines, and Nigeria).[62]

But the power of the factors that "push" people on a mass scale to leave their homelands (e.g., poverty, overpopulation, unemployment, political corruption, and the lack of economic opportunity) cannot alone explain the scale of illegal immigration to the United States. After all, aside from Mexico and some of the countries of the Caribbean region, there are other industrialized nations that are often nearer to the homelands of those persons who have illegally immigrated to the United States. The answer lies in the fact that immigration policy in the post-1965 era up until 1986 lacked any semblance of deterrence.

Other industrial nations of the free world typically had in place work permit systems, and national identification systems, and they quickly adopted legal sanctions against employers who hired illegal immigrants when confronted with their presence.[63] The United States did not. It was illegal for aliens to enter the United States without inspection or to "overstay" nonimmigrant visas (and in most cases even to seek work as a nonimmigrant) but it was not illegal for an employer to hire such persons (knowingly or not). Indeed, the Immigration and Nationality Act of 1952, as a concession to Texas agricultural employers, included a specific provision that exempted anything that employers did in their role as employers from constituting the illegal act of "harboring" an illegal immigrant. This became known as the infamous "Texas Proviso." Moreover, when an illegal immigrant was apprehended in the United States, they were given the right to contest the charge (but they would have to post bail); or remain in custody and, if found guilty in a legal proceeding, face formal deportation (which usually precludes any future right to legally immigrate to the United States); or they could elect to take "a voluntary departure" from the country. About 95 percent of those apprehended in this era elected that last option. If they chose voluntary departure and if they had been apprehended near a border (usually the Mexican border), they were escorted to the border and released. Frequently this meant that they simply turned around and sought to reenter again, making the whole process a mockery. If they were actually apprehended in the interior of the nation and chose the voluntary departure option, they usually were simply released and told to leave unless some criminal activity was also involved. It is unlikely that many did. In some cases, if the INS had available funds, it would pay the transportation costs of these persons back to their homelands but such funds were often not available. Again, the whole process had the appearance more of a sad joke than of serious deterrence policy. Furthermore, throughout this period, the Border Patrol which was responsible for monitoring the border region was chronically understaffed with fewer than 2,000 members, no more than 400 of whom were on duty on any eight-hour shift on any given day but who were expected to patrol the 1,500-mile border with Mexico and the 4,000-mile border with Canada), and was underfunded relative to its assigned duties.

Legislative Reaction to Mounting Illegal Immigration

The initial reaction to the rapid escalation in the number of apprehensions of illegal immigrants was to do nothing. Indeed, for ten years following the passage of the Immigration Act of 1965, the powerful chairman of the Senate Judiciary Committee (who had also appointed himself Chairman of its Subcommittee on Immigration), James O. Eastland (D-Miss.), refused even to convene a meeting of the Subcommittee where any reform legislation had to originate. Thus, efforts by the House of Representatives in the early 1970s, led by Peter W. Rodino (D-N.J.), to repeal the "Texas Proviso" and to enact sanctions against employer who hired illegal immigrants were to no avail. Both times the House passed such legislation during that decade, the bills died in the Senate.

Perceiving that illegal immigration was reaching a crisis stage, President Jimmy Carter sent to Congress a legislative proposal on August 4, 1977, "to help markedly reduce the increasing flow of undocumented aliens in this country and to regulate the presence of millions of undocumented aliens already here."[64] It included an employer sanctions program; enhanced funding for border enforcement; temporary legalization status for illegal immigrants who had been in the country for over five years; and a proposal to increase the country ceiling for legal immigrants from 20,000 a year from Canada and Mexico to a combined level of 50,000 based on demand (which at the time would have meant about 42,000 visas a year for Mexico since Canadians were using only about 8,000 visa slots a year). Lacking a consensus on the merits of these ideas, the Carter proposals were not acted upon by Congress. In 1978, when Congress added the amendment that established the single worldwide ceiling on immigration, it included in the legislation a provision to establish the Select Commission on Immigration and Refugee Policy (SCIRP).

The Report of the Select Commission

SCIRP, as noted in Chapter 1, was given the mandate to examine the immigration policy of the nation in its entirety. Illegal immigration, it was felt, could best be addressed as part of a comprehensive examination and possible overhaul of the entire immigration system. A cynic, however, might conclude that Congress wanted to bide time rather than react to the Carter proposals which various special interest groups in the nation felt were controversial.

When the Commission released its final report on March 1, 1981, it proposed significant changes in all facets of the nation's immigration policy.[65] But its recommendations pertaining to illegal immigration drew the most attention and reaction. Succinctly stated, SCIRP called for the enactment of civil and criminal sanctions against employers who hire illegal immigrants (which meant the repeal of the "Texas Proviso"); the coupling of sanctions with some form of secure identification system for job applicants (but the Commission could not agree on what the nature of the identification system should be); enhanced border enforcement to preclude some illegal entry; and an amnesty for those illegal immigrants who were in the United States as of some unspecified date set several years prior to the enactment of employer sanctions (in order not to set off any massive onslaught of persons seeking to qualify for a future eligibility deadline).

By the time that the Select Commission issued its report, however, the Carter Administration had been voted out of office. The incoming Reagan Administration had not considered immigration reform to be a high priority. Its initial reaction was to be wary of the subject. Hence, it set up its own Task Force to study the recommendations of the Select Commission. Ultimately, a legislative package was put forth by the Administration but its provisions were far more timid than those of the Select Commission.[66] Consequently, the Reagan proposals were put aside by Congress and a bipartisan bill was drafted by Senator Alan Simpson (R-Wy.) and Representative Romano Mazzoli (D-Ky.). This bill embraced the key recommendations of the Select Commission and also proposed a number of other policy changes.

The original Simpson-Mazzoli bill was comprehensive in its design. It sought changes in all of the component parts of the nation's immigration and refugee policies. Again, however, it was the proposals pertaining to illegal immigration that attracted the most critical attention. In particular, two key elements—employer sanctions and amnesty—were the targets of attack. In general, people who supported one, opposed the other but the key to the bill's passage rested upon their linkage. Other controversial amendments were added to the bill during the subsequent legislative process, pertaining to attempts to add a foreign worker program for agricultural workers and new provisions to prohibit employment discrimination on the basis of alienage. These amendments contributed to the strident nature of the subsequent debate.[67] The upshot was that the bill passed the Senate, but died on the floor of the House of Representatives in December 1982. An attempt to pass a very similar bill in 1984 also failed in the House of Representatives after passing in the Senate.

The Immigration Reform and Control Act of 1986 (IRCA)

With the perception that the problems of the nation's immigration system were worsening, a new tack was taken in 1986: piecemeal reform. Illegal immigration was selected as the first issue to be addressed under this new legislative strategy. This time different bills were introduced in the Senate and the House of Representatives. Senator Simpson introduced a bill that included the three key provisions: employer sanctions, amnesty, and enhanced border enforcement. His bill did include revisions in the existing H-2 provisions (see Chapter 4) that would make it easier for agricultural employers to employ temporary foreign workers in the form of nonimmigrant workers. This was intended to ameliorate some of the opposition of southwestern agribusinesses who feared the loss of a substantial number of workers if they could no longer hire illegal immigrants from Mexico. On the Senate floor, Pete Wilson (R-Cal.) offered an amendment to add an entirely new temporary worker program for agricultural workers. Ultimately, it was done. It would have permitted up to 350,000 temporary harvest workers of perishable commodities to be admitted for each of three years after this proposed bill went into effect. The amended bill passed the Senate in September 1985.

In the House, a bill cosponsored by Representatives Peter Rodino and Romano Mazzoli was introduced in September 1985. It too contained provisions that were similar to the three key provisions in the Simpson bill. It also had provisions to make it easier for H-2 workers to be brought into the United States. It did not contain any provisions for any new temporary worker program although it provided for a transitional temporary worker program for agriculture whereby the number of workers would be annually reduced over a three year phase-out period.

For the next ten months, there was no visible action taken on the House bill. Behind the scenes lengthy negotiations took place over the issue of the temporary foreign worker provisions. Involved were proponents of farm workers; supporters of agricultural business interests; and advocates of a compromise solution between these two contending groups in order that the immigration reform bill could be debated. Finally, in early June 1986, Congressman Charles Schumer (D-N.Y.), a leader of the compromise group, announced that agreement had been reached on a plan to end the stalemate.[68] Essentially, his amendment stated that the Attorney General could grant lawful permanent-resident status to any illegal immigrants who could prove they had been working in perishable agriculture for at least twenty full days between May 1, 1985 and May 1, 1986. Called the Special Agricultural Worker program (SAW), it was, in essence, another amnesty program. It also provided that if a substantial number of SAW workers subsequently quit working in agriculture, their numbers could be "replenished" by other workers recruited from foreign countries who could subsequently apply for permanent-resident alien status if they worked in agriculture for a set time period. These persons would be known as Replenishment Agricultural Workers (or RAW workers).

The rationale for providing the opportunity for illegal immigrants who had recently been employed in agriculture to become permanent-resident aliens was multifold. It overcame the southwestern growers' opposition to the possibility that employer sanctions would make several hundred thousand of their current employees ineligible to be retained. These agricultural employers had continued to be adamant in their assertions that citizen workers could not be attracted to meet their seasonal demand for workers to pick perishable crops. Of equal importance was the fact that the SAW program also overcame the fears of supporters of immigration reform who strongly opposed the idea of a guestworker program (e.g., the Wilson Amendment to the pending Senate bill). By allowing those illegal immigrants who had been employed in agriculture to have a right to obtain resident aliens status by virtue of their past employment record and, if they chose, to become naturalized citizens later, these workers would quickly acquire most of the protections and freedoms available to nonagricultural citizen workers. Given resident alien status, SAW workers would be able to qualify for some social entitlement programs in the off-season. Moreover, they would not be forced to remain agricultural workers (i.e., they would not be tied to particular employers as "serfs") if better job opportunities elsewhere should become available to them. For those who remained in agriculture, it would be easier for them to be unionized if they knew that they could remain permanently in the United States. Thus, this ingenious compromise provided a balance between the demands of growers for an adequate supply of labor and the insistence of unions and various Hispanic groups that agricultural workers be protected from the opportunities for exploitation that were traditionally associated with temporary-worker programs in the agricultural industry in the past.

The immediate reaction to the Schumer Amendment, however, was far from positive. It became a subject of intense controversy. Nonetheless, it accomplished its primary purpose: it broke the logjam in the House Judiciary Committee that had prevented IRCA from reaching the floor. On June 25, 1986 the Committee voted to add the Schumer amendment, with only slight modification, to the bill. The revised version specified that permanent-resident alien status would be provided to illegal immigrants if they had worked in agriculture for U.S. employers for not less than sixty days during the twelve months that preceded May 1, 1986. At this point, however, Congressman Mazzoli threatened to abandon the entire bill. Calling the amendment "unparalleled, unprecedented, and unacceptable," he pessimistically predicted that "passage of the Schumer Amendment ensures that bill's doom."[69] Nonetheless, the next day the Judiciary Committee voted to send the amended bill to the floor of the House.

For a time, it seemed that Mazzoli's prediction would prove true. The bill was not taken up by the House Rules Committee until late September 1986. When it was, House minority whip, Trent Lott (R-Miss.), called the Schumer Amendment "the most controversial issue" in the entire bill and Representative Dan Lungren (R-Cal.), a strong supporter of immigration reform, called the amendment "an abomination" that would "kill the bill."[70] When the debate rules were established, however, they forbade any amendments to be made from the floor to the fragile terms of the Schumer Amendment. Other key provisions of the bill—employer sanctions and amnesty—could be debated on the floor and were subject to possible deletion—but no feature of the SAW and RAW programs could be discussed. Their fate was linked to the passage of the overall bill.

A resolution to adopt the debate rules, however, was defeated on the House floor on September 26, 1986. With Congress planning to adjourn during the next week, the prospects for an immigration reform bill appeared to be lost again. All fingers of blame immediately pointed to the provision in the rules that prohibited debate on the Schumer Amendment.

Amid an outcry of critical editorials from the nation's print media in the days that immediately followed the defeated vote on the rules, a completely unexpected window of opportunity for the resurrection of immigration reform was suddenly created. The Congress had not yet passed a military appropriation bill which contained several controversial foreign policy provisions. In addition, President Reagan had not yet signed another controversial bill pertaining to the creation of a large environmental "superfund" and there was congressional fear that, if Congress adjourned, he would kill the bill with a pocket veto. It was at this point that officials in the White House suddenly announced on October 7, 1986 that President Reagan would meet personally with Soviet Premier Mikhail Gorbachev in Reykjavik, Iceland on October 11 and 12. Hence, Congress could not force the showdown on the appropriation bill while the President was preparing for this critical meeting or was actually out of the country at a summit meeting on the possibility of setting an agenda for nuclear disarmament. Thus, an unexpected pause in its planned activities was forced on Congress. Adjournment had to be postponed. With nothing else to do, behind the scenes negotiations on the immigration bill were quickly renewed. A minor change was made in the provisions of the Schumer Amendment. The number of days an illegal immigrant who had worked in agriculture in the year preceding May 1, 1986 needed to be eligible for eventual adjustment of status to become a resident alien was increased from sixty to ninety days. Given the inability to act on the other critical issues, the Houses of Representatives reversed itself on October 9, 1986 and voted to accept the debate rules it had rejected only the week before. Fourteen amendments to IRCA would be allowed to be debated (four of which were subsequently adopted) but there could not be any debate on any of the Schumer provisions. A marathon session began and, late in the evening of October 9, 1986, the House passed the Immigration Reform and Control Act (i.e., the Simpson-Rodino Act).

A Senate-House conference committee was quickly constituted and it reached agreement on October 14, 1986. In the conference, the Senate proposals for the Wilson program and the House proposal for a three-year transitional farm-worker program were deleted; the House proposal with the Schumer provisions was retained. Both houses of congress voted to accept the conference report and the historic bill was signed into law by President Reagan on November 6, 1986.

The passage of IRCA produced the most extensive legislation in the area of employment law in the United States in two decades (i.e., since the adoption of the Occupational Health and Safety Act of 1970). From the day it was signed by the President, its provisions affected every employer and every jobseeker. Among its multiple provisions were strictures designed to prohibit employers from hiring illegal immigrants. The "Texas Proviso" was repealed. An escalating series of civil penalties, with provisions for criminal penalties for employers who repeatedly violated its provisions, were established.

IRCA also provided four separate amnesty programs that varied widely in their respective number of potential beneficiaries. The largest—the general amnesty—stated that any illegal immigrant living in the U.S. prior to January 1, 1982 and not falling into any of the excludable categories could register within a twelve-month period that began six months after this IRCA provision took effect (i.e., after May 5, 1987).

Applicants who could prove their eligibility were granted a temporary-resident alien status. After eighteen months in that status, they had one year to file to adjust their status to become permanent-resident aliens. As of December 1, 1991, 1,760,201 persons filed for coverage by the general amnesty. Of these, 94.8 percent were approved and granted temporary-resident status. Of the 1,580,558 persons who had followed through with an application for permanent-resident status as of that date, 1,526,814 were approved (or 96.6 percent).[71]

The second amnesty was the aforementioned SAW program whose applicants had to have worked in perishable agriculture for ninety days in the year ending May 1, 1986. The number of SAW applicants far exceeded what anyone expected. A total of 1,272,978 persons filed for the SAW amnesty of which 997,429 (or 88 percent) were approved. SAW applicants who had worked in the United States in the years 1984–1986 were immediately eligible for permanent-resident status; those who had worked only in 1986 were granted temporary-resident alien status for a year, after which they automatically acquired permanent-resident status. Due to the enormous number of SAW applicants as of early 1992, the replenishment (i.e., RAW) program had, as of early 1992, not yet been deemed necessary to implement.

The other two amnesties were smaller scale. One provided specific amnesty to the previously discussed "Cuban-Haitian entrants" who entered during the "Mariel era." The other involved an update in the legal registry date from June 1, 1948 to January 1, 1972. The registry date provisions allows the Attorney General, at his or her discretion, to adjust the status of persons who had illegally entered prior to that date to become permanent-resident aliens without having to meet the various eligibility standards of the other amnesty programs.

In addition to the great number of persons who were the direct beneficiaries of the amnesty programs, substantial family reunification obligations are associated with each person who is granted a permanent-resident alien status. Many spouses and children of such amnesty recipients were already in the United States. The general amnesty under IRCA, however, did not cover any persons who had entered after 1982 so there was concern that some family members could be deported. In February 1990, the INS reversed its previous position that made no exceptions to enforcing this policy. The INS announced that a "family fairness" policy would be put into place that modified its original stance.[72] Both the children and spouses of amnesty recipients would be granted a temporary-resident status and be permitted to work if they were residing in the country prior to November 6, 1986. The change did not affect the status of children over the age of eighteen or family members who arrived after that cutoff date. But even most of these persons will eventually be eligible to legally immigrate to the United States once the amnesty recipient either receives permanent-resident status or later qualifies to become a naturalized citizen.

IRCA also included provisions that strengthened the existing law on employment discrimination on the basis of national origin, since it expanded the nation's civil rights law by prohibiting discrimination on the basis of alienage (i.e., on the basis of citizenship). An interesting feature of this provision, however, is that it specifically states that employers may always give hiring preference to a citizen job-applicant if the citizen and noncitizen applicants are viewed as being equally qualified. Such absolute preferences for one group relative to another are not available under the other protected categories specified in the Civil Rights Act. The protection against citizenship discrimination applies to the public as well as to the private sector. But in the public sector an important exception is made that limits its scope. This is that, in government employment, certain jobs may be designated by law, regulation, executive order, or government contract to be filled only by citizens. There are many such restrictions at both the federal and state levels of government that legally remain in effect.[73]

Lastly, IRCA did include provisions to make it easier for employers to hire temporary workers under the H-2 provisions for nonimmigrant admissions. Agricultural workers were separated into a new H-2A section in the hope that, in the future, agricultural employers, when confronted with real labor shortages, would make use of this program rather than agitate for a new temporary worker program as they had done throughout the debates on immigration reform in the 1980s. Section H-2B was reserved for requests from nonagricultural employers for temporary foreign workers to meet specific labor market shortages.

The Continuation of Illegal Immigration

Despite the enactment of IRCA, there are few signs that illegal immigration to the United States has abated. As noted in Table 6.4, apprehension rates only slightly declined after IRCA went into effect, but by 1990 they were generally back at pre-IRCA levels. Indeed, every indication is that the illegal immigration is again flourishing.[74] Aside from the substantial "push" factors involved in the process of generating illegal immigrants in the source countries (i.e., unemployment, poverty, overpopulation, political corruption, human rights abuses, and a pervasive spirit of hopelessness) which IRCA cannot address, it remains the case that enforceability of the nation's immigration laws is still a major problem.

The new employer-sanctions program contains an enormous loophole. IRCA did not require that a counterfeit proof identification system be established to verify eligibility to work. Employers are not responsible for the authenticity of the documents that are offered by job applicants. They are only required to make a "reasonable" effort to attest to their validity. As a consequence, counterfeit documents—which were always a problem—have become a thriving urban enterprise.[75] The INS has had to devote an inordinate amount of its staff and limited resources toward document validation which has never been the agency's strong suit. Furthermore, the proposed increases in federal funds authorized in the law to support INS border enforcement activities never materialized. In fact, the actual appropriations were reduced.[76] Lastly, there are no fines placed on the illegal immigrants, themselves, who are found to be employed. As Barry and

Carmel Chiswick have noted, "it is obvious that any attempt to enforce the immigration laws with virtually no cost to the lawbreakers is destined to perpetuate the revolving-door."[77] They asked rhetorically "why are we as a nation so reluctant to impose on illegal border-crossers the types of penalties that we routinely accept for ourselves when we violate the laws of the land?"

It is also the case that the SAW program under IRCA was massively abused. The legislation placed the complete onus on the INS to prove that the documents that were presented by applicants were fraudulent rather than on the applicant to prove they were valid. As the number of SAW applicants far exceeded any of the pre-IRCA predictions of the number of eligible agricultural workers, it is not surprising that the SAW program has been aptly described as being "one of the most extensive immigration frauds ever perpetuated against the United States Government."[78]

There is one other aspect of IRCA that has contributed to further illegal immigration. Namely, prior to its passage, it was legal for the INS to go into open farm fields that were the private property of growers without first obtaining a search warrant from a court specifying that there was "probable cause" that illegal immigrants were at work. The legal premise was that fields were open space and are different from buildings and homes where privacy protections require the issuance of warrants before they may be entered by authorities. IRCA responded to the pressure of agribusiness by requiring that the INS had to secure such a warrant in advance of entry onto such open fields. But in rural areas that are distant from courts, it is simply not feasible to locate farmworkers who may be illegally employed; go back to a city where a court is located; make a case for a warrant; and return to the original rural location and expect to find the illegal immigrants still there.   Hence, the use of "field raids"—which prior to 1986 had been highly a successful strategy for apprehending large numbers of illegal immigrants—has essentially been abandoned. With these barriers to enforcement, it is not surprising that Philip Martin and Gary Thompson found in 1990 that IRCA has failed "to convert the agricultural labor market into a legal market.["][79]

Thus, illegal immigration has been a major contributor to the mass immigration phenomenon that has occurred since 1965. It appears that it will continue to be until Congress takes seriously the steps needed to make the nation's immigration laws enforceable. IRCA was a first step but it is not the last.

The Accelerating Increase in Nonwork-Related Legal Immigrant Admissions

One of the many unexpected consequences of the Immigration Act of 1965 has been the steady increase of legal immigrants that are admitted

Table 6.5 Annual Legal Immigration to the United States By Major Immigrant Categories During Fiscal Years 1965-90[a]

Year	Total	Immediate Relatives[b]	Relative preference[c]	Occupational Preference[d]	All other
1990	1,536,483	231,680	214,550	53,729	1,268,204
1989	1,090.924	217,514	217,092	52,775	603,543
1988	643,025	219,340	200,772	53,607	169,306
1987	601,516	218,575	211,809	53,873	117,259
1986	601,708	223,468	212,939	53,625	111,676
1985	570,009	204,368	213,257	50,895	101,489
1984	543,903	183,247	212,324	49,521	98,811
1983	559,763	177,792	213,488	55,468	113,015
1982	594,131	168,398	206,065	51,182	168,486
1981	596,600	152,359	226,576	44,311	173,354
1980	530,639	151,131	216,856	44,369	118,283
1979	460,348	138,178	213,729	37,709	70,732
1978	601,442	125,819	123,501	26,295	325,827
1977	462,315	105,957	117,649	21,616	217,093
1976	398,613	102,019	102,007	26,361	168,226
1976-TQ	103,676	27,895	28,382	5,621	41,778
1975	386,194	91,504	95,945	29,334	169,411
1974	394,861	104,844	94,915	28,482	166,620
1973	400,063	100,953	92,054	26,767	180,289
1972	384,685	86,332	83,165	33,714	181,474
1971	370,478	80,845	82,191	34,563	172,879
1970	373,326	79,213	92,432	34,016	167,665
1969	358,579	60,016	92,458	31,763	174,342
1968	454,448	43,677	68,384	26,865	315,522
1967	361,972	46,903	79,671	25,365	210,033
1966	323,040	39,231	54,935	10,525	218,349
1965	296,697	32,714	13,082	4,986	245,915

[a] The categories listed are generally used to describe large groups of immigrants. During 1965-90, minor changes were made in the qualifications for some immigrant classes making up these categories.

[b] Spouses of citizens, children (unmarried and younger than 21) of citizens, and parents of citizens 21 or older.

[c] The 1st, 2nd, 4th, and 5th categories of the immigrant preference system. The 1st preference allows the entry of unmarried sons and daughters (older than 21) of U.S. citizens. The 2nd preference covers spouses and unmarried sons and daughters of aliens lawfully admitted for permanent residence. The 4th preference allows for the entry of married sons and daughters of U.S. citizens. The 5th preference deals with the brothers and sisters of U.S. citizens, provided they are at least 21 years old.

[d] The 3rd and 6th categories of the immigrant preference system. The 3rd preference allows for the admission of members of the professions and scientists or artists of exceptional ability. The 6th preference covers skilled or unskilled occupations for which labor is in short supply in the U.S. TQ=Transitional quarter when the federal goverment altered its fiscal year from ending on June 30 to ending on September 30.

Source: U.S. Immigration and Naturalization Service.

on grounds unrelated to specific employment needs of the labor market. Table 6.5 vividly reveals this trend. The column labeled "occupational preferences" (or "employment-related" admissions) shows the annual number of persons admitted under the two preference categories reserved for labor market needs since 1965. Clearly, the "employment-related" preferences have been the smallest component of the total admission flow. The actual number of persons admitted under the "occupational preferences" over the years from 1965 to 1990 has been even far smaller than the numbers indicated in Table 6.5. This is because "accompanying family members" of those admitted under the "occupational preferences" are counted individually in these same numbers. For example, the 52,775 persons admitted in 1989 under the occupational preferences include not only the one person who received a specific labor certification to be admitted but also any spouse and all minor children who accompany the visa recipient. Hence, the data in Table 6.5 significantly overstate the actual number of persons admitted because they have needed skills or are qualified to be employed in a shortage occupation.

As is clear in Table 6.5, the vast preponderance of the legal admissions to the United States since 1965 have entered under the "relative preferences" (or "family-related preferences") or as their "immediate relatives." They have been allowed to legally immigrate because they are in some way related to someone who is already a U.S. citizen or permanent-resident alien. This does not automatically mean, of course, that those admitted under the "relative preferences" are lacking in needed skills, educational abilities or work experiences that are consistent with emerging labor demand requirements. Rather, it means that, if they have these abilities or characteristics, it is entirely incidental to the reason they were admitted. Likewise, the local labor market where those admitted for family reasons seek to find employment is more likely to be located where their U.S. relatives live rather than to be determined by prevailing local labor market conditions or actual employment trends.

The number of immediate relatives, as shown in Table 6.5, in the "fourth wave of mass immigration" has also revealed a significant growth trend. In part, this pattern indicates an increasing trend for whole families to immigrate together (in contrast to the immigration pattern of single men that dominated the "first," "second," and "third" waves of mass immigration that were discussed in Chapter 3). This means that there is no longer any proper analogy with the "birds of passage" phenomenon that characterized those earlier waves of mass immigration; the "fourth wave" immigration is more likely to settle permanently.[80] Therefore, as we have

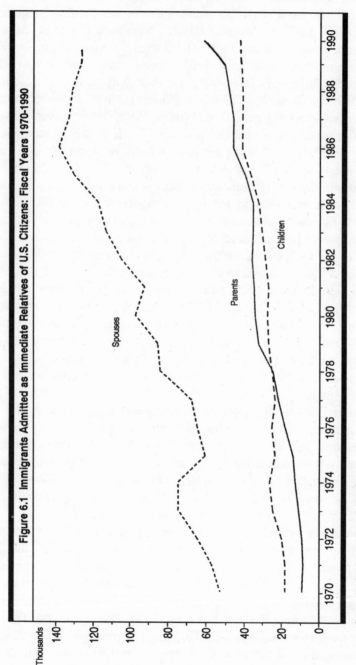

Figure 6.1 Immigrants Admitted as Immediate Relatives of U.S. Citizens: Fiscal Years 1970-1990

Source: Immigration and Naturalization Service.

noted in Chapter 2, the high emigration rates of the past periods of mass immigration are unlikely to be a characteristic of the current wave of mass immigration. Figure 6.1 shows the trends of the component groups that comprise the "immediate relatives" category from 1970 to 1990. Spouses are by far the largest segment of this group, with parents of adult U.S. citizens increasing rapidly. A substantial number of children are also part of the legal immigrant flow of the "fourth wave" which means greater pressure on local communities to provide educational, health, and housing opportunities in the local labor markets where their parents have settled.

As for the last column in Table 6.5, titled "all others," it reflects the growing scale of adjustments to permanent-resident alien status of persons originally admitted as refugees and asylees; or of nonimmigrants who have subsequently become eligible for immigrant status (e.g., they may have married a U.S. citizen or been a beneficiary of a change in legislation); or who have become eligible for any of the various amnesty programs created under IRCA for persons who entered illegally. The surge, for example, in the numbers in this column in 1989 and 1990 is principally the result of the effect of the amnesty program under IRCA of persons shifting from temporary- to permanent-resident status. Here again, virtually all of these admissions have been made without any concern for the human capital endowments of those admitted or the prevailing labor market conditions in the local labor markets where they have settled.

The Immigration Act of 1990

In accordance with the political strategy of pursuing piecemeal reform, the legal immigration system became the next component to be addressed after IRCA was passed in 1986. The Select Commission, in its aforementioned report in 1981, stated that "we recommend the closing of the back door to undocumented/illegal immigration" and "the opening of the front door a little more to accommodate legal immigration in the interest of this country."[81] The Commission, however, called for a "cautious approach" to the topic and specifically stated that "this is not the time for a large-scale expansion in legal immigration."[82] Specifically it proposed that the number of legal immigrant visas granted each year be raised to 350,000 (plus immediate family relatives who would remain exempt from the numerical ceiling). Included within the slight increase in the number of visas was the recommendation that a new category of "independent immigrants" be created and that it be assigned a proportion of these new visas (no specific number was cited). This new category would allow some legal admissions of persons who could not otherwise qualify on the basis of having either family relatives in the United States or having needed work skills.

In 1987, steps to reform the legal immigration system were begun by Congress. In sharp contrast to the common definition of the issues involved in addressing the problem of illegal immigration, there was no clear agreement among policymakers about the ideal composition or the desirable level of legal immigration. It was not surprising, given the preference system created in 1965, that family reunification considerations had come to dominate the admission flow. But as John Higham observed, the dominance of the family reunification preferences was "discouraging the diversity, fluidity, and innovation that immigration traditionally fostered."[83] He explained that:

In the name of family reunification, the new preferences have given a high claim on admission to certain relatives of immigrants already legally established in the United States. The family reunification preferences have tended to preempt the annual quotas. In doing so they reinforce and perpetuate existing patterns of migration. Instead of opening a way for prospective leaders, striking out on their own to make a new life, we have with the best of intentions granted a preference to followers, pursuing the family chain.[84]

In searching for alternatives, there were some who felt that it was time to give greater emphasis to the economic effects of the level of annual immigration and the human capital endowments of those who are admitted. But others were far more concerned with another of the unexpected consequences of the 1965 legislation—namely, the fact that its country-neutral and family-based features led to a major shift in the immigrant-sending regions away from Europe in favor of a small number of Asian and Latin American countries. By the late 1980s about 85 percent of all the legal immigrants to the United States were coming from Asia and Latin America. The countries of Mexico, the Philippines, Korea, Cuba, Vietnam, India, Dominican Republic, and China had become the dominate source countries. Only about 10 percent of immigrants were coming from Europe, the continent that had dominated all earlier mass immigrant flows. Nothing in the earlier debates in 1965 had anticipated such a possible outcome. Thus, one of the leaders of the new reform movement, Senator Edward Kennedy, candidly stated at the beginning of hearings in 1987 on prospective changes that: "One of the issues...that I am particularly concerned about is...how we correct the unexpected imbalances stemming from the 1965 Act—the inadvertent restriction on immigration from the 'old seed' sources of our heritage."[85]

The ensuing bill, coauthored by Senators Kennedy and Simpson, sought to address these concerns. Their bill, which overwhelmingly passed the Senate on March 15, 1988, sought to place a cap on legal immigration at 590,000 a year. The cap would be on the sum of both the number of family-related immigrants admitted under the preference system and the number of immediate family members. The two never before had been linked in law. It proposed a separate admission track for "independent immigrants" be created for those who could not otherwise be admitted under either the family or the occupational preferences. A total of 50,000 visas were suggested to be made available for such immigrants and they would be granted on the basis of a point system that rewarded certain factors such as training, age, occupational demand, and English-speaking ability. Originally, there were points to be given if the applicant came from a list of thirty-four countries that had been "adversely affected" by the Immigration Act of 1965 (i.e., mostly European countries). This latter consideration was subsequently dropped after it was publicly criticized for reintroducing national origin considerations. The Senate bill, however, was not acted upon by the House of Representatives although it did hold hearings on the subject.

In the next session of Congress, the Kennedy-Simpson Bill was reintroduced and passed on July 13, 1989 by the Senate. Among its multiple provisions, this revised version called for raising the ceiling on legal immigration to 630,000 persons a year and it also proposed that a cap be placed on the total number of family-related immigrants and immediate family members who could be admitted.

In the House of Representatives, a different bill was prepared by the subcommittee on immigration now chaired by Congressman Bruce Morrison (D-Conn.) of the Judiciary Committee. The House bill was even more expansive in its provisions than the Senate bill. It called for an increase in legal immigration to 844,000 for two years before falling back to a level of 776,000 a year with no cap on family-related and immediate relatives. It also sought to expand the coverage of the definition of "immediate family members" who could be admitted each year without limits to members of families of permanent-resident aliens. It had provisions for the admission of 75,000 "diversity immigrants" (i.e., persons from thirty-four countries that had low levels of immigration in recent years) as well as for "investor immigrants" (i.e., persons who agreed to invest in job-creating business ventures as a condition of their entry). There were also extensive changes in the various nonimmigrant worker programs as well as a host of other changes in the prevailing immigration statutes that ranged from concern for battered spouses of immigrants to tighter antidiscrimination provisions under IRCA as well as a proposed extension in the time beneficiaries of IRCA's amnesty program would have to convert from temporary- to permanent–resident status. On October 3, 1990, the House of Representatives passed, with some floor modifications, the Morrison bill.

With enormous differences between the bills that had been separately passed in the Senate and the House, it did not seem that a compromise was likely. It was an election year and Congress was anxious to adjourn. Moreover, a key supporter of the legislation in the Senate, Alan Simpson, announced on September 24, 1990 that he could no longer support the key feature of both bills—the substantial increases in the level of legal immigration. Simpson noted that recently released apprehension data showed that illegal immigration was again soaring. He reiterated the fact that the Select Commission (of which he had been a member) had proposed only "slight" increases in legal immigration and that it was predicated on the assumption that "the back door" of illegal immigration would be closed. He stated that "we must face the fact that we have not yet closed the back door."[86] He added that "in fact, we are still leaving the back door open while considering prying open the front door much wider" and he concluded that, "I just do not believe it would presently be in the national interest to approve of the increases in legal immigration that are now contemplated by proposed legislation." He then introduced a bill that provided for the strengthening of IRCA's provisions by addressing the issue of the use of false documents by illegal immigrants and requiring the INS to construct new physical barriers or to upgrade existing barriers at key entry points for illegal immigrants on the southern border. He indicated that these concerns should be the *quid pro quo* for passage of the pending legislation with its proposed substantial increases in legal immigration levels. His proposals, however, were ignored.

It was at this point that politics once more overwhelmed any rational examination of the goals of the legal immigration system. With two bills as diverse as those pending in the Senate and the House, there seemed to be little chance that the differences could be reconciled in the few weeks remaining in the 101st congressional session. Moreover, the dominant issue that laid claim to national attention at the time was the fact that

Congress and the Bush Administration were at loggerheads over the federal budget for Fiscal Year 1991 that had already begun on October 1, 1990. The Democrats in Congress were determined to force President Bush to accept a series of tax increases as a part of a budget package that included some restraints on government social spending. President Bush threatened to shut down the federal government if his budget proposals that did not include new taxes were rejected. When the new fiscal year began and no budget agreement had been reached, some federal agencies were briefly closed only to be reopened for short periods when the President accepted temporary budget extensions. Without going into greater detail, the point is that the media and public attention was riveted on the terms of the budget fight while, behind the scenes, attempts were being made to craft a new legal immigration law from the separate immigration bills that each chamber of Congress had passed. On October 19, 1990, an informal agreement was reached between the leaders of the legal immigration reform movement.[87] In the traditional spirit of the political process, when time pressures force closure, differences were split and whole sections of one bill were also accepted on the condition that whole sections of the other bill were accepted. Efforts to tighten illegal immigration provisions of IRCA were dropped. Several new provisions that had not been part of either of the previous bills were added in an effort to gain quick support (e.g., the repeal of a number of exclusionary provisions for immigrants and nonimmigrants and the addition of a new temporary "safe haven" provision for foreign persons who might need such protection but who do not qualify as refugees). In the following week, the compromise bill, which was 277 pages long, was hastily crafted and, before the bill had even been voted upon by either chamber, a conference bill was pasted together on October 24, 1990. The resulting product, which it is doubtful any member of Congress had actually read, was passed by the House of Representatives on October 26, 1990 and by the Senate on October 27, 1990—the same day that Congress finally passed the Budget Reconciliation Act of 1990 and adjourned. President Bush signed the Immigration Act of 1990 into law on November 29, 1990 with its effective date set for October 1, 1991.

In terms of historical significance, the Budget Reconciliation Act, which was the focal point of public attention throughout the early weeks of October 1990, will not even warrant a footnote. The Immigration Act of 1990, however, received virtually no public scrutiny at all during those critical weeks, yet it is destined to make landmark changes in U.S. society. It may, in fact, rank as one of the major legislative actions of the decade of the 1990s. For the Immigration Act of 1990 not only expands the scale of legal immigration by 35 percent over the already high level in existence at the time of its passage, but it also cements into existence the phenomenon of mass immigration as an ongoing feature of American life for as long as it remains in effect.[88]

As this chapter is devoted to a discussion of how mass immigration was revived, a discussion of the major provisions of the Immigration Act of 1990, which will govern the future, will be deferred to Chapter 8.

The Increasing Utilization of Nonimmigrant Workers

Paralleling the increase in legal immigrants, refugees, asylees, and illegal immigrants in the population and labor force since the mid-1960s, there has also been a less publicized growth in the use of nonimmigrant aliens as workers in the U.S. economy. Since the Immigration Act of 1924, all noncitizens entering the United States at any time must be classified as being either an "immigrant" or a "nonimmigrant." The "immigrant" classification is fairly straightforward. It consists essentially of permanent-resident aliens who have been abroad for a temporary period for business or pleasure. It can be more complicated in the special case of border commuters who are permanent-resident aliens but who actually live in either Canada or Mexico and who commute on a regular basis to jobs in the United States.[89] But since 1929, the U.S. Supreme Court has upheld the notion that border commuters can be treated as "immigrants" when they enter the United States even though everyone acknowledges it is "amiable fiction" that they are returning from a temporary trip abroad.[90]

But putting aside the border commuter issue, the "nonimmigrant" classification is a residual grouping. It collectively embraces all other persons who are not U.S. citizens but who seek to enter the United States for a temporary period of time but not for permanent residence. Nonimmigrants were first defined in U.S. law in 1819 but it was the Immigration Act of 1924 that set forth the process of defining separate admissions classes that were expanded in number and later broken into subclasses by the Immigration and Nationality Act of 1952. This latter legislation also created an unofficial convention whereby each of these separate classes and subclasses are now identified by the letter and numbers of the sections and subsections of this Act under which they are defined.

The number of nonimmigrants entering the United States each year is staggering in its size. In 1990, it reached a new record high of 17.5

million persons (a 6.3 percent increase over the preceding year). In most instances, the presence of nonimmigrants in the United States is encouraged. For example, the largest grouping by far is composed of tourists (i.e., B-2 visa holders) who come for pleasure. Another important visitor grouping are foreign persons who come to conduct business (i.e., B-1 visa holders). Collectively these two classifications account for about 85 percent of all of the nonimmigrant visas issued each year. For most nonimmigrant admissions classifications, the policy of the United States is one of an "open door," which means there are no restrictions on their numbers although there are strict limitations on how long they can remain, whether they can extend their stays, and, in some cases, who is eligible to receive such a visa. Most nonimmigrants are not allowed to be employed while in the country so there is no labor market effect associated with their presence except for the stimulative effects on domestic employment opportunities that their spending provides.

Some other nonimmigrant classifications permit such persons to be employed but, because of the nature of their work, they do not compete with domestic workers. These are nonimmigrants, for example, who work for foreign governments (e.g., ambassadors, diplomats, consular officers) and their attendant employees; or officers and employees of international organizations (e.g., the United Nations); or members of the foreign news media who cover events in the United States.

But there are also certain groups of nonimmigrants who are permitted to work under specified conditions in the United States in occupations and industries where the domestic work force is employed. Most of these nonimmigrant workers can be admitted only if qualified citizen workers cannot be found. But typically, merely perfunctory checks are made to test for citizen availability. Supposedly the nonimmigrant workers are admitted only for temporary periods, but their visas can be extended in some cases for up to five or six years. Table 6.6 shows these selected classifications and the number in each category admitted in 1974 and in 1990. It should be noted, however, that just because they are permitted to be employed does not mean that all of these nonimmigrants actually exercise that option. The best estimate is that about half of the nonimmigrant visa holders listed in Table 6.6 are actually in the U.S. labor force at any given time (i.e., about 435,000 persons). Some classifications, such as foreign students (i.e., F-1 visa holders), have restrictions on the number of hours a week and the circumstances under which they may work. Treaty traders and investors (i.e., E visa holders) are not technically considered to be "employed" but it is widely acknowledged that, for all intents and purposes, many are employed since they are permitted to establish businesses in the United States. Others, such as exchange visitors (J visa holders) are permitted to study, teach, conduct research, or participate in cultural exchanges, all of which often involve a substantial paid-work component.

Table 6.6 Nonimmigrants Admitted to the United States Under Classifications that Permit Nonimmigrants to be Employed, Fiscal Years 1974 and 1990

Category	Classification	Number in 1974	Number in 1990
Treaty Trader or Investor	E	36,853	147,536
Student	F-1	109,197	319,467
Temporary Worker a.) Of Distinguished Merit or Ability	H-1	15,074	100,446
b.) Other Temporary Worker	H-2	40,883	41,266*
c.) Industrial Trainee	H-3	4,414	3,168
Exchange Visitor	J-1	50,911	174,247
Financé of U.S. Citizen	K-1	8,248	6,545
Intra Company Transfer	L-1	12,478	63,180
TOTAL		278,058	855,855

*As a result of legislative changes in 1986, the H-2 classification was divided into two subclassifications, H-2A for agricultural workers (18,219 visa holders in 1990) and H-2B for Nonagricultural workers (23,047 visa holders in 1990).

Source: U.S. Immigration and Naturalization Service.

There are two other nonimmigrant classifications that have sustained substantial growth and about which there has been considerable concern with respect to their direct impact on the U.S. workforce. One of these is intracompany transfers (i.e., L-1 visas) who are permitted to provide temporary managerial, executive, and technical services to international corporations operating within the United States. As foreign ownership of U.S.-based firms—often previously owned by U.S. enterprises—has soared in the 1980s (and, as will be discussed in Chapter 7, is expected to continue into the foreseeable future), there has been concern that many foreign enterprises are filling the top jobs in these newly acquired firms with L-1 visa holders brought on a rotational basis from homelands.[91]

Responding to these charges, a subcommittee of the House Government Operations Committee chaired by Representative Tom Lantos (D-Cal.)

conducted hearings on the subject in 1991. It heard extensive testimony about the existence of a "glass ceiling" in Japanese-owned companies operating within the United States whereby U.S. citizens can see top management jobs in these enterprises but are not allowed to hold them. These accounts led Representative Lantos to conclude that U.S. workers are "crying out in anguish as American citizens are discriminated against within their own country."[92]

The other nonimmigrant classification that has sustained consistent growth is that of temporary workers (i.e., H visa holders). These visa holders span the gamut of occupations. They range from agricultural workers, to nurses, to engineers, to athletes, to entertainers.[93] There has been extensive debate, however, over the need to use nonimmigrant workers in unskilled and low-wage labor markets (e.g., agriculture). It is difficult to argue in these latter circumstances that there are not members of the domestic labor force who need jobs and who would seem to be able to meet the minimal hiring standards associated with such jobs. Employers, however, argue that the very fact that these are temporary jobs, often seasonal in nature, and located in specific geographical areas (sometimes isolated rural settings as in the case of agriculture) makes it impossible to attain or to depend on citizen workers to fill them. The central issue of concern is whether the availability of H-2A workers, for instance, reduces the incentives of employers to raise wages in order to attract domestic agricultural workers.

In another industry, the extensive use of H-1 workers as a means of supplying foreign nurses to work in the United States set off a firestorm of protest—both in favor and against their presence—throughout the 1980s. Nursing has been identified as a growth occupation that is assoc-iated with the anticipated future expansion of the health care industry. It is also an occupation in which, it was alleged, throughout the 1980s that there was an extreme shortage of labor (i.e., the unemployment rate for nurses was 1.4 percent in 1989). Consequently, many hospitals and other health organizations turned to the H-1 program in the 1980s as a means to find trained nurses.

On the supply side, there are a number of foreign countries that have turned the training of women as nurses into an export industry. The prin-cipal country involved in this process is the Philippines. Other coun-tries—such as Ireland, Canada, the United Kingdom and Jamaica—where English is also the primary language and where high unemployment rates prevail—have also proved to be fruitful sources of recruits. As a consequence, in 1989, there were 24,417 foreign nurses in the United States working under H-1 visas (and of these 72.6 percent were from the Philippines).[94] It was believed that 60 percent of all such foreign nurses were employed in the New York City and northern New Jersey area in 1989. Indeed, in New York City, one of every three nurses was believed to be on an H-1 visa. At the time, H-1 workers could work for five years before their visas expired and they were expected to return to their homelands. As more hospitals hired H-1 workers and as the years passed, the inevitable time came when the visas were about to expire for a large number of these foreign nurses. There was an outcry from the employers in the health care industry about the possible effect of such a substantial loss of trained personnel.

While it is sometimes the case that nonimmigrant workers use their entry as an opportunity to adjust their status to become permanent-resident aliens, this was not possible for most of the Filipino nurses. The reason was that if they applied for such a change of status they would have to wait until an opening existed in the two occupational preference categories of the legal immigration system at that time. Also they were subject to the annual ceiling on immigration from any one country. In the case of the Philippines—which had a massive backlog of would-be immigrants to the United States for all of the preference categories, the waiting time for status conversion in 1989 was estimated to be 16.3 years in the professions category (i.e., the third preference) and 4.5 years in the skilled or unskilled category (i.e., the sixth preference) of the Immigration Act of 1965 that was in effect at that time.[95]

As a consequence, the Immigration Amendments of 1988 were enacted which allowed foreign nurses who were facing the expiration of their five-year H-1 visas to remain in the country for one additional year. In 1989 the Immigration Nursing Relief Act was passed, providing special permanent-resident alien status to all individuals (as well as any accompanying sponsors and children) who entered the United States prior to January 1, 1988 with an H-1 visa and who were employed as registered nurses. In other words, the foreign nurses were allowed to convert their status without being subject to the lengthy waiting times, and they would not be charged against the existing worldwide or individual country ceilings.

To qualify for future access to such foreign nurses, the medical facility for which the foreign nurses work is required to certify that the employment of such foreign nurses will not adversely affect the wages and working conditions of registered nurses similarly employed. Furthermore, it must certify that it has taken and will continue to take significant steps to recruit and to train registered nurses who are United States citizens or permanent-resident aliens. A new H-1A temporary visa classification was established for foreign registered nurses to use when recruited by a qualifying health institution in the United States.

Without prolonging the discussion, there are other instances where U.S. firms have felt it to be to their advantage to recruit H-1 workers in various scientific and professional occupations. They claim that they are unable to find similarly qualified workers from the available labor force because the waiting times are so long it is not possible to recruit someone through the limited number of occupational preferences available each year under the legal immigration system. Given the sizable increase in nonimmigrant workers (see Table 6.6), the growing use by employers of nonimmigrant workers is symptomatic of the fact that something is grossly wrong with the legal immigration system, which gives dominant preference to family reunification as the principle entry route. Efforts by employers to meet legitimate shortages of labor through the use of the legal immigration system are often forestalled.

There is also another way to interpret the increasing tendency of U.S. employers to rely on nonimmigrant workers for professional, managerial, and technical workers. Namely, given the declining quality of both the nation's educational system and its paucity of adequate occupational preparation opportunities for young people, many employers are simply finding it easier to recruit foreign workers who are already trained and who may already have relevant work experience.

The employment of nonimmigrant workers can serve U.S. employers as a preferential alternative to setting up their own training systems or waiting for elusive educational and training reforms promised by politicians to be initiated to upgrade the nation's human resource development capabilities. Nonimmigrant workers are proving to be an attractive option but their increasing usage does not augur well for the future employment opportunities for the nation's labor supply—especially its youth—who could be prepared for these same jobs.

Concluding Observations

Without the benefit of careful design and with little congressional regard for the ensuing unexpected consequences, all the major components of the nation's immigration policy have contributed to the return of mass immigration. Even after a presidential commission concluded that immigration was "out of control," the subsequent policy responses enacted under the banner of "immigration reform" during the 1980s have not addressed any of the fundamental policy deficiencies. Indeed, the main consequence of these reform measures is that they make certain that mass immigration will continue to be the ongoing experience of the U.S. economy.

Of equal significance is the issue of the composition of the inflow. Immigration policy has been written largely to placate special interest groups. It has, in the process, become essentially a political policy that manifests little concern for any of its economic consequences. But paralleling the years since 1965 in which mass immigration has resumed, the labor market of the United States has entered a period of radical transformation. Both the demand and the supply of labor are being buffeted by unprecedented pressures of change. As will be discussed in the next chapter, the failure to appreciate the scope of these change-creating forces and to adjust immigration policy to fit this new American reality has turned immigration into a source of problems instead of an avenue for answers.

Notes

1. Demetrios G. Papademetriou, "Contending Approaches to Reforming the U.S. Legal Immigration System." Paper presented at the New York University—Rockefeller Foundation Conference on "Migration, Ethnicity, and the City," The Arden House Homestead, New York (November 2–4 1990), p. 46.

2. Leon F. Bouvier, *Peaceful Invasions: Immigration and Changing America* (Washington, D.C.: Center for Immigration Studies, 1991), p. 18.

3. Robert L. Bach, "The New Cuban Immigrants: Their Background and Prospects," *Monthly Labor Review* (October, 1980), p. 44.

4. Because only those refugees who were admitted to the United States under the preference system were automatically eligible to become immigrants after a residency period, special legislation was required to grant immigrant status to all persons who were admitted under the parole authority. The parole authority was originally intended to apply only to individuals, but with the extension of this authority to massive numbers of refugees, individual admission requirements would have caused lengthy

waiting periods, during which the person involved would have been in limbo waiting for a visa slot to open; they could neither have worked, nor have been eligible for most assistance services. Hence, special legislation was separately enacted for members of those groups that received parole admissions. These enactments per-mitted these refugees to become permanent-resident aliens outside the normal immigration channels.

5. *Silva V. Levi*, No. 76, C4268 (N.D., Ill. Apr. 1, 1978).

6. Robert Sherrill, "Can Miami Save Itself?" *The New York Times* (July 19, 1987), pp. 18 ff.

7. Julia V. Taft, David S. North, and David A. Ford, *Refugee Resettlement in the U.S.: Time for a New Focus* (Washington, D.C.: New Trans Century Foundations, 1979), p. 103.

8. U.S. Congress, Senate Committee on the Judiciary, *Review of U.S. Refugee Resettlement Programs and Policies*, (Washington, D.C.: U.S. Government Printing Office, 1980), p. 14.

9. Ibid.

10. U.S. Congress, Senate Committee on the Judiciary, *U.S. Immigration Law Policy, 1952-1979*, op. cit., p. 79.

11. U.S. Department of State, Office of the U.S. Coordinator for Refugee Affairs, "Proposed Refugee Admissions and Allocations for Fiscal Year 1983" (Washington, D.C., 1983, mimeographed), p. 14.

12. U.S. Congress, Senate Committee on the Judiciary, *U.S. Refugee Resettlement Programs*, op. cit., p. 38.

13. The Refugee Act of 1980 specified that all refugees who were admitted to the United States would be allowed to adjust their status to that of permanent-resident aliens after one year. This change cut in half the two-year waiting period that had been imposed for the various ad hoc refugee admission programs enacted since the 1950s.

14. U.S. Congress, Senate Committee on the Judiciary, *Caribbean Refugee Crisis: Cubans and Haitians* (Washington, D.C.: U.S. Government Printing Office, 1980), p. 47. The quotation is from the prepared statement submitted to the committee by Ambassador-at-Large Victor H. Palmieri on May 12, 1980.

15. For a more detailed discussion of this entire episode, see Felix Roberto Masud-Piloto, *With Open Arms: Cuban Migration to the United States* (Totowa N.J.: Rowman & Littlefield, 1988).

16. U.S. Congress, Senate Committee on the Judiciary, *Caribbean Refugee Crisis*, op. cit., p. 30.

17. Sherrill, op. cit., p. 20.

18. "Carter and the Cuban Influx," *Newsweek* (May 26, 1980), p. 23.

19. "Eighteen Nations Move to Assist Exodus," *New York Times* (May 10, 1980), p. A-11.

20. Senate Committee on the Judiciary, *Caribbean Refugee Crisis*, op. cit., p. 42.

21. Ibid.

22. For greater detail, see Vernon M. Briggs, Jr., *Immigration Policy and the American Labor Force* (Baltimore: Johns Hopkins University Press, 1984), pp. 210-216.

23. *Jean V. Nelson*, No-84-5240 (1985), 105 *Supreme Court Reporter*, 2992.

24. Anthony DePalma, "For Haitians, Voyage to Land of Inequality," *New York Times* (July 16, 1991), pp. A-1 and A-7.

25. Ibid., p. A-1.

26. Ibid., p. A-7.

27. "Communique," New York City, N.Y. (December 14, 1984). A xerox copy of the agreement signed by representatives of Cuba and the United States on immigration matters.

28. Clifford Krauss, "U.S. Taking Steps to Bar New Wave of Cuban Emigres," *New York Times* (August 4, 1991) p. A-18.

29. Barbara Crossette, "Issue of Haitians Raises Debate on Asylum Policy," *New York Times* (December 2, 1991), p. A-11.

30. Barbara Crossette, "Forced Return of Haitians Fleeing By Boat to U.S. is Halted by Judge," *New York Times* (November 20, 1991), pp. A-1 and A-11.

31. Howard W. French, "Haitians Win Stay on Forced Return," *New York Times* (December 5, 1991), p. A-10.

32. Howard W. French, "U.S. Begins Forcible Return of Haitians Who Fled Coup," *New York Times* (November 19, 1991), pp. A-1 and A-18.

33. Ibid.

34. Crossette, "Issue of ...," op. cit., p. A-11.

35. Ronald Smothers, "Ban on Sending Haitians Home is Upset," *New York Times* (December 18, 1991), p. A-3.

36. Charles Maechling, Jr. "Reagan's Anti-Human Rights Policy," *New York Times* (Sept. 4, 1983), p. E-15 [In this article, the quoted material that is cited is from an internal memo from Under Secretary of State Richard Kennedy to Secretary of State Alexander M. Haig, Jr.].

37. Ibid.

38. Larry Rohter, "Central American Plight Is People in Abundance," *New York Times* (September 9, 1987), p. A-1.

39. "Immigration Rules Are Eased for Nicaraguan Exiles in U.S.," *New York Times* (July 9, 1987), p. A-8.

40. *I.N.S. v. Cardoza-Fonseca*, (1987), *Supreme Court Reporter* 1207.

41. Robert Pear, "Reagan Rejects Salvadorean Plea on Illegal Aliens," *New York Times* (May 5, 1987), p. A-1 and A-12.

42. For a discussion of this movement, see Ignatius Bau, *This Ground is Holy: Church Asylum and the Central American Refugees* (Mahwah, N.J.: The Paulist Press, 1985); for an assessment, see David Simcox "Refugees, Asylum, and Sanctuary: National Passion vs. National Interest," *U.S. Immigration in the 1980s* (Boulder, Co.: Westview Press, 1988), pp. 52-58.

43. E.g., See Wayne King, "Activists Vow to Continue Aiding People from Central America," *New York Times* (January 16, 1985), pp. A-1 and A-10:, and Peter Applebome, "In Sanctuary Movement, Unabated Strength but Shifting Aims," *New York Times* (October 27, 1987), pp. A-18; and "Sanctuary Leaders Say Aid to Aliens Goes On," *New York Times* (May 7, 1989), p. A-35.

44. Jeffrey Schmalz, "Nicaraguan Influx Tests Miami's Hospitality," *New York Times* (November 20, 1988), pp. A-1 and A-36.

45. Jeffrey Schmalz, "Dreams and Despair Collide as Miami Searches for Itself," *New York Times* (January 23, 1989), pp. A-1 and B-8; see also Jeffrey Schmalz "Miami's New Ethnic Conflict: Haitians vs. American Blacks," *New York Times* (February 19, 1989), pp. A-1 and A-38; and Sherrill, op. cit.

46. Jeffrey Weiss, "Racial Violence Subsides in Miami," *Dallas Morning News* (January 19, 1989), pp. A-1 and A-6.

47. "Miami Riots Spread to Other City Areas," *Dallas Morning News* (January 18, 1989), pp. A-1 and A-16.

48. Roberto Suro, "U.S. to Detain Refugees in Tents Beginning Today" (February 2, 1989), pp. A-1 and 21.

49. *American Baptist Churches, et al. v. Thornburgh, et al.*, Civ. No. C85-3255 RFP (December 19, 1990), Stipulated District of California; see also Katherine Bishop, "U.S. Settles Suit on Ousting Aliens," *New York Times* (December 20, 1990), p. B-18.

50. Robert Pear, "U.S. Issues Asylum Rules Praised As Fairer to Aliens," *New York Times* (July 19, 1990). p. A-16.

51. Department of State, *World Refugee Report*: 1988 (Washington,

D.C.: U.S. Department of State Publications, 1987), p. 55.

52. "Israel Asks U.S. Not to Admit Jews as Refugees," *New York Times* (February 23, 1987), p. A-23.

53. Michael R. Gordon, "Schultz Holds Off on Soviet Emigres," *New York Times* (July 22, 1988), p. Y-5.

54. Celestine Bohlen, "Europeans Confer on Emigre Limits," *New York Times* (January 27, 1991), p. A-9.

55. Robert Pear, "Soviet Armenians Let in Improperly, U.S. Officials Say," *New York Times* (May 29, 1988), p. A-17.

56. *Matter of Chang* (1989). See *Interpreter Releases* (July 10, 1989) pp. 751-754.

57. "Chinese Couple Qualifies for Refugee Status," *New York Times* (May 13, 1990), p. A-28.

58. Robert Pear, "Bush Rejects Bill on China Students," *New York Times* (December 1, 1989), p. A-9; see also Thomas Friedman, "Bush is Set Back on House Override of Veto on China," *New York Times* (January 25, 1990), pp. A-1 and A-6.

59. *Employment and Training Report of the President: 1978* (Washington: U.S. Government Printing Office, 1978), pp. 111-112.

60. Ellis W. Hawley, "The Politics of the Mexican Labor Issue, 1950-1965," in *Mexican Workers in the United States* edited by George C. Kiser and Martha Woody Kiser (Albuquerque, N.M.: The University of New Mexico Press, 1979), p. 101.

61. For a more detailed discussion of problems with illegal immigration data, see Vernon M. Briggs, Jr.*Immigration Policy...*, op.cit.,pp. 131-137; see also National Research Council, *Immigration Statistics: A Story of Neglect* (Washington, D.C.: National Academy Press, 1985).

62. For a more detailed discussion of how the forces of illegal immigration became entwined with other economic and military relationships, see Briggs, *Immigration Policy...*, op.cit, pp. 154-156.

63. Mark J. Miller and Demetrious Papdametriou, "Immigration Reform: The United States and Western Europe Compared," in *The Unavoidable Issue: U.S. Immigration Policy in the 1980s*, edited by Demetrious Papademetriou and Mark Miller (Philadelphia: Institute for the Study of Human Issues, 1983), Chapter 10.

64. U.S. Congress Senate Committee on the Judiciary, *U.S. Immigration Law and Policy: 1952-1979* (Washington, D.C.: U.S. Government Printing Office, 1979), p. 75.

65. Select Commission on Immigration and Refugee Policy, *U.S.*

Immigration Policy and the National Interest (Washington, D.C.: U.S. Government Printing Office, 1981).

66. For details, see Briggs, *Immigration Policy...*, op.cit, pp. 89 and 174.

67. See the background discussion of both of these issues in Vernon M. Briggs Jr. "The 'Albatross' of Immigration Reform: Temporary Worker Policy in the United States" *International Migration Review* (Winter, 1986), pp. 995-1019 and Vernon M. Briggs, "Employer Sanctions and the Question of Discrimination," *International Migration Review* (Winter, 1990), pp. 803-815.

68. Robert Pear, "Schumer Offers Plan for Importing Farm Workers," *New York Times* (June 10, 1986), p. 19.

69. "House Committee Clears Immigration Reform Bill," *Daily Labor Report*, No. 124 (Washington, D.C.: Bureau of National Affairs, 1986), p. A-3.

70. Robert Pear, "House Panel is Setting Terms for Debate on Aliens," *New York Times* (June 26, 1986), p. 31.

71. U.S. Immigration and Naturalization Service, "Provisional Legalization Application Statistics" (December 1, 1991), Xeroxed Material, p. 1.

72. Michael Isikoff, "INS Policy on Families is Reversed," *Washington Post* (February 3, 1990), p. A-1 and A-4.

73. Briggs, *Immigration Policy...*, op.cit., Chapter 4.

74. For a discussion of how the employment data indicate a rise in illegal entry, see, Paul Flaim, "How Many New Jobs Since 1982? Data from Two Surveys Differ," *Monthly Labor Review* (August 1989) p. 14; See also Herb Lash, "Skirting the Law, Mexicans Flock to New York City," Associated Press Story in *Ithaca Journal* (September 28, 1991) p. A-11; and Bill Nicholas, "Arrests Show Immigration Problem Worsens," *USA Today* (August 8, 1991), p. 5-A; and Tim Golden "Mexicans Head North Despite Rules on Jobs," *New York Times* (December 13, 1991), pp. A-1 and A-28.

75. E.g., see Robert Suro, "Traffic in Fake Documents is Blamed on Illegal Immigration Rises," *New York Times* (November 26, 1990), p. A-14 and Richard Stevenson, "Growing Problems: Aliens with Fake Documents," *New York Times* (August 4, 1990), p. A-8.

76. U.S. General Accounting Office, *Border Patrol: Southwest Border Enforcement Affected by Mission Expansion and Budget* (Washington, D.C.: U.S. General Accounting Office, 1991).

77. Barry R. Chiswick and Carmel U. Chiswick, "'Illegals' Should Pay for Breaking the Law," *Los Angeles Times* (October 9, 1985), p. 20.

78. Robert Suro, "False Migrant Claims: Fraud on a Huge Scale," *New York Times* (November 12, 1989), p. A-1.

79. Gary D. Thompson and Philip L. Martin, "Immigration Reform and the Agricultural Labor Force," *Labor Law Journal* (August, 1991), p. 532.

80. E.g., see, Seth Mydans, "More Mexicans Come to U.S. to Stay," *New York Times* (January 21, 1991), p. A-14.

81. Select Commission, op.cit., p. 3 [Emphasis is supplied].

82. Ibid., p. 8.

83. John Higham, "The Purpose of Legal Immigration in the 1990s and Beyond," *The Social Contract* (Winter 1990-91), p. 64.

84. Ibid.

85. Congressional Research Service, "Immigration: Numerical Limits and the Preference System," *Issue Brief* (March 28, 1988), p. CRS-3. The report was prepared by Joyce Vialet of the CRS staff.

86. U.S. Congress, Senate, *Congressional Record*, 2nd Sess., 101st Cong. (September 24, 1990), (Washington, D.C.: U.S. Government Printing Office, 1990) p. S13,628.

87. Robert Pear, "Lawmakers Agree on Immigration Rise," *New York Times* (October 21, 1991), p. A-26.

88. Vernon M. Briggs Jr., "The Immigration Act of 1990: Retreat from Reform," *Population and Environment* (Fall, 1991), pp. 89-93.

89. Briggs, *Immigration Policy...* op.cit.. pp. 231-236.

90. *Karnuth V. Albro*, 279 U.S. 231 (1929).

91. E.g., see Peter T. Kilborn, "U.S. Workers Say Japanese Keep Them Out of Top Jobs," *New York Times* (June 3, 1991), p. A-1 and p. B-6.

92. "U.S. Workers Tell House Subcommittee of Discrimination by Japanese-Owned Firms," *Daily Labor Report* (August 9, 1991), p. A-11 and p. A-12.

93. For a more in depth discussion of the complex subject of nonimmigrant labor policy, see Briggs, *Immigration Policy...* op.cit., Chapter 4.

94. U.S. General Accounting Office, *Health Care: Information on Foreign Nurses Working Under Temporary Work Visas*, (Washington, D.C.: U.S. General Accounting Office, 1989), p. 7.

95. Ibid., p. 8.

SEVEN

Oversight: The Economic and Social Transformation of the U.S. Labor Market

Paralleling the timespan marked by the post-1965 revival of mass immigration, the labor market of the United States entered a period of economic transformation. Both the nature of the demand for labor (i.e., the evolving employment patterns) and the supply of labor (i.e., the evolving labor force) have been significantly affected. The gradual pace of labor market changes that characterized past stages of economic development has given way to a rapid and abrupt succession of new trends. In such an economic environment, the old, comfortable assumption that the labor market can easily adjust to such changes is no longer valid.

As outlined in the previous chapter, immigration policy since 1965 has been implemented in a manner totally oblivious to these new economic trends. The "fourth wave" of mass immigration was spawned—and is perpetuated—by public policies designed primarily to serve political goals. Only by pure luck would such a politically driven immigration policy produce consequences congruent with the profound economic changes in progress over this same timespan. The nation was not so fortunate.

As if the adjustment difficulties associated with economic transformation were not a sufficient challenge, it also happens that the post-1965 era has also been a period of social revolution within the United States. New public attitudes have been created concerning the labor market participation of various population segments in the economy. The year 1965 marked not only the time when the nation's immigration laws were revamped but it was also the year in which the equal employment opportunity provisions (i.e., Title VII) of the Civil Rights Act of 1964 actually went into effect (i.e., on July 1, 1965). That historic legislation sought to end the overt racial discrimination haunting this nation since its birth. It was originally conceived as a response to the demonstrated needs of black Americans for equal inclusion into the nation's economic life. But as its goal was to achieve equal employment opportunity, the language of the Act did not specifically mention blacks. Instead, it was written in much broader terms so as to protect all groups from the pernicious effects of unfair hiring and employment practices. Consequently, other racial, ethnic, and religious groups as well as women in general quickly seized its provisions as a source of leverage for social change. Subsequently, in its ongoing quest to stretch the boundaries of freedom, the nation has also enacted the Age Discrimination in Employment Act of 1968 to protect older workers and the Americans with Disabilities Act of 1990 to protect physically and mentally impaired workers in their respective efforts to find and to maintain employment. Thus, as the nation has struggled with providing greater access to the labor market for groups that were hitherto largely ignored or purposely restricted from achieving such opportunities, it has also simultaneously dramatically enlarged the flow of immigration workers into the same labor market. There has been no recognition in the immigration reform legislation debates of any need to reconcile efforts to afford greater opportunities for these citizen groups with the increased competition for employment and job preparation opportunities of the expanded immigrant flow that has occurred over these same years. Indeed, the Immigration Reform and Control Act (IRCA) of 1986 even went so far as to create yet another protected group. It extended antidiscrimination protection in employment to cover alienage—that is, to include noncitizens who are eligible to work (e.g., permanent-resident aliens and certain nonimmigrant foreign workers) for the first time in U.S. history.

Thus, the period of labor market transformation—with its efficiency concerns for labor market adjustment—has exactly paralleled the time period in which the United States initiated its equal employment opportunity endeavors that are intended to achieve equity goals. Under such circumstances, immigration policy should have been designed to assist the nation to achieve both of these high priority domestic goals. Such has not been the case. Immigration policy has been allowed to function without regard to either its efficiency or equity implications. It has become a political "wildcard" that is unaccountable for its economic or social consequences.

Postindustrialism and the Changing Patterns of Employment

While most social scientists feel it is risky to attempt to place exact dates on when social systems move into entirely new eras, Daniel Bell has written that "symbolically at least" the "birth years" of the "postindustrial society" were from 1945 to 1947.[1] It was in these years, beginning with the dropping of the atom bomb at Hiroshima; spanning the development of the electronic computer in 1946; including the publication of Norbert Wiener's classic book *Cybernetics* (which set forth the mathematical foundations of electronic communication and automatic control that launched the computer revolution); and encompassing the pioneering work by Vannevar Bush and his associates that culminated in the creation in 1950 of the National Science Foundation (which has institutionalized the massive federal government financial support for scientific endeavors over the ensuing years), that this new era was spawned in the United States.

Although sociologists may wrangle over the precise timing and particular events that were the most prominent contributions to the beginning of postindustrialism, the economic indicators show that in the years following the end of World War II the employment patterns of the nation have been fundamentally altered from anything that had hitherto existed. These years mark the inflection point whereby entirely different employment patterns from the past began to emerge. These patterns are the manifestation of the new era of labor market transformation that is in full stride in the 1990s.

Industrial Shifts

The most significant sign of the advent of postindustrialism has been the general stagnation (in absolute terms) and the sharp decline (in relative terms) of employment in the goods-producing sector of the economy. This sector (which includes agriculture, manufacturing, mining, and construction) had been the historic employment base since this nation was born. It should be recalled that it was the growth of the goods-producing sector, as discussed in Chapter 3, that accommodated the preponderance of the immigrants of the three waves of mass immigration that occurred in the nineteenth and early twentieth centuries. Since the 1950s however, the goods-producing sector has ceased providing increases in employment opportunities. While continuing to be a vital source of value-added to the nation's gross national product, the high levels of output in the goods-producing sector no longer require the input of increasing numbers of workers. Indeed, many goods-producing industries now require fewer production workers to produce expanded levels of output.

Agriculture, the only goods-producing industry that was in long-term employment decline prior to World War II, has continued its employment shrinkage. In 1947, there were 10.3 million workers employed as agricultural workers. By 1989 there were only 2.8 million farm workers. The decline has been the greatest for those in the unskilled farmworker occupations. Consequently, this critical industry—once the haven for the employment of mass numbers of unskilled and poorly educated workers—has not produced a net new job in over forty years. To the contrary, it has been a negative source of employment over this entire period.

The displaced agricultural workers—who far outnumber those displaced to date from other goods-producing industries, but for whom no publicly supported displaced-worker policy has ever been enacted—have been forced to seek employment on a catch-as-catch-can basis in the nonagricultural sector. Most of those who have been displaced have been non-Hispanic whites but a disproportionate number of these displaced farm workers have been blacks from the rural Southeast and Mexican Americans from the rural Southwest.

Aside from the agricultural sector, Table 7.1 shows that manufacturing, employment has essentially stagnated; mining has declined (except for the period around 1980 when energy shortages briefly revived mining as a source of jobs); and only the construction industry has shown any long-term growth trend. But construction is notoriously sensitive to cyclical swings so that it cannot be counted upon to provide increasing numbers of jobs at any particular time. Table 7.2 shows that em-ployment in the goods-producing industries has dramatically fallen from 41.6 percent of total nonfarm employment in 1950 to 22.7 percent in 1990.

The rapid fall-off in employment in the goods-producing sector has been caused by the confluence of several broad economic forces. First, there has been a shift in spending patterns that is one of the hallmarks of the postindustrial economy. Since the demand for labor is derived from the demand for goods and services, changes in expenditure patterns can alter industrial employment patterns. Indeed, employment projections based on the assumption that employment trends follow spending trends are among the safest of all economic forecasts. Following World War II, the United States has entered a new phase of economic development. It is the mature stage of being a mass consumption society.[2] One of the distinguishing features of such a society is the expansion of personal consumption beyond levels required to provide basic food, shelter, and clothing requirements and into a vast array of new economic wants. In

Table 7.1. Employees on Nonfarm Payrolls, by Major Industry, Ten-year Intervals, 1950-1990 (in thousands)					
Industry/Year	1950	1960	1970	1980	1990
Goods Producing Mining	901	712	623	1,027	735
Construction	2,333	2,885	3,536	4,346	5,205
Manufacturing	15,241	16,796	19,349	20,285	19,064
Service Producing Transportation, Communications, and Public Utilities	4,034	4,004	4,504	5,146	5,838
Wholesale Trade	2,518	3,004	3,816	5,275	6,361
Retail Trade	6,868	8,388	11,225	15,035	19,790
Finance, Insurance, and Real Estate	1,919	2,669	3,687	5,160	6,833
Personal Services	5,382	7,423	11,641	17,890	28,209
Government	6,026	8,353	12,561	16,241	18,295
Total	45,222	54,234	70,920	90,405	110,330

Source: Economic Report of the President: 1991

its first century as a nation, the expenditure patterns of the economy of the United States indicated an emphasis on nondurable goods (food and fiber). Agriculture, as a result, was the major employment sector.

During the last quarter of the nineteenth century and throughout the first half of the twentieth century, the economy shifted its expenditures toward durable production. Manufacturing gradually emerged as the major employment sector. It was during the 1920s that manufacturing employment surpassed agricultural employment for the first time. In terms of its percentage of total nonfarm employment, manufacturing peaked during the World War II years at about 41 percent. By 1953 manufacturing was employing about the same absolute number of workers as during World War II, but its percentage of total nonfarm employment was 35 percent.

Beginning in the mid-1950s, a perceptible shift in expenditures toward services emerged and the growth in service employment commenced in earnest. By 1990, 77.3 percent of the nonagricultural labor force were employed in the service industries (see Table 7.2). Moreover, the U.S. Department of Labor has projected that 90 percent of the jobs to be created in the 1990s will be in the service industries.[3]

Table 7.2 Total and Percentage of Employees on Nonfarm Payrolls, by Goods Producing and Service Producing Sectors, for Ten-Year Intervals, 1950-1990 (in thousands)

Sector/Year	1950	1960	1970	1980	1990
Goods Producing	18,775	20,393	23,508	25,658	25,004
Service Producing	26,447	33,841	47,412	64,747	85,326
Total	45,222	54,234	70,920	90,405	110,330
Percent in Goods	41.6	37.6	33.1	28.4	22.7
Percent in Services	58.4	62.4	66.9	71.6	77.3
Total (percent)	100.0	100.0	100.0	100.0	100.0

Source: Economic Report of the President: 1991

In addition to spending shifts, the advent of computer controlled technology in the decades following World War II has created automatic production systems that have reduced the demand for unskilled and semiskilled workers in the goods-producing sectors.[4] An electronic "mind" has been created for coordinating, guiding, and evaluating most routine production operations. With the introduction of a vast array of mechanical and electrical substitutes for the human neuromuscular system, it is now possible to link these new computer-driven machines together into self-regulating systems that can perform an enormous variety of work tasks. Norbert Wiener, the intellectual father of the cybernetic revolution, described in 1950 what the anticipated employment effects of computer technology would be. He wrote:

Let us remember that the automatic machine, whatever we may think of any feelings it may or may not have, is the precise economic equivalent of slave labor. Any labor which competes with slave labor must accept the economic conditions of slave labor.[5]

Thus, Wiener observed, "in all important respects, the man who has nothing but his physical power to sell has nothing to sell which is worth anyone's money to buy."[6] His words have proved to be prophetic. Indeed, the technology of manufacturing production has changed so rapidly that even the descriptive word "manufacturing" itself has become obsolete. As the linguist Bill Bryson has observed, "manufacture, from the Latin root for hand, once signified something made by hand; it now means virtually the opposite."[7] Moreover, the application of computer technology has not been restricted only to the goods-producing sectors. It has also made rapid inroads into the service sector of the economy as well.

What a far cry are the evolving employment patterns associated with the era of computer technology from those of the nineteenth and early twentieth centuries when the nation last experienced periods of mass immigration. In those times, the need was for physical labor to do the manual work associated with the needs of an expanding goods-producing sector—agriculture, manufacturing, mining, and construction. But the mass immigration of the post-1965 era is occurring against an entirely different economic backdrop. With the new technology, high-paying jobs for poorly skilled and inadequately educated workers are largely becoming a thing of the past. As former Secretary of Labor William E. Brock aptly said, "the days of disguising functional illiteracy with a high-paying assembly line job that simply requires a manual skill are soon to be over. The world of work is changing right under our feet."[8] The new technology is creating additional jobs but the growth is concentrated in occupations that generally reward extensive training and education in both the goods-producing and service-producing sectors of the economy.[9] Conversely, it is rapidly eliminating the need for workers in occupations that lack such prerequisites in both employment sectors.

Occupational Shifts

Looking specifically at the rapidly changing occupational structure of the U.S. economy, the effects of the transformation process are startlingly apparent. Table 7.3 shows the percentage of employees in the private sector who were employed in nonproduction or supervisory occupations for the decades from 1950 to 1990. In rough terms, these figures indicate white-collar employment. Without exception, the ratio of employment in nonproduction occupations to total employment has increased over each decade in every industry. The percentages are especially noteworthy in the goods-producing industries. Conversely, of course, these trends mean that production and nonsupervisory jobs, which are often described as being blue-collar occupations, are vanishing. Such jobs in the past often provided high pay, good fringe benefits, and job protections for workers with relatively low human capital endowments. In many instances, the workers in these jobs benefited from being unionized. In fact, from the mid-1920s until the mid-1960s, these blue-collar jobs in the goods-producing sector were the heart of the union movement in the private sector of the economy. Unionism, which flourished after mass immigration ended in the 1920s, soared to 35.8 percent of the nonagricultural labor force in 1945. It was still as high as 33.2 in 1958. Since then it has

Table 7.3 Percentage of Employees in Private Sector Who Are Employed in Non-Production or Supervisory Occupations (percentage terms)

Industry/Year	1950	1960	1970	1980	1990
Goods Producing					
Mining	9.4	19.9	24.1	25.8	28.0
Construction	11.1	14.7	16.7	21.3	23.0
Manufacturing	17.8	25.1	27.5	29.9	32.1
Service Producing					
Transportation, Communication, and Public Utilities	N.A.	N.A.	13.3	16.6	16.9
Wholesale Trade	9.6	13.9	16.6	18.2	19.8
Retail Trade	5.6	7.5	9.1	10.2	11.5
Finance, Insurance, and Real Estate	17.1	18.4	21.0	24.3	27.4
Personal Services	N.A.	N.A.	9.2	11.0	12.8

N.A. = Not Available

Source: U.S. Department of Labor.

fallen off precipitously. By 1990, it was down to 17 percent. The changing industrial and occupational structure is one reason for the rapid decline in unionism in the United States, but so has been the return of mass immigration as well as increasing management resistance to unions.[10]

Looking more specifically at occupational growth in the U.S. economy from 1978 to 1990 (a timespan when the overall number of employed persons increased by an incredible 22.1 percent), professional, technical, and administrative occupations experienced the greatest growth by far. As shown in Table 7.4, these three occupations accounted for a phenomenal 52 percent of the total number of jobs created over that timespan. These occupations tend to have the highest educational and training requirements of the entire workforce. On the other end of the spectrum, the relatively unskilled occupations of private household workers, laborers, and farm workers all sustained negative growth rates and declining shares of the nation's workforce. Although there was an academic debate during the 1980s over whether the types of jobs that were being created required more or less skills, the decade is over. The evidence clearly shows that the types of jobs that are increasing in the United States are those with the highest education and skill requirements while those jobs that are declining are overwhelmingly the ones that require the least in the ways of human capital preparation.[11] A confirmation of these trends has also been found with regard to the movement of real wages. Workers in the occupations that require extensive education and skill preparation received higher wages over the decade of the 1980s while those that did not require such prerequisites sustained declining real wages over this timespan.[12] The real wage trends, therefore, indicate the existence of labor shortages among the ranks of the higher-skilled work-force coexisting with labor surpluses among the less-skilled labor force.

The emergence of the service economy has imposed an entirely different set of job requirements on the actual and potential labor force. While the technology of earlier periods of U.S. economic history stressed physical and manual skills for job seekers (when the goods-producing industries were expanding), the emerging service-producing economy since the 1960s creates jobs that stress mental, social, linguistic, and communication skills. A premium is placed on cognitive skills such as reading, writing, numeracy, and fluency in English. Thus, the emerging employment structure is in the process of debunking a pervasive myth that service sector jobs are dead end and low-paying. Some are, of course, but so are some jobs in the goods-producing sector (e.g., many in agricultural as well as in textile and garment manufacturing). The reality is that 80 percent of the professional and managerial jobs in the entire economy are to be found in the service sector. While it is true that there are growing employment opportunities in such low-paying service industries

as fast-foods and nursing home care, there are also substantial employment increases being realized in high-paying jobs in computer services,
legal services, and advertising as well as in average-paying jobs in
insurance, wholesale trade, and auto repairing.

Table 7.4 Actual Percentage Growth and Percentage Share
for Major Occupational Groups in U.S. Economy
between 1978 and 1989 (percentage terms)

Major Occupation	Percentage Increase (or decrease) from 1978 to 1990	Share of Employed Increase (or decrease)
Executive, Manager and Administrator	-56.7	25
Professional	42.3	22
Technical	45.8	5
Sales	36.7	18
Administrative Support	18.4	13
Protective Services	35.9	2
Private Household	-26.1	-1
Other Services	24.3	12
Precision Production and Craft	13.9	8
Machine Operator	-10.0	-4
Transportation Operatives	7.9	2
Laborers	-3.9	-1
Farm, Forestry and Fish Workers	-7.9	-1
Total Occupational Growth for U.S. Economy (percent)	22.1	100

Source: John H. Bishop and Shani Carter, "The Deskilling vs. Upskilling Debate: The Role of BLS Projections." Ithaca: Center for Advanced Human Resource Studies, 1990. Working Paper # 90-14.

In its projections of occupational growth to the year 2000, the U.S.
Department of Labor forecasts that the managerial, professional, and tech-
nician occupations—all requiring postsecondary levels of education and

training—are expected to continue to grow much faster than the projected average growth rate for total employment.[13] Of the twenty occupations projected to be the fastest growing in the 1990s, half are related to the growing computer and health fields. The shift to a service-based economy is leading to a general upgrading of the skill and educational requirements of the labor force from what had ever previously existed. Conversely, of course, those occupations that require minimal skills and education have sharply contracted and are projected to continue to do so.

Geographical Shifts

The U.S. economy is also in the midst of a major geographic shift in its employment patterns. The distribution and growth of nonagricultural employment in the United States is uneven.[14] The regions of greatest employment growth in the 1970s and 1980s were in the South Atlantic (from Delaware to Florida), West South Central (from Arkansas to Texas), and the Pacific Coast regions. The areas of greatest decline have been in the mid-Atlantic (New York, New Jersey, and Pennsylvania) and East North Central (the Great Lakes area from Wisconsin through to Ohio) regions. The employment shifts reflect the broader movement of the population away from the Northeast and Midwest to the South and West.

The 1990 census also revealed another important population development. For the first time in the nation's history, more than half of the nation's population lived in the thirty-nine large metropolitan areas with a population of one million persons or more.[15] In 1950, 30 percent of the population lived in such areas; in 1980, 46 percent did; and in 1990 slightly over 50 percent did. Of these thirty-nine large metropolitan areas, 90 percent grew in size over the decade of the 1980s. The greatest growth came in the metropolitan areas in the South Atlantic states (e.g., nine of the twelve fastest growing metropolitan areas in the nation were in Florida) and the Pacific Coast states. The greatest growth in metropolitan areas, however, was in the suburbs and not the central cities of metropolitan areas. Of the five largest metropolitan areas that lost populations, four (Pittsburgh, Buffalo, Cleveland, and Detroit) were in the former manufacturing heartland region near the Great Lakes. The only other metropolitan area to decline was New Orleans. Implicit in the growth of all metropolitan areas, of course, is the decline in nonmetropolitan (i.e., rural) areas.

The perceptible shifts of employment and population growth from the Northeast and Midwest to the South and West are the product of a number of historic differences. Among these are differences in regional income, wages, and cost of living, as well as changes in the importance of certain geographic features and natural resource endowments. Nonetheless, within the context of these long-term influences, there are also several other change-creating pressures at work. The rapid shift to a service economy has implications for the location of jobs. Goods-producing industries tend to cluster in specific geographic areas. During their growth phase, for instance, employment in the automobile industry was concentrated in Michigan—especially in the Detroit area; the steel industry was concentrated in Western Pennsylvania, Western New York, Northern Ohio, and Northern Indiana; and the rubber industry was in Ohio. Thus, if workers wished to find jobs in these industries they had to migrate to these areas. But the key characteristic of services is that they must be produced locally. Thus, the shift from goods to service industries has contributed to a general decentralization of employment away from the historic concentration in the urban Midwest and urban Northeast to other regions.

It is also the case that the urban cities of the interior regions of the United States were not only tied heavily to many manufacturing industries but their economies were also linked disproportionately to agriculture. When these goods-producing industries began to decline in terms of their employment needs, their urban labor markets also felt the impact of the employment erosion. On the other hand, coastal cities of the nation were more dependent on service industries (e.g., banking, insurance, finance, legal services, and advertising) in particular and have benefited from their rapid growth in the 1970s and 1980s.

Shifting national defense expenditures have also affected the geography of jobs within the manufacturing sector. Historically, through the Korean Conflict of the 1950s, major nonpersonnel defense expenditures were made on steel and wheeled vehicles as well as armaments. Their production was typically concentrated in the existing manufacturing centers in the urban Midwest and urban Northeast. Since the 1960s, however, the bulk of nonpersonnel expenditures has shifted toward missiles, rockets, and aircraft. These weapons often require that some phase of their construction be accomplished out-of-doors and that they be tested either over water or in remote areas with low populations. The result has been a shift in employment opportunities in the defense industries to the Southeast and Southwest.   In 1988, for example, California received $30 billion under federal procurement contracts—over twice the amount of the next-highest recipient state, which was Virginia with $12 billion, and almost three times the third-highest, which was Texas with $10 billion. Of these federal procurement contracts, about 75 percent are directly related to defense contracts. Because present-day military weaponry has become so dependent on electronics, much of the related production costs are associated with research and development expenditures as well as highly technical production techniques. The 1991 war with Iraq clearly proved the dominance of "silicon over steel" as the weapon technology for the future. These defense contractors, however, are not the same industries as those that were prominent in the World War II and Korean Conflict eras. They disproportionately require more highly skilled workers and they tend to be located along the coastal states of the Southeast and West.

There is another aspect of defense-related employment that portends significant changes for the 1990s. Namely, there is the real prospect of significant declines in military personnel and probable reductions in overall military outlays.[16] The end of the Cold War relations between the East and the West and the startling political changes in Eastern Europe of the late-1980s and in the former Soviet Union in the early 1990s precipitated a move to reduce the scale of the national defense program. The brevity of the war with Iraq in 1991 meant that the political momentum favoring military reductions is back on track. Budgetary plans already approved by Congress and President George Bush in the Budget Reconciliation Act of 1991 call for a 25 percent reduction in the nation's Armed Services by 1995 (a reduction from about 2.1 million to about 1.6 million military personnel). Related reductions in support material and in the size of previous military orders are also anticipated. For present purposes, these reductions—assuming they are actually carried through—will mean that the volunteer military will provide fewer opportunities for participation in the next decade and it will be much more selective as to whom it admits and retains. In 1991, for example, 97 percent of those serving in the military had at least a high school diploma. The military force in 1995 will be the smallest in size since before the Korean Conflict in 1950. Thus, it will be the burden of the civilian sector to absorb many of those young people for whom the military in the past provided an alternative port of entry into the world of work. Likewise, should nonpersonnel military cutbacks also occur, the closing of military bases and the reduction in work by private sector defense contractors will also cause disruptions in many communities and place added responsibilities on civilian-oriented industries to employ workers from the defense sector. Should defense contractors actually reduce their employment levels, these displaced workers—many of whom are semiskilled, skilled, and highly educated workers—will be available to fill similar needs elsewhere in the civilian sector where shortages are anticipated. It will require, however, a guided human resource policy that includes retraining and, possibly, relocation assistance to minimize the adjustment costs. It may also mean that there will be far less need for skilled immigrant workers in the 1990s if these reductions in defense employment actually materialize.

The Internationalization of the U.S. Economy

The post–World War II era has also witnessed the introduction of another significant and entirely new force that is rapidly increasing and exerting unprecedented influences on the U.S. economy, its workforce, and its communities: international competition. In 1946, the dollar value of merchandise trade for the United States was $11.7 billion in exports and $5 billion in imports, for a favorable net balance of $6.7 billion. By 1989, these figures had risen to $360.4 billion in exports versus $475.3 billion in imports, for a deficit trade balance of $114.9 billion.[17] The lion's share of the increase in all of these numbers occurred since the mid-1970s. Prior to 1971, the United States had been a net creditor nation for over seventy years; since then, it has not only become a net debtor nation, but it is the world's largest net debtor nation.

Explaining the sharp growth in international trade is the fact that the United States has embarked upon a foreign trade policy that departs from anything that it ever pursued before. The United States economy was not built on the principles of free trade. Indeed, the nation's rise to world dominance was based precisely on the fact that it did not depend upon the control of foreign markets but, rather, on production for its vast home market. The pace of U.S. economic development was also greatly stimulated in the twentieth century by the expanded production demand associated with two world wars that were fought on foreign shores. In the process, the United States economy generated a disproportionate number of high-wage and high-income jobs that became the envy of the world, and at the same time, developed a mass domestic market, especially for expensive and technologically advanced goods and services, which were produced by the highly heterogeneous industrial structure.

As discussed earlier in Chapter 3, high protective tariffs were a fact of life throughout the nation's history up until the 1930s. The lack of any numerical ceiling on immigration prior to the 1920s meant that the labor market was subject to extensive worker competition. But the product market during those earlier waves of mass immigration was securely protected from competition throughout that entire period. With the enactment of the Smoot-Hawley Tariff in 1930, U.S. tariffs reached their highest levels in history. As a direct consequence of its passage, twenty-five other countries quickly retaliated by raising their tariffs on U.S. exports. This legislation has been blamed, in part, for the worsening and prolonging of the Great Depression that began only a few months before its passage.

With the election of President Franklin Roosevelt in 1932, U.S. tariff policy underwent a dramatic revision. Protectionism *per se* was repudiated. A new era of reciprocal trade agreements was launched. It allowed bilateral agreements to be arranged whereby favorable tariff reductions of up to 50 percent of existing levels were permitted by the United States on a reciprocal basis with other specific nations. World War II, however, interrupted this trend. During the war, foreign trade came to a virtual halt but the productive capabilities of the U.S. economy were increased dramatically. Moreover, the economies of all other major industrial powers at the time were devastated by the destruction of the fighting. The United States emerged from the war as the leading industrial power in the world. In 1950, the United States accounted for 50 percent of the world's total production of goods and services. It was from this position of unrivaled economic strength that the United States slowly began the process of abandoning its protectionist tradition. It was in the national interest to do so.[18] The United States was instrumental in the adoption in 1947 of the General Agreement on Tariffs and Trade (GATT) in which signatory nations pledged to reduce the tariff barriers to world trade.

It was not until the Trade Expansion Act of 1962, that the actual process of general tariff reduction commenced. This led to the "Kennedy Round" of international trade negotiations in 1964 and, later, the "Geneva Round" in 1979, which produced significant tariff reduction by member nations. In the wake of these and subsequent multi-lateral negotiations and agreements, U.S. exports have soared—but so have imports.

As other nations gradually regained and expanded their productive capabilities after World War II, they were gradually able to reclaim production for much of their own domestic markets. Further, because the U.S. unilaterally opened its marketplace for their entry, they have been able to select and to pick-off certain sectors of the U.S. economy for competition with their specifically tailored export policies. Even some less economically developed nations have been able to join the feast. Unconstrained at home by environmental and worker protection laws comparable to those in the United States, many nations can choose particular segments of the U.S. economy that are susceptible to competition from their less-costly production requirements. Or, alternatively, these nations can successfully attract formerly U.S.-based enterprises to relocate to their countries and then export back to the U.S. the output that once was domestically produced at higher costs.

The way free trade is usually portrayed in the textbooks is as a perpetual self-balancing barter process. No nation theoretically can buy more than it can sell. Each individual nation supposedly specializes in those products and services in which competitive market forces reveal it to have a comparative advantage. In practice, of course, the balance of U.S. trade has become—and remains—in a chronic deficit state. Few, if any other nations, are content to allow market forces to shape their destinies. Indeed, most modern nations rely on industrial policies that are explicitly designed by their respective governments to create rather than to reveal comparative trade advantages.

By the mid-1980s, the U.S. economy was reeling from "industrial import shock."[19] Manufacturing in the United States has sustained the greatest impact of this new competition. By the mid-1980s 70 percent of U.S. manufacturing industries had direct foreign competition—many for the first time. U.S. agriculture has also found itself confronted with mounting competition from foreign imports at home and with stiff competition from other nations for export markets. The reduction in trade barriers has also led many U.S. businesses to abandon their role as potential exporters. Whereas they once produced their goods and services within the country, many now prefer to relocate their production facilities abroad and import some of their output back to this country.[20] Frequently, the plant relocations are to less-developed countries where not only are wage rates a fraction of what they are in the United States but there are few, if any, enforceable regulations pertaining to employment standards or environmental protections.

There has also been another development that has been a direct consequence of the pursuit of active free trade policies. It is the growing tendency for some foreign companies to establish their own operational branches in the United States or to buy existing enterprises located within the United States. As of 1988, for instance, almost 11 percent of the "value added" in U.S. manufacturing came from foreign-owned enterprises employing three million workers (or roughly 15 percent of the manufacturing workforce).[21] The trend has been greatly encouraged by the large U.S. trade deficit which has virtually flooded the world with dollars. It has been exacerbated by the conscientious decisions of the Reagan and Bush Administrations to allow the value of the dollar to fall relative to other major foreign currencies. The purposeful devaluation of the dollar was intended to make U.S. products cheaper and to serve to stimulate exports. But as Japan's Vice Minister of Finance and International Affairs, Makato Utsumi has observed, the falling value of the dollar has "not put American products on sale but put America on sale."[22] Under these circumstances, it becomes easier by the day for foreign businesses to buy U.S. assets.

The rapid internationalization of the U.S. economy has meant that this is the first generation of U.S. businesses and workers who have had to compete in such a global environment. When GATT was signed, it was anticipated that a parallel agreement on the protection of employment standards in signatory nations would be adopted at a later date. It has yet to happen. Subsequent legislation, such as the Caribbean Basin Initiative of 1983 and the Trade and Tariff Act of 1984, contain general homilies requiring that "internationally recognized worker rights" are to be assured as a consequence of reducing trade barriers but there is no effective agency or mechanism in place to enforce such principles and, to date, little political will to find such a means.[23] Cost-cutting, often unilaterally imposed, has become the order of the day in many U.S. enterprises which are now confronted with strong competition from foreign imports. Such endeavors usually involve efforts to cut employment levels, to reduce worker benefits, and to invoke higher productivity requirements on those employees who remain or who are subsequently hired. Thus, the international competition has contributed to a dramatic reshaping of the economic environment at the workplace.

The United States is the largest single marketplace in the world and serves as a natural magnet to attract exports of other nations. Most other nations—especially the major industrial powers—have comprehensive trade policies in place that encourage export industries while affording protection to nonexporting industries. Most of the major industrial nations also have parallel human resource development strategies that provide retraining, educational up-grading, and relocation assistance to workers along with the general community readjustment assistance programs to ease the transitional process for the members of their local labor forces who are adversely affected by trade policy. Lacking such formal public policies and with little historical experience to provide guidance, many U.S. communities and U.S. workers have had to fend for themselves. The results have not been altogether positive.[24]

The Growing Size and Changing Composition of the Labor Force

As for the supply side of the U.S. labor market, the labor force is also in the midst of a prolonged period of unprecedented growth and radical change in its composition. The "fourth wave" of mass immigration, as discussed in Chapter 6, is significant for both its numerical size and the diversity of the personal characteristics of its participants. Both features are major contributors to even larger trends of similar natures that have characterized the overall labor force since the mid-1960s.

Before discussing "the labor force" and the data that are used to analyze its behavior, it is essential to review briefly the specific meaning of the term as defined by "official" government agencies who collect, tabulate, and publish such information. For as is too often the case, the general public's understanding of key terms used to discuss popular concepts is based on personal perceptions of what they mean. But such common sense reasoning can be deceptive. For data collectors (i.e., government agencies) encounter a multitude of circumstances when it comes to measuring who is employed and who is not; who wants to be employed and who does not; who is available to be employed and who is not; and who is actively seeking employment and who is not. Thus, these agencies, of necessity, have adopted statistical definitions that are designed for their collection convenience and for their consistency over time. Economic statistics are measurement tools. They should not be confused, as they often are, with being actual indicators of social welfare.

Bearing this disclaimer in mind, the civilian labor force consists of all persons in the noninstitutionalized population over sixteen years of age who have a job plus those who meet a specific definition as being unemployed. The unemployed are those persons in the noninstitu-tionalized population who are sixteen years of age or older who do not work one hour a week for pay and who are willing, able, available, and "actively seeking" work. The civilian labor force, however, does not include those persons who want to work but who, because of the state of the economy, have abandoned active search for a job because they believe such efforts would be fruitless. Such potential labor force participants are called "discouraged workers." Research has shown that the more people who are unemployed at any given time, the more other people tend to be discouraged (and vice versa). It also reveals that women, in general, as well as younger and older men are most likely to be affected by the "discouraged worker" phenomenon. On the other hand, the definition of the civilian labor force does include as being employed all persons who desire to work full-time but who can only find part-time jobs because of prevailing economic conditions. Thus, the official definition of the civilian labor force has serious limitations. Indeed, the definition as to who should be included in the labor force and who should not, as well as who is employed or unemployed and who is not, is periodically a heated subject of both political and professional controversy.[25]

Beginning in the mid-1960s and accelerating in the decades that have followed, the labor force of the United States entered a period of protracted growth. No singular characteristic of the labor force of the United States stands out more clearly when compared to all other major industrial powers. Table 7.5 shows the actual size and growth of employment and unemployment between the United States as compared with the other nine industrial powers of the free world. It indicates that over the twelve-year interval from 1976 to 1988, the U.S. labor force grew by 25.5 million workers (or by an astounding 26.5 percent). This quantitative growth exceeded the combined total growth of the other nine nations by more than one-third. Moreover, over this timespan, the United States was the only individual nation to sustain a decline in the number of people who were unemployed. For all other industrialized nations, a substantial portion—depending which individual nation is examined—of their labor force growth was the result of an increase in unemployment. For the United States, actual employment grew by a phenomenal 26.2 million workers over this timespan. In annual terms, this was a net addition of about 2.2 million employed workers a year. At no previous time in the nation's history has the labor force annually grown by such an equivalent number. No other country that competes with the United

Table 7.5 Changes in Labor Force, Employment, and Unemployment in 10 Industrialized Nations Between 1976 and 1988
(number in thousands)

Country	Labor Force			Employment			Unemployment		
	1976	1988	Change	1976	1988	Change	1976	1988	Change
United States	96,158	121,669	25,511	88,752	114,968	26,216	7,406	6,701	-705
Canada	10,203	13,275	3,072	9,477	12,245	2,768	726	1,031	305
Australia	6,244	7,974	1,730	5,946	7,398	1,452	298	576	278
Japan	53,100	60,860	7,760	52,020	59,310	7,290	1,080	1,550	470
France	22,010	23,590	1,580	21,020	21,180	160	990	2,410	1,420
Germany	25,900	28,580	2,680	25,010	26,770	1,760	890	1,810	920
Italy	20,300	22,660	1,850	19,600	20,870	1,270	700	1,790	1,090
Netherlands	4,890	6,560	1,670	4,630	5,940	1,310	260	620	360
Sweden	4,149	4,540	391	4,083	4,467	384	66	73	7
United Kingdom	25,290	28,150	2,860	23,810	25,740	1,930	1,480	2,410	930

Note: All data for foreign nations are adjusted to approximate U.S. definitions.

Source: U.S. Department of Labor.

States has been confronted with such pressure to accommodate annually so many new job-seekers over this timespan. Germany, as the result of the unique reunification process that began in late 1989, is the only other industrial power in the 1990s that is likely to confront significant labor force growth pressures. But West Germany's unemployment in the 1980s was considerably higher than that of the United States, and given the poor economic state of what was formerly East Germany, it is likely that a substantial portion of unified Germany's labor force growth in the 1990s will be in the form of unemployment.

As for the near future, substantial absolute growth in the U.S. labor force is projected to continue throughout the 1990s. As shown in Table 7.6, the "official" moderate growth projections for the twelve-year period from 1988 to 2000 call for a net increase of 19.5 million new job-seekers (or a 16.0 percent rate). It is true that the projected annual growth rate of 1.2 percent for the 1988 to 2000 period represents a decline from the actual annual rate of 2.0 percent for the 1976 to 1988 period. But this projected rate translates into an annual average flow of 1.6 million additional job-seekers a year (or 19.5 million workers for the period). Except for the 1976 to 1988 period, this projected moderate growth—if it actually happens—would be the largest increase in labor force size over such a twelve-year timespan in the nation's history.

Moreover, all previous projections of labor force growth by the Bureau of Labor Statistics (BLS) have seriously erred on the conservative side. It is highly likely that this will again be the case with these projections for the year 2000 because the moderate growth projections were based on a number of faulty assumptions—all pertaining to the anticipated effects of immigration. One certain source of error was the assumption by BLS that illegal immigration would decline from 200,000 persons a year to 100,000 persons a year during the 1900s when, as discussed in Chapter 6, just the opposite is occurring. Indeed, the estimate of a net flow of 200,000 illegal immigrants a year into the U.S. population—which of necessity could only be crudely approximated—was derived from data from the 1980 census.[26] A subsequent study in 1989 by BLS, however, noted that the "rather strong indication of an upsurge in illegal immigration in the mid-1980s has not yet been taken into account in constructing the official population estimate for the nation."[27] That study, which found employment in the United States to be growing faster than the Census data predicted, bluntly stated that there is absolutely no basis for any assumption that the earlier estimate of 200,000 illegal aliens a year was

Table 7.6 Civilian Labor Force and Participation Rates by Sex, Race, and Hispanic Origin, 1976 and 1988, and Moderate Growth Projection to 2000

Group	Participation rate (percent)			Employment Level (in thousands)			Change (in thousands)		Percent Change		Growth rate	
	1976	1988	2000	1976	1988	2000	1976-88	1988-2000	1976-88	1988-2000	1976-88	1988-2000
Total, 16 and over	61.6	65.9	69.0	96,158	121,669	141,134	25,511	19,465	26.5	16.0	2.0	1.2
Men, 16 and over	77.5	76.2	75.9	57,174	66,927	74,324	9,753	7,397	17.1	11.1	1.3	.9
Women, 16 and over	47.3	56.6	62.6	38,983	54,742	66,810	15,759	12,068	40.4	22.0	2.9	1.7
Whites, 16 and over	61.8	66.2	69.5	84,767	104,756	118,981	19,989	14,225	23.6	13.6	1.8	1.1
Men	78.4	76.9	76.6	51,033	58,317	63,288	7,284	4,971	14.3	8.5	1.1	.7
Women	46.9	56.4	62.9	33,735	46,439	55,693	12,704	9,254	37.7	19.9	2.7	1.5
Blacks, 16 and over	58.9	63.8	66.5	9,565	13,205	16,465	3,640	3,260	38.1	24.7	2.7	1.9
Men	69.7	71.0	71.4	5,105	6,596	8,007	1,491	1,411	29.2	21.4	2.2	1.6
Women	50.0	58.0	62.5	4,460	6,609	8,458	2,149	1,849	48.2	28.0	3.3	2.1
Asian and other, 16 and over	62.8	65.0	65.5	1,826	3,709	5,688	1,883	1,979	103.1	53.4	6.1	3.6
Men	74.9	74.4	74.6	1,036	2,015	3,029	979	1,014	94.5	50.3	5.7	3.5
Women	51.6	56.5	57.5	790	1,694	2,659	904	965	114.4	57.0	6.6	3.8
Hispanics, 16 and over	60.7	67.4	69.9	4,279	8,982	14,321	4,703	5,339	109.9	59.4	6.4	4.0
Men	79.6	81.9	80.3	2,625	5,409	8,284	2,784	2,875	106.1	53.2	6.2	3.6
Women	44.1	53.2	59.4	1,654	3,573	6,037	1,919	2,464	116.0	69.0	6.6	4.5

Note: Persons of Hispanic origin may be of any race.

Source: U.S. Department of Labor.

a constant for the decade. Indeed, the early 1980s was a period when unemployment was rising to levels that had not been seen since the depression decade of the 1930s. Hence, the study observed, "in subsequent years, when the demand for labor increased considerably, the new inflow of illegal aliens is likely to have reached much higher levels."[28] The relevant conclusion, therefore, was that "because most illegal aliens enter the country to take a job, a substantial underestimation of the increase in their numbers would inevitably lead to a substantial underestimation of employment growth in the data."[29]

Another factor that will cause the labor force projections cited in Table 7.6 to be significantly understated is that the annual figure used as the basis for legal immigration was 400,000 persons. The actual figure was running closer to 550,000 a year in the late 1980s and early 1990s and, as the provisions of the Immigration Act of 1990 go into effect, the level should rise to 700,000 a year. There were no provisions made in the projection for the family reunification implications of the various amnesty programs enacted in 1986 under IRCA that will occur in the 1990s. Also, the immigration estimate did not make any allowance for the admission of refugees, whose numbers are likely to average over 100,000 a year throughout the 1990s. And lastly, no estimate was made of the increasing number of nonimmigrant foreign workers who are legally permitted to work in the United States under the terms of their visas. These workers, averaging about 435,000 workers a year in the late 1980s, are certain to swell in the years ahead as a result of the new provisions of the Immigration Act of 1990.

Accordingly, when the projected labor force growth for the period 1988 to 2000 becomes an actual number, the total will certainly exceed the projected growth total of 19.5 million new workers shown in Table 7.6 by several million. The actual number should be closer to the aforementioned record-setting 25.5 million worker figure of the 1976 to 1988 period. Thus, there is no reason for any concern about any general "shortage of labor" developing because of an alleged slackening in the growth of the labor force in the 1990s. The labor force would have grown close to record numbers regardless of whether the Immigration Act of 1990 was enacted. The issue of a potential "shortage of labor" raised by advocates to argue for passage of the Immigration Act of 1990 was a red herring. The existence of surplus labor is the most likely scenario for the 1990s.

The Causes of Labor Force Growth

There have been three ongoing factors that have contributed to rapid growth of the labor force. Each of these pressures is also exerting significant influences on the gender, age, and ethnic composition of the labor force. In the process, a new labor force is being constituted with characteristics unlike any previous labor force in the nation's history and unlike that of any other major industrialized nation. The remaking of the U.S. labor force, however, is taking place in an era when older issues that remain unsolved still have a powerful claim for both priority and remediation. It is in this social context that these new transforming forces are of special significance.

One of the new pressures is, of course, the return of mass immigration to the U.S. economy. As it was the subject of the detailed discussion in Chapter 6 and its effects for the 1990s will be the subject of Chapter 8, the influence of mass immigration will not be repeated here, but its effects must be kept in mind. The other two powerful forces for growth and change in the population and labor force are the unprecedented number of women who have sought entry into the labor market, and the maturing of the post–World War II "baby boom" population cohort.

The Growth in the Female Labor Force

More women in both absolute and relative terms have been entering and staying longer in the labor force than at any previous time in the nation's history. The movement has been so abrupt and so large that it can fairly be described as a "social revolution" in its own right. As shown earlier in Table 7.6, two out of every three new labor market entrants since 1976 have been women, and the same pattern is forecast to continue through to the year 2000.

Although there is an enormous variation in the female labor force participation rates among the states of the union (i.e., they range from a high of 67 percent in Alaska to a low of 43 percent in West Virginia in 1990), there can be no mistake about the long-term trend. The labor force participation rate of all women has risen from 33.9 percent in 1950 to 57.5 percent in 1990. It is projected to rise even further to 62.6 percent in the year 2000 (see Table 7.6). In total, women constituted 45.3 percent of the civilian labor force in 1990 and it is projected that this percentage will increase to 47 percent by 2000.

The contributing factors for this growth rest with the rapidly increasing participation rate of married women in general and women with children in particular. It is their labor market behavior that represents the dramatic departure from the past. Single adult women without children were usually in the labor market, but married women and women with children were not.

The reasons for the sudden acceleration of women in the labor market are still the subject of debate. The movement was completely unpredicted by demographers and labor market forecasters in the 1960s. The mechanization of housekeeping tasks since the end of World War II combined with the growing acceptance of family planning and the availability of new methods to permit the timing of birth occurrences created an opportunity for the social change to occur. The momentum to alter the status of women in the workplace was provided in the 1960s by the civil rights movement. Women were not initially included in the Civil Rights Act of 1964 but, as the result of an amendment offered by opponents to the bill as a possible ploy to defeat the legislation, prohibitions against sex discrimination in employment were included in the final version of the legislation. The moral force of the law, combined with the creation of a legal enforcement mechanism, provided the emerging feminist movement with a lever to attack barriers that had previously prevented women from fully participating in the labor market. The pattern of change was subsequently enhanced by the prolonged period of high inflation that occurred during the 1970s and early 1980s. The decrease in real family incomes forced many women to find jobs in order to maintain their family's previous standards of living. Simultaneously, over this same timespan there has been a surge in the number of female heads of households. In 1989, 16.2 percent of all families were so constituted—up from 10.8 percent in 1970. For black families, the percentages increased from 28.3 percent in 1970 to 42.8 percent in 1989. Aside from single adult women, other factors such as widowhood, divorce, and pregnancies outside of marriage have caused an increasing number of other women to be the sole breadwinners for their families. Many such women have been forced to seek employment whether they wished to do so or not.[30]

An important population corollary to the growth of female participation in the labor market is the decline in family size. The number of children per family in the United States has fallen from 3.2 in 1930 to about 1.8 in the mid-1980s. A sustained rate of 2.1 children per family is needed for population replacement. The most significant encouragement to smaller families has been provided by the entry of married women into the labor force. In the future, it is highly unlikely that women will abandon the financial and personal independence that they have come to experience. This is especially the case since divorce has become so common. Thus, high labor force participation by women is likely to be a permanent feature of the U.S. economy along with the pattern of smaller families.

The Maturing of the Population

The rapid growth of the labor force has also been significantly affected by the age distribution of the U.S. population. There has been a large "bulge" in the age range between twenty-five and forty-four years of age during the years from 1971 through 1989. Not only has it been the largest cohort of the population, but it is also the most rapidly growing in absolute numbers. The bulge is a direct result of the labor force entry of the post–World War II baby boomers (those born between 1946 and 1964) who have now matured into prime working-age adults. Of the nation's population in 1990, 32 percent were in this age cohort. Regardless of gender or race, persons in the twenty-five to forty-four years of age cohort of the population have the highest labor force participation rates of the entire labor force. If ever a person is going to seek work, it is most probable he or she will do so between these ages. Thus, the bulge is a "good" problem for an economy to be confronted with—especially when its implications are compared to the earlier period when this age group was primarily in its youth (before 1980) or what lies ahead when this cohort enters its retirement phase (after 2001).

It is also of critical significance to note that the racial and ethnic composition of the "baby boom" population is also affecting the composition of the labor force. Although family size is generally decreasing for all major racial and ethnic groups, the decline began earlier and has been more rapid for non-Hispanic whites than for minority groups. When combined with the effects of "fourth wave" mass immigration, the racial and ethnic composition of the United States population is undergoing rapid change. Indeed, the 1990 Census figures show that "the racial composition of the American population changed more dramatically in the last decade [i.e., the 1980s] than at any time in the twentieth century."[31] During the decade of the 1980s, the overall population of the

United States increased by 9.8 percent while the white population grew by 6.0 percent; the black population by 13.2 percent; the Hispanic population by 53.0 percent; the Asian population by 107.8 percent; and the Native American population by 37.9 percent. The actual and projected effects of population change on the anticipated growth of the labor force can be dramatically seen in Table 7.6. The labor force growth rates of black, Hispanic, and Asian workers (there is no such data for Native Americans) considerably exceeded that of whites in the 1980s and are expected to continue this pattern throughout the 1990s and into the twenty-first Century.[32]

The Growth in Labor Force Participation

One of the most consequential results of the aforementioned growth of the labor force has been the rising overall labor force participation rate in the United States. In 1989, this overall rate reached the highest level in U.S. history—66.5 percent before slipping a notch to 66.4 percent in 1990 (the result of rising cyclical unemployment during the last half of that year). Except for Sweden and Canada, no other major industrial country has a labor force participation rate that comes close to that of the United States. As shown in Table 7.6, the U.S. Department of Labor projects that labor force participation will regain its upward momentum and rise throughout the 1990s to a projected rate of 69 percent in the year 2000. In laymen's terms, this means that of the entire noninstitutionalized population over the age of sixteen, 69 percent will be in the labor force (i.e., they will either be employed or unemployed as "officially" defined). Thus, the consequence of rising labor force participation will be that the labor force will continue throughout the 1990s to sustain substantial aggregate growth pressures. In this context it should also be recalled that the projection for continued labor force growth shown in Table 7.6 is based on the moderate growth projection of the U.S. Department of Labor and that the projection was based on questionable estimates of anticipated immigration influences that seem far too low.

The Major Exception: Male Blacks

Buried within the statistical data contained in Table 7.6 is one deeply worrisome exception. It pertains to the low labor force participation rate of black males relative to white males. Historically through the 1940s, the black male labor force participation rate consistently exceeded that of white males. But since the 1950s, the white male rate has passed the black rate and the gap between the two has widened. In 1990, the white male rate exceeded the black male rate by 6.8 percent (76.9 percent to 70.1 percent). The wide gap exists for every age grouping. Indicative of the significance of this decline in black male participation is the fact that the absolute number of black women in the labor force in 1990 exceeds that of black men (6,785,000 black women to 6,708,000 black men). It is the only racial group in the U.S. labor force where this occurs and, as is also shown in Table 7.6, it is projected to worsen throughout the 1990s. Black women, therefore, are the nation's largest minority group in the labor force. On the surface, there appears to be no reason why white males should have a significantly higher participation rate for every age cohort than black males or why white males should have a considerably higher overall rate. In fact, given that the black population is considerably younger than the white population, (i.e., the median age of the white population in 1988 was 33.2 years old while for blacks it was 27.5 years old), standard labor market analysis would predict that the black male labor force participation rate should be higher than the comparable white rate. However, blacks are clustered disproportionately in the central cities of twelve major cities outside the South, in most central cities of the South, as well as being scattered throughout the large geographic area of the rural South (the only region with a significant rural black presence). Jobs in these locations are frequently scarce. Moreover, black male workers have been disproptionately displaced by the decline in manufacturing industries and production-related occupations because they were disproportionately employed in these sectors.[33]   But jobs in the expanding service industries and white-collar occupations are especially hard to find if one has few skills and little education and if there are limited opportunities to acquire skills or to develop latent abilities. Qualifying for jobs is made more difficult if there are lingering vestiges of racial discrimination.

There is, of course, an ominous societal implication to these low black male participation rates. An inordinately high number of black males are incarcerated in federal and state prisons as well as local jails. Such persons, of course, are not even included in the labor force participation data because the data are based only on the noninstitutionalized proportion of the black male population. The low participation rate reflects, in part, the fact that black male unemployment is about twice that of white males. But low participation rates mean that a significant number of black males have simply stopped looking or seldom have tried to actively seek work. The question then is, if these adult black males are not at work, or in school, or in the military, what are they doing to survive? The answer, of course, is that an urban subclass of adult black males who function outside the normal labor market has been formed and institutionalized.[34] It exists through reliance on irregular activities such as casual "off the books" work and antisocial behavior such as crime. It may also entail such self-destructive activity as alcoholism and drug abuse. Helping those black male adults who can be reached to enter the regular labor market and preventing many black male youths from succumbing to nonparticipation in the labor market is a major policy challenge for the 1990s. It should have been for the preceding three decades.

One reason why black male labor issues have not been adequately addressed—especially since they were highlighted in the 1960s by both the Civil Rights movement itself and the aforementioned findings of the National Advisory Committee on Civil Disorders (see Chapter 5)—has been the availability of the large flows of immigrant workers over the succeeding decades into most of the same urban labor markets where the urban black population is concentrated. As Elizabeth Bogen has succinctly observed, post-1965 mass immigration, like the earlier waves of mass immigration experiences, "is overwhelmingly an urban phenomenon."[35] The 1980 Census disclosed that 92 percent of the foreign born population lived in metropolitan areas compared to 74 percent of the native born. More to the point, 40 percent of the foreign-born population of the nation lived in only five metropolitan areas (New York, Los Angeles, Chicago, San Francisco, and Miami) where as only 11 percent of the native-born population did so. As regards the central cities, eight (the five listed in the preceding sentence plus Houston, San Diego, and Philadelphia) accounted for 26 percent of the entire foreign-born population. All eight of these central cities also have substantial black populations. Given the high levels of immigration that occurred during the 1980s, it is certain that the 1990 Census data, when available, will show even higher concentrations of foreign-born in these eight central cities and, probably, several others as well.

Given the scale of "fourth wave" immigration and, as matters now stand, the fact that the inflow is going to continue, the entry of immigrants into these central city areas has increased the competition for jobs available. Under these conditions, an inordinate number of black males apparently have despaired from seeking work in the regular economy. Competition from immigrants is not the only factor that might explain the low labor force participation rates of black males but it must be included within any such list of negative influences. Proving displacement, however, is an impossible chore because it is not possible to measure what would have happened absent mass immigration. Would blacks have continued to migrate into the cities to fill jobs if immigrants had not moved in? Would blacks have stopped moving out of urban areas if mass numbers of immigrants had not moved in? Any adequate discussion of job displacement must include estimates of both of these factors—but none do. What is clear is that black migration out of the South—which began only after earlier waves mass immigration ended prior to World War I, has been reversed during the 1980s for the first time in U.S. history.

As Raymond Frost has found, "there is a competitive relationship between immigration and black migration out of the South...When the rate of immigration declines, black migration to the North and West increases; when the rate of immigration increases, black migration declines."[36] Black migration out of the South to the North and West fell during the decade of the 1970s to the lowest level (i.e., 313,000 persons) since the 1911 to 1920 era while it actually became negative (−444,000 persons) during the 1980s (which meant there was a net outflow of blacks back to the South).[37]

The worsening plight of black males is, of course, also affecting black females in particular and black family structure in general. Up until the 1950s, black women married at higher proportions than did white women. By 1991, the proportion of black women who do not ever marry had reached an incredible figure of 25 percent of all black women.[38] This figure is three times higher than the comparable percentage for white women. The major explanation for the disparity rests with the fact that the pool of black men who are able to earn a living through work in the regular economy that is sufficient to support a family is rapidly shrinking. It is not only the negative effects of high unemployment and the inordinately high incarceration rates of black men, but also because the death rate—especially from homicide—for urban black males is soaring (estimated to be a one-in-ten chance of being killed in 1991).[39] The consequential effect on black family structure has been devastating. In 1990, 57.6 percent of all black births were out of wedlock (compared to 17.2 percent for whites and 23.2 percent for Hispanics).[40] Female heads of household with families, especially those who are from minority groups, are usually condemned to lives of poverty as are their offspring.

The economic status of blacks is a complicated issue but it is, given the legacy of slavery and *de jure* segregation, a problem that the citizens of the United States are obligated to resolve. Any public policy—including immigration policy—needs to be carefully examined to be certain that it does not in any way reduce the domestic pressures to address the needs of native-born blacks. To date, no comprehensive attempt has been made to do this. Because immigration policy has been designed primarily to meet political objec-tives, policymakers have largely ignored any concern of the economic impact of mass immigration on local labor markets. Not only have the economic interests of blacks been largely ignored but so have the interests of the nation's workforce in general. But for blacks in particular, it is very likely that immigration policy has become the latest manifestation of institutionalized racism. Immigration policy was not purposely intended to harm black Americans, but it has done just that. The longer it is allowed to function as a political policy, the worse are the economic prospects for blacks.

Labor Market Turmoil

When the national trends representing the demand for labor (i.e., the evolving employment patterns) are combined with those portraying the supply of labor (the emerging labor force characteristics), there are ample indications that the labor market is in disequilibrium.[41] Although adjustment problems are not restricted only to minorities, there are clear racial and ethnic patterns associated with who is having the worst difficulties.

While free markets have historically experienced cyclical fluctuation in economic activity that results in unemployment, Figure 7.1 shows that economic volatility has been far less of an issue since World War II than it was prior to it. On the other hand, Figure 7.1 also shows that the post–World War II economy has witnessed a gradual trend of rising unemployment rates; a phenomenon that has become associated with each succeeding period of economic prosperity (i.e., in each nonrecessionary period). Implicit in this pattern are indications that the effects of structural changes in the labor market are becoming more difficult to overcome.

In 1987, the U.S. Department of Labor issued a report entitled *Workforce 2000* that warned that the United States was facing the prospect of a serious crisis in the work place.[42] For many of the reasons

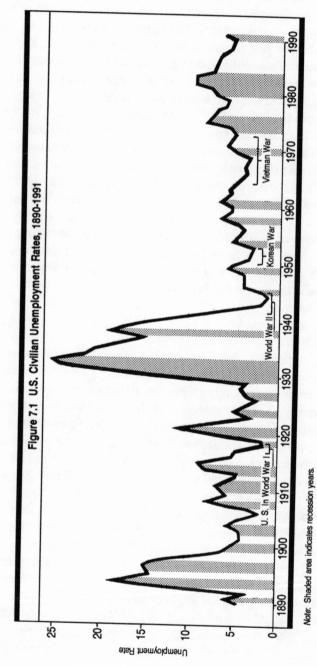

Figure 7.1 U.S. Civilian Unemployment Rates, 1890-1991

Note: Shaded area indicates recession years.

Source: U.S. Department of Labor.

outlined earlier in this chapter, a mismatch was developing between therequirements of jobs that were expanding and the qualifications of the future workforce to meet them. In 1989, a follow-up study concerned with how the nation should respond to this mismatch was conducted by the Commission on Workforce Quality and Labor Market Efficiency. This Commission found that, in fact, "the crisis envisioned in *Workforce 2000* has already begun to emerge."[43] It stated that:

> Increased demand for highly skilled workers, combined with an aging labor force, has already created shortages of skilled workers, shortages that are likely to grow for many years. At the same time, many low skilled workers are having increasing difficulty finding employment.[44]

The Commission spoke of a "skills gap" that was developing due largely to the lack of preparedness of the new labor force entrants as well as the tendency toward rapid obsolescence of the skills of much of the experienced workforce. The retraining of the experienced labor force, however, was hindered by the fact that the basic reading and computational skills that an effective program requires have prerequisites that "are well beyond those currently possessed by many experienced workers." It further noted that "at least 20 million, and possibly as many as 40 million, adults today experience substantial literacy problems."[45] In accepting the report, Elizabeth Dole, then the U.S. Secretary of Labor, described the United States labor force being "woefully inadequate" for the demands expected of it.[46] The Commission warned that if comprehensive education and training reforms were not soon initiated, job vacancies for skilled workers would coexist with unemployed job seekers, a disproportionate number of whom would be minorities. Moreover, the report indicated that under such circumstances, employers will actively recruit skilled immigrant and nonimmigrant workers or be tempted to relocate abroad where they can find the skilled workers they need. Such outcomes, the Commission voted, "could lead to social and political conflict" within the nation by those individuals and groups who are left out.

In the same vein, still another labor market analysis was issued in mid-1990 by the Commission on the Skills of the American Labor Force for the National Center on Education and the Economy. It was cochaired by two other former U.S. Secretaries of Labor, William E. Brock (during part of the Reagan Administration) and Ray Marshall (during all of the

Carter Administration). It found that the economic expansion of the mid-1980s was due largely to the aforementioned growth in the size of the labor force but that real wages for 70 percent of the workforce had actually declined considerably (i.e., by more than 12 percent) since 1969. Hence, in most families it was essential that there be two wage earners to make ends meet. The Commission's analysis blamed the decline in labor force productivity on the decline in real wages. It too had a warning that if substantial changes in human resource development did not occur, "either the top 30 percent of our population will grow wealthier while the bottom 70 percent become progressively poorer or we will all slide into poverty together."[47] Interestingly, this Commission found that many U.S. firms did not perceive a skills shortage to exist although most, however, complained about the "quality" of job applicants (by which they meant their social behavior, reliability, appearance, personality, and work ethic). The Commission blamed much of the fact of the low productivity on the organization of work in the United States, which has been premised on breaking complex jobs into simple rote tasks that a worker is expected to repeat almost endlessly. Under this arrangement, little attention has been focused either on the educational quality of the workforce or to its formal training. Indeed, the Commission found that only one-half of one percent of U.S. employers accounted for 90 percent of all the funds spent on formal work training. Over two-thirds of these funds are spent on workers who already have college degrees. On-the-job training is the way most workers actually learn their jobs. The result is that a huge, multilayered bureaucracy is required to supervise what the workforce does. The result of such an organizational structure is low productivity and an emphasis on low wages as the means to compete. As Co-Chairman Brock stated in a separate interview about the Commission's findings,

The choice is between high skills and low wages. We [i.e., the United States] seem to be continuing to compete on the basis of wages which means that the effort will constantly be to pull wages down instead of building skills up. We are making the wrong choice.[48]

The Commission found that other industrialized nations place much greater emphasis on high educational standards for virtually all of their students; have superior school-to-work transitional systems; have comprehensive human resource development systems in place that provide training, labor market information, job search, and income maintenance programs for those who become unemployed; have generalized company-based training programs for upgrading workers and preventing skill obsolescence financed by general tax revenues or payroll tax schemes; and all have achieved national consensuses about the desirability of high productivity work organizations and high wage economies. None of these attributes are current features of the U.S. economy. Moreover, none of these other industrialized countries saw immigration as a means of bolstering the skill and educational levels of their respective workforces. Instead, they have decided to invest in their citizens through these human resource development policies and have adopted or strengthened restrictions on immigration.

It is also the case that most of these other industrialized nations (the exception being Japan) have experienced higher unemployment rates than the United States since the mid-1970s. These nations, however, consider periods of high unemployment to be the ideal time to focus on expanded training and education needs of the workforce while people are out of work. When the economy improves, the workforce is prepared.[49] In the United States, unfortunately, just the opposite philosophy prevails. There is a tendency in the U.S. to reduce both public and private training during periods of high unemployment due to the belief that it makes little sense to engage in such activities when there is a shortage of available jobs. Consequently, when the economy picks up, the unemployed workers are not prepared for the jobs that become open and frustrated employers pressure the government for more liberal immigration policies for legal immigrants and nonimmigrants. The losers of course, are U.S. workers who belatedly have to find ways to become qualified—if they can—for jobs if they are still available.

Thus, although the two reports vary in their assessment of the existence of skill shortages, they come to exactly the same policy conclusion. The Commission of Work Force Quality found that employment prospects are bleak for the substantial number persons who are inadequately educated and poorly trained. Likewise, the Commission on Skills of the American Workforce concluded that this same portion of the workforce can only expect falling real wages if the prevailing organization of work, with its disregard of human resource development policies, is perpetuated.

While there are some shortages in U.S. occupations that require extensive educational and skill preparation, there is absolutely no indication that the United States will be confronted with the prospect of a general shortage of labor. What it does have is a substantial pool of workers whose human resource potential has been ignored or underdeveloped. Nor is there any shortage of unskilled workers. In fact, no technologically advanced nation that has from 20 to 40 million adult workers who are functionally or marginally illiterate need have any fear of a shortage of unskilled workers in its immediate future. Indeed, the major labor market problem for the 1990s will be what to do with the nation's surplus of unskilled workers.

It is within the context of this economic environment that the "fourth wave" of mass immigration began—and continues.

Notes

1. David Bell, "The Nature of Modernity," "Preface" to Leon Barit, *The Age of Automation* (New York: Mentor Books, 1964), pp. X-XI.

2. W.W. Rostow, *The Stages of Economic Growth* (London: Cambridge University Press, 1971), 2nd Edition, Chapter 6.

3. Valerie Personick, "Industry Output and Employment Through the End of the Century," *Monthly Labor Review* (September 1987), pp. 30-45.

4. Richard M. Cyert and David C. Mowery (eds.), *Technology and Employment* (Washington, D.C.: National Academy Press, 1987), Chapter 4; and Edward A. Feigenbaum and Pamela McCorduck, *The Fifth Generation* (Reading, Mass: Addison-Wesley Publishing Company, 1983), Chapter 2 and 3.

5. Norbert Weiner, *The Human Use of Human Beings: Cybernetics and Society* (New York: Avon Books, 1967), p. 220. [This is the paperback version of the original book that was published in 1950 by Houghton Mifflin Company].

6. Ibid., p. 209.

7. Bill Bryson, *The Mother Tongue: English and How It Got That Way* (New York: Morrow and Company, Inc., 1990), p. 78.

8. William E. Brock, U.S. Secretary of Labor, "Address to the National Press Club," Washington, D.C. (March 5, 1987), p. 8. [xerox copy].

9. Cyert and Movery, op.cit, Chapter 5.

10. F. Ray Marshall and Vernon M. Briggs, Jr., *Labor Economics: Theory, Institutions, and Public Policy*, 6th Edition (Homewood, Ill.: Richard D. Irwin, Inc. 1989), Chapter 12.

11. John H. Bishop and Shani Carter, "The Deskilling vs. Upskilling Debate: The Role of BLS Statistics" (Ithaca: Center for Advanced Human Resource Studies, 1990), Working Paper # 90-14, pp. 5-6 and Table 1, p. 31. See also John Bishop and Shani Carter, "How Accurate are Recent BLS Occupational Projections?" *Monthly Labor Review* (October 1991), pp. 37-43.

12. Bishop and Carter, "The Deskilling vs. Upskilling Debate," op.cit, pp. 2-3.

13. George T. Silverstri and John M. Lukasiewicz, "A Look at Occupational Employment Trends to the Year 2000," *Monthly Labor Review* (September, 1987), pp. 46-63.

14. Philip L. Rones, "An Analysis of Regional Employment Growth, 1973-85," *Monthly Labor Review* (July 1986), pp. 3-13.

15. Barbara Vobejda, "Half of Population Lives in Urban Areas," *Washington Post* (February 21, 1991), p. A-1 and A-12.

16. Norman Saunders, "Defence Spending in the 1990s: The Effect of Deeper Cuts," *Monthly Labor Review* (October 1990), pp. 3-13.

17. *Economic Report of the President: 1991* (Washington D.C.: U.S. Government Printing Office, 1991), Table B-102, p. 402.

18. Ray Marshall, "Labor Market Implications of Internationalization," in *The Internationalization of the U.S. Economy: Its Labor Market Policy Implications*, edited by Vernon M. Briggs, Jr. (Salt Lake City: Olympus Publishing Company, 1986), pp. 7-27.

19. Milton D. Lower, "Labor Market Impact of 'Industrial Import Shock'," Ibid., pp. 38-50.

20. Louis Uchitelle, "Trade Barriers and Dollar Wings Raise Appeal of Factories Abroad," *New York Times* (March 26, 1989), p. A-1 and p. A-23.

21. Hobart Rowen, "Thinking of 'Us' as U.S. Workers, Not as U.S. Firms," *Washington Post* (March 25, 1990), p. H-1.

22. D.E. Sanger, "Tokyo's Top Official for Overseas Trade is Critic of the U.S.," *New York Times* (August 8, 1989), p. D-1.

23. Howard D. Samuel, "Social Goals and International Trade: A New Dimension," in *The Internationalization of the U.S. Economy,* op. cit., pp. 27-37.

24. John M. Culbertson, *The Trade Threat and U.S. Trade Policy* (Madison: 21st Century Press, 1989); see also, Gordon L. Clark, *Unions and Communities Under Seige* (New York: Cambridge University Press, 1989).

25. Definitional details and a review of the related policy issues appear in National Commission on Employment and Unemployment Statistics, *Counting the Labor Force* (Washington, D.C.: U.S. Government Printing Office, 1979).

26. Jeffrey S. Passel, "Estimating the Number of Undocumated Aliens,"*Monthly Labor Review* (September 1986) p. 33.

27. Paul O. Flaim, "How Many New Jobs Since 1982? Two Surveys Differ," *Monthly Labor Review* (August 1989), pp. 13-14.

28. Ibid., p. 14.

29. Ibid.

30. Howard V. Hayghe, "Family Members in the Work Force," *Monthly Labor Review* (March 1990), pp. 14-19.

31. Felicity Barringer, "Census Shows Profound Change in Racial Makeup of the Nation," *New York Times* (March 11, 1991) p. A-1.

32. Ronald E. Kutscher, "New BLS Projections: Findings and Implications," *Monthly Labor Review* (November 1991), pp. 6-7.

33. Lori G. Kletzer, "Job Displacement, 1979-86: How Blacks Fared Relative to Whites," *Monthly Labor Review* (July 1991), pp.

34. William Julius Wilson, *The Truly Disadvantaged: The Inner City, the Underclass, and Public Policy* (Chicago: The University of Chicago Press, 1987); See also, Louis Uchitelle, "America's Army of Non-Workers," *The New York Times* (September 27, 1987), pp. F-1 and F-6.

35. Elizabeth Bogen, *Immigration in New York* (New York: Praeger Publishers 1987), p. 60.

36. Raymond M. Frost, *Challenge: The Magazine of Economic Affairs*, (November-December 1991), p. 64. [Note: the available data cited is only for nine years of the 1980s].

37. Ibid.

38. Barbara Vobejda, "25% of Black Women May Never Marry", *Washington Post* (November 11, 1991), p. A-1 and A-12.

39. Ibid., p. A-12.

40. Robert Pear, "Bigger Number of New Mothers are Unmarried," *New York Times* (December 4, 1991), p. A-20; See also Paul Taylor "Nonmarital Births: As Rates Soar, Theories Abound," *Washington Post* (January 22, 1991), p. A-3.

41. See, for example, Edward B. Fiske, "Impending U.S. Jobs Disaster: Work Force Unqualified to Work," *New York Times* (September 25, 1989), p. A-1.

42. Hudson Institute, *Workforce 2000: Work and Workers for the Twenty-first Century* (Indianapolis: Hudson Institute, 1987).

43. Commission on Workforce Quality and Labor Market Efficiency, *Investing in People* (Washington, D.C.: U.S. Department of Labor, 1989), p. 1.

44. Ibid., p. 2-3.

45. Ibid., p. 3. See also Jonathan Kozol, *Illiterate American* (Garden City, N.Y.: Anchor Press, 1985).

46. "U.S. Study Says Work Force is Suffering from Shortages," *New York Times* (September 2, 1989), p. A-9.

47. Commission on the Skills of the American Workforce, *America's Choice: High Skills or Low Wages* (Rochester, N.Y.: National Center on Education and the Economy, 1990), p. 1.

48. Gisela Bolte, "Will American's Work for $5 a Day?" *Time* (July 12, 1990), p. 12.

49. Robert Haveman and Daniel Saks, "Transatlantic Lessons for Employment and Training Policy," and Bernard Casey and Gert Bruche, "Active Labor Market Policy: An International Overview," *Industrial Relations* (Winter 1985), pp. 20-36 and 37-61 respectively.

EIGHT

The National Interest: Synchronization of Immigration Policy with Economic Circumstances

With the labor market in a state of transformation, immigration is the one element of change that could be designed to respond directly to the emerging economic circumstances. Immigration could be used to assist the labor force during this transition period by filling some legitimate occupational shortages. On the other hand, given the scale and scope of these structural changes, immigration policy should never be permitted to function in a manner that worsens the economy's adjustment process. As has been shown, unfortunately, the potential benefits of immigration have not been utilized while its counterproductive tendencies have been permitted to flourish. The main reason for the perpetuation of this paradox is the reluctance of policymakers to acknowledge that immigration is an economic phenomenon and its regulation is an instrument of economic policy.

Most immigrants (as broadly defined to include legal immigrants, illegal immigrants, refugees, and asylees) as well as those nonimmigrants who are legally permitted to work must seek employment to support themselves and their families. Ultimately, most of their accompanying spouses and children will eventually seek employment if, indeed, they do not do so immediately following entry. Those immigrants who do not work usually must be supported by other citizens and resident aliens who do. Hence, there are always labor market implications associated with the number of immigrants who enter, the human capital attributes that they

Table 8.1 Percent Distribution Of Immigrants, By Major Occupation Group At Time Of Arrival, Selected Years 1970-1990

Fiscal year	Total	Professional, technical and kindred workers	Executive, Administrative, and Managerial	Administrative Support	Sales workers	Precision, Production, Craft and Repair	Operatives, and kindred workers	Laborers exc.farm and mine	Private household	Service workers (exc. priv household)	Farmers and farm managers	Farm laborers and foreman	No occupation[1]
1970	373,326	12.3	1.6	3.7	.7	7.5	4.9	3.8	2.7	2.5	1.0	1.2	57.9
1975	386,194	9.9	2.6	3.8	.9	5.5	4.8	3.4	1.5	4.2	.2	1.6	61.3
1979[2]	530,639	8.6	4.0	4.6	1.0	4.4	6.6	3.0	1.9	3.5	.2	2.1	59.8
1985	570,009	7.3	3.6	3.4	2.1	4.6	8.5		7.5		1.9		61.1
1989	1,068,342	4.2	3.0	4.2	2.0	6.4	15.7		12.8		2.9		48.5
1990	1,536,483	4.4	3.0	3.7	2.0	7.3	15.9		14.9		6.8		41.7

[1] Includes dependent women and children and other aliens without occupation or occupation not reported.
[2] Occupational data for 1980 and 1981 were lost in data processing by INS (see 1981 Statistical Yearbook of the INS [Washington D.C.: U.S. Government Printing Office, 1982] p. VII). Hence, 1979 data are used.

Source: U.S. Immigration and Naturalization Service.

individually and collectively bring with them, and the effects their presence imposes on the people and communities where they settle.

As there was no anticipation that mass immigration would begin in the mid-1960s or that it would continue unabated after that time, there was also no concern manifested by policymakers about the human capital characteristics of the preponderance of those who came and who continue to come. Unfortunately, the simultaneous transformation of the U.S. economy has created new patterns of employment. Thus, comparisons about the adjustment experiences of past eras of mass immigration with that of "fourth wave" immigrants are largely irrelevant. The U.S. economy has never before confronted such rapid and significant shifts in its industrial, occupational, and geographic employment patterns nor has it experienced such growth and compositional changes in its labor force. Even greater changes are anticipated in the 1990s. At a time when the citizen and resident alien labor force is experiencing significant adjustment difficulties, the revival effects of mass immigration simply cannot be ignored.

With immigration currently accounting for 30-40 percent (depending on what estimate of illegal immigration is applied) of the annual growth of the U.S. labor force, it is essential to know how the labor market transformation process relates to immigration. As a purely discretionary act of the federal government, the flow of immigrants is the one aspect of labor force growth and compositional change that public policy should be able to control and shape to serve the national interest.

The Incongruity of "Fourth Wave" Immigration with Emerging Economic Trends

Aside from the sheer scale of the "fourth wave" of mass immigration, the next most significant characteristic of this phenomenon is the fact that the human capital characteristics of the immigrant flow are completely counter to evolving employment trends of the economy. Table 8.1 shows the occupations of the immigrants at the time of arrival for selected years since 1970. The administrative data shown in Table 8.1 are admittedly crude but they are relevant for showing broad trends and rough orders of magnitude. The data reflect what an admission system that is not based on work-related needs has produced. When this occupational data on immigrants are compared with the occupational growth data for the U.S. economy shown earlier in Table 7.4, they are virtually mirror-opposites.

Since the "fourth wave" of immigrants began, the proportion of immigrants whose occupations at the time of arrival were in the professional, technical, or managerial occupations has declined sharply although it is precisely these occupations that have sustained the greatest growth over this time interval. Likewise, the preponderance of the occupations of the new immigrants has been in the blue-collar occupations (operatives, laborers, and farm workers) and low-wage service and household workers—precisely the occupations that are in the sharpest decline over this time period. It is not surprising, therefore, that research by George Borjas and Barry Chiswick on the economic impact of immigrants has found that the human capital characteristics of the immigrant population—especially those who have entered since 1970—are rapidly declining.[1] Thus, precisely at the time that every labor market indicator shows that the nation needs a more highly skilled and better educated labor force, its immigration policy is pouring large numbers of unskilled, poorly educated workers with limited English-speaking ability into the central cities of many of its major urban labor markets. The perpetuation of such an incongruence cannot possibly be in the national interest.

It should be noted that the data in Table 8.1 probably overstate the occupational characteristics of the total flow of "fourth wave" immigrants. For as noted in Chapter 6, the data do not include the characteristics of the ongoing infusion of illegal immigrants; or those who enter as refugees (mostly from Third World nations) but who have not yet adjusted their status to become permanent-resident aliens; or those who legally work as nonimmigrants. Studies that have focused on determining the characteristics of illegal immigrants have found them to be overwhelmingly employed in blue-collar and service occupations of the low-wage sector of the economy and to have minimal human capital endowments.[2] These findings have been confirmed in the data that have been collected on those 2.6 million illegal immigrants who benefited from the legalization of their status that was provided by the Immigration Reform and Control Act of 1986.[3] Likewise, the data on the human capital characteristics of the refugee flows since the late-1970s also reveal minimal human resource characteristics for the vast majority of those who have entered.[4] The occupational data for nonimmigrants, as could be expected, are quite mixed as they have been employed in a variety of occupations ranging from farm workers, to nurses, to engineers, to scientists, to executives, to managers, to professors. Indeed, a major reason for the growth in the use of nonimmigrant workers is that there have been so few work-based visas available under the prevailing legal immigration system. The increasing dependence of U.S. employers on nonimmigrant workers is itself a symptom that something is fundamentally wrong with the current system. It implies that the legal immigration system lacks the direction and the flexibility to respond to legitimate shortages of qualified workers needed to fill real job vacancies.

Given the substantial size of the overall immigrant inflow associated with the ongoing "fourth wave" of immigration and their overwhelming tendency to concentrate locationally in the urban areas (especially the central cities) of about six major states (California, New York, Texas, Florida, Illinois, and New Jersey), there must be parallel concern about their impact on the employment opportunities of citizens and resident aliens who also seek employment in these same major labor markets. Not only the actual effects of increased competition for jobs and social services are important, but there is also the issue of the opportunity cost of what has transpired. What would have happened had immigrants not congregated in significant numbers in these specific labor markets? Would public and private policies necessary to develop the human resource potential of citizen workers have been spurred (as they were during World War II) to provide quality education and training opportunities if the alternative of immigrant labor were less available? Would the adjustment process associated with the transformation of the economy have led to greater inflows of displaced citizens and resident aliens into these same local labor markets if immigrant labor were not there? Would there have been less outflow of citizens and resident aliens from these same labor markets had it not been for the immigrant inflows?

There have been a number of studies that have tried to determine the multiple effects of "fourth wave" immigration on specific labor markets and on the U.S. economy.[5] But given the severe limitations of available data as well as the multiple influences other than immigration that also affect employment patterns and job-seeking, the significance of these findings are often open to question. For example, two major studies of the impact of immigration on California, one by the Rand Corporation and another by the Urban Institute, claimed to find only minor adverse effects.[6] These studies, however, were severely criticized by former Secretary of Labor, Ray Marshall, who convincingly showed that "their conclusions often do not follow from their evidence."[7] From his analysis of both of these studies, Marshall found that "there can be little doubt that immigration displaces workers," that "no study of the effects of immigration is able to hold everything constant," and that "elementary economics suggests that at a time of high unemployment, increased labor supplies depress wages and reduce employment opportunities for legal residents unless you completely segregate labor markets."[8] Likewise, the usefulness of impact studies is restricted by the fact that they cannot measure what would have happened if the immigrants were not present. As mentioned above and as Marshall included in his criticisms of the aforementioned studies, there is no way for a local labor market study to measure the effects on citizen and resident alien workers who have left high immigrant-impacted communities for just that reason. Moreover, as industries and occupations have declined in other geographic regions, there would have been alternative adjustment patterns if it were not for the fact that many of the nation's largest urban labor markets had become mass immigrant centers in the interim.

Without being diverted into the quagmire of a review of the diverse and limited findings of the existing literature that have sought to measure the impact of immigration, it suffices to review and compare the aforementioned occupational data shown in Tables 8.1 and 7.4 to see that there is a clear incongruity. Moreover, in the high-immigrant impact states, there is mounting concern being manifested that immigration is causing severe adjustment difficulties even if academic impact studies (which by defini-tion must lag years behind actual events) have yet to discern such effects.[9] All of the key studies to date used 1980 census data. And until at least 1993, when the 1990 census data on the foreign born will be available, they cannot be updated to capture the effects of the decade in which the greatest mass immigration in the nation's history occurred. Besides, even those studies that have not quantified employment displacement and wage depression effects or the disproportionate use of social services by immi-grants, cannot be interpreted as saying those effects are absent. Given the severe data and major methodological difficulties inherent in studying this complex economic phenomenon, such effects may very well be present but have, as yet, eluded capture.

The Contrast with Earlier Waves of Mass Immigration

As has been shown earlier, mass immigration in the nineteenth and early twentieth centuries was essentially congruent with the economic circumstances of those times. As the nation was expanding its physical size, it needed more workers to build its nonagricultural workforce.

Unskilled workers were required and mass immigration provided them. It was not necessary that they be well-educated or trained or fluent in English—and most immigrants were not. There were alternatives to the mass immigration of those eras—namely, efforts could have been made to tap the domestic pools of unskilled workers (that is, blacks, native Indians, and Mexican Americans in particular as well as rural workers in general). But those options were not immediately pursued.

It was not until mass immigration was stopped by public policy intervention in the 1920s that any serious effort was made to draw upon domestic labor surpluses. Fortunately, during the forty-year period from the mid-1920s to the mid-1960s, the labor market was still in need of vast numbers of unskilled and poorly educated workers to meet most of its employment needs. Thus, during these years, historic changes occurred that opened employment opportunities to previously excluded segments of the population. But when mass immigration was inadvertently revived in the years since the mid-1960s, there was little recognition in the ensuing immigration policies that the nation was entering an era of economic transformation. On the demand side of the market, unskilled jobs that pay high wages are rapidly disappearing in the wake of automation and international competition. High-skilled jobs are increasing but they typically require extensive preparatory training and education. Unfortunately, the United States has a substantial number of displaced workers from the declining sectors as well as new job entrants who are inadequately prepared to qualify for jobs in the expanding sectors. Moreover, while no population segment has been immune from the effects of these changes, it is clear that racial and ethnic minorities in particular, and women in general, have been the most adversely affected. It is highly ironic, therefore, that the commitment to achieve equal employment opportunity had just been codified by the Civil Rights Act of 1964 when the Immigration Act of 1965 unwittingly launched the "fourth wave" of mass immigration. Thus, the most important domestic priority of that era—the obligation to alter the patterns of employment that were the legacy of past toleration of employment discrimination—has been greatly hampered in succeeding years, by the rapid contraction of jobs in the sectors where these groups were concentrated before they were adequately prepared to compete for new jobs in the expanding employment sectors.

The mass immigration that has ensued since the mid-1960s has taken place with little regard as to how it might affect these unprecedented labor market adjustment needs.

Table 8.2 The Preference System Created Under The Immigration Act of 1990 (In Effect As Of October 1, 1991)

Category and Preference	Fiscal Years 1992 - 1994	Fiscal Years 1995 and beyond
I. Family Immigration (total)	520,000	480,000
A) Immediate Relatives (projected)	239,000 (unlimited)	254,000 (unlimited)
B) Preference System	226,000*	226,000*
1) Unmarried adult children of U.S. citizens	23,400	23,400
2) Immediate family members of permanent residents	114,200*	114,200*
3) Married Adult children of U.S. citizens	23,400	23,400
4) Brothers and Sisters of U.S. citizens	65,000	65,000
C) Additional Family Legalizations (for relatives of IRCA amnesty recipients)	55,000	NONE
II. Independent Immigration (total)	180,000	195,000
A) Employment Based Immigration	140,000	140,000
1) Priority Workers (workers of extraordinary ability)	40,000	40,000
2) Professionals (with advanced degrees)	40,000	40,000
3) Skilled workers, professionals, and other workers (unskilled)	40,000 (10,000 limit on unskilled)	40,000 (10,000 limit on unskilled)
4) Special immigrants	10,000	10,000
5) Investor immigrants	10,000	10,000
B) Diversity Immigrants	40,000 (16,000 must be Irish)	55,000
Total Immigration	700,000	675,000

* As the immediate family members are exempt from numerical limitation, the limitation on family immigration is determined by subtracting the Immediate Relative total of the **previous** year from the Worldwide total of family-sponsored immigrants, but the family preference may not fall below 226,000. Hence, the indicated numbers are "pierceable" -- they may be exceeded if the immediate family members are greater than is projected.

Source: Public Law 101.

The Immigration Act of 1990

As indicated in Chapter 6, the Immigration Act of 1990 was "unexpect-antly passed" on the last day that the 101st Congress was in session behind the smokescreen of a protracted budget battle between the President and Congress.[10] It had been the subject of very little public debate and the final version was the product of substantial last-minute behind-the-scenes political compromises over the terms of the two different bills that were pending in the House of Representatives and the Senate. The legislation was signed into law by President George Bush on November 29, 1990 and went into effect on October 1, 1991. The Congressional Research Service has stated that "the Immigration Act of 1990 represents a major overhaul of immigration law."[11]

Yet despite the fact the new law does make numerous procedural chang-es in immigration policy, its central feature is the fact that it dramatically increases the level of immigration while maintaining essentially the same policy thrusts as the law it replaced. Moreover, the alleged responsiveness of the new law to labor market needs is largely illusory. For the Immigration Act of 1990 actually perpetuates all of the negative attributes of the Immigration Act of 1965. As a consequence, the nation's immigration policy remains highly mechanistic, legalistic, nepotistic, and inflexible. It is still essentially a political policy. Its design continues to reflect a disregard for the economic transformation that is restructuring U.S. employment patterns and reconstituting the labor force.

The key provisions of the Immigration Act of 1990 are set forth in Table 8.2. As this legislation will form the core of the nation's immigra-tion policy for the foreseeable future, its features require brief elaboration.

An Increase in the Level of Legal Immigration

The most distinguishing characteristic of the Immigration Act of 1990 is that it raises the annual level of legal immigration by about 35 percent over the levels occurring at the time of its passage. For fiscal years 1992 through 1994, the annual admission level will be 700,000 persons. Beginning in 1995 it will be 675,000 persons. The chosen numbers do not reflect any concern for actual labor market needs of the nation nor are they the product of any careful labor market studies. Rather, they are the consequence of a political compromise that "split the difference" between two separate bills that were pending in each Congressional house.[12]

Ostensibly, a unique feature of this legislation is that it places a "cap" on total immigration that was not present under the previous Immigration Act of 1965. But as will be discussed shortly, the new legislation also contains provisions that make the cap "pierceable" under certain circumstances. Moreover, there are other special provisions of the legislation that all result in additional inflows of immigrants outside the "cap." For example, additional immigrant visas are to be given to 12,000 Hong Kong nationals who work for multinational firms in the United States, to 1,000 displaced Tibetans, and to 1,000 persons from "adversely affected" nations who "won" visas in a special visa lottery under IRCA but for whom visas were not actually available. There also are provisions for "safe haven" for 450,000 Salvadoreans believed to be living in the United States to remain for up to eighteen months but who it is doubtful will ever leave given the length of time that many have already been in the country. The Act also created a potentially open-ended category of "safe haven" protection for people from any country to be granted by the Attorney General to nationals from countries facing "armed conflict," natural disasters, or where other countries notify the United States that they cannot handle any large return of their citizens who fled from earlier armed conflicts. Hence, the "cap" is anything but firm in its definition.

The law also replaces the previous annual country ceiling of 20,000 visas with a requirement that no one country can receive more than 7 percent of either the family-based or employment-based visas in a single year. The result is that the new country ceiling is 25,620 visas but, it too has some exceptions (for example, 75 percent of the visas allocated to spouses and minor children of permanent-resident aliens are not counted toward a country's numerical limitation).

Family-Related Admissions Remain the Dominant Entry Route

As shown in Table 8.2, 465,000 of the immigrants from 1992 to 1994 will be admitted on the basis of family reunification. Immediate family members (spouses, children, and adult parents) of each visa holder are admitted without limitation, as was the case under the previous law. The number of remaining visas go to four categories of family-related immigrants (these categories are essentially the same as under the Immigration Act of 1965). The exact number of available visas each year for these categories is determined by subtracting the number of immediate relatives admitted during the previous year from the total of 465,000 visas that are allowed. The new law, however, stipulates that at least 226,000 visas each year must be reserved for these four family preference categories (this is 10,000 more family-related visas than were available for these four categories under the immigration system it replaces). Moreover, for the initial three-year period, 55,000 additional visas are available for spouses and children of aliens whose status was legalized by the amnesty provisions of IRCA in 1986. These persons would have eventually been eligible to adjust their status but this provision expedites the process. It simply recognizes that many family members of newly legalized aliens are already in the country (albeit illegally) but, rather than force families to be broken up, they are being allowed to adjust their status more quickly. This is in accord with the INS policy of "family fairness" that was put into practice in 1990. It should also be noted that, if by chance, the aforementioned subtraction process that determines the number of visas available for family preference results in a number below 226,000 in the years up until 1994, this minimum number of family-related visas are guaranteed by reducing the 55,000 visas available for IRCA family members by that difference.

Beginning with fiscal year 1995, the overall level of family-sponsored immigrants goes up to 480,000 visas. There are no more visas available for IRCA family members. The number of immediate family members of each visa recipient remains unlimited. Hence, the numbers of visas available to the family-preference immigrants will be determined each year by subtracting the number of immediate family members from the 480,000 figure. But, the number of family-preference visas still may not be lower than 226,000 visas each year. If the number would be less than 226,000 (as it is certain to be), then the overall cap of 480,000 is to be "pierced" to accommodate the required minimum of family preference immigrants. Hence, the new law introduces a new oxymoron—the "pierceable cap"—into the nation's immigration lexicon.

Employment-Based Immigration is Increased

Much of the political rhetoric surrounding the passage of the Immigration Act of 1990 dealt with allegations that the nation was facing the prospect of a general labor shortage in the 1990s. The issue was a myth. Nonetheless, the Immigration Act of 1990 did significantly increase the number of visas that could be issued based on employment needs. The number of employment-based visas was increased from 54,000 to 140,000 visas a year over the levels in effect since 1965 and the number of work-related admission preferences was increased from two to five (see Table 8.2 and compare with Appendix B).

The first employment-based preference provides 40,000 visas annually for "priority workers." These are persons of extraordinary ability as demonstrated by national or international acclaim; "outstanding" professors and researchers to enter senior positions; and executives and managers of multinationals who have at least one year of experience with such firms. A U.S. Department of Labor officials explained, perhaps hopefully, that priority workers will be "international superstars, your basic Einsteins."[13] With the exception of the first grouping, the other two groupings must have a U.S. employer before they can be admitted.

The second preference provides 40,000 visas a year for professionals with advanced degrees and aliens of exceptional ability. These persons must have a U.S. employer and they must receive a labor certification (see Chapter 5) before they can be admitted, although both requirements can be waived by the Attorney General.

The third preference provides annually for 40,000 visas for "skilled workers, professionals, and other workers." All such immigrants are required to have a U.S. employer and a labor certification before they can be admitted. A skilled worker must be in an occupation that requires at least two years of training in advance. Professionals must have at least a bachelor's degree. "Other workers" is a grouping for persons who are "unskilled" and their numbers cannot exceed 10,000 visas a year.

A fourth preference was created for "special immigrants" of whom 10,000 visas a year are reserved. Special immigrants are ministers of religion, persons working for religious organizations, foreign medical school graduates, retired persons from international organizations, and employees of the U.S. government abroad.

The fifth preference is for a new grouping called "investor immigrants." Of these, 7,000 visas are for investors of $1 million or more in urban areas and 3,000 for investors of $500,000 or more in rural areas. The investment must provide jobs for at least ten U.S. workers.

The Addition of a New Entry Route: Diversity Immigrants

One of the legislative motivations that culminated in the Immigration Act of 1990 was concern that the "country-neutral but family-based" immigration system created in 1965 had inadvertently foreclosed entry from the nations that had provided the bulk of earlier waves of mass immigration (most particularly but, not exclusively, persons from countries in Europe). Reflecting these views, the legislation created an entirely new admission category for "diversity immigrants." For the years 1992 through 1994, a transitional program will provide 40,000 visas a year for natives of thirty-four specified countries "adversely affected" by the 1965 legislation (see Appendix C). Of these, 16,000 (or 40 percent) are specifically reserved for persons from one country, Ireland.

The 40,000 visas are to be awarded each year as the result of a lottery process. When the first lottery was held in October, 1991, more than nineteen million appli-cations were submitted (many were multiple applications from the same persons).[14] The entire process was chaotic. Over 7.4 million applications were disqualified because they arrived too early and over two million were disqualified because they arrived too late. Aside from the 16,000 visas specifically reserved for people from Ireland, the next most popu-lous countries of lottery winners were (in order of magnitude) persons from Poland, Japan, Great Britain, Indonesia, Argentina, Germany, France, Italy, Norway, and Czechoslovakia. Beginning in 1995, the pro-gram changes as "diversity immigrants" will no longer be restricted to the aforementioned thirty-four countries but, instead, there will be 55,000 visas selected each year by lottery from a random drawing of applicants from countries determined in advance by the Attorney General to have had low immigrant admissions in recent years.

The Creation of "Safe Haven" Provisions

The Act of 1990 grants the power to the Attorney General to provide a "safe haven" (i.e., the authority to provide extended voluntary departures) and to issue work authorizations to foreign nationals already in the United States who are from countries facing ongoing armed conflict, suffering natural disasters, or whose governments are unable to handle the return of their nationals who fled and so notify the United States government. The potential scope of these provisions is unknown and unpredictable. Also, the Act specifically mandates that "safe haven" be provided to persons from El Salvador in the United States since September 19, 1990 for a period of up to eighteen months. While in the United States, they are to be granted work authorizations. It is unlikely that many of those Salvadoreans who register under this program will ever leave.

Expanded Nonimmigrant Provisions

The legislation expanded the number of nonimmigrant categories while narrowing some categories and expanding others. As for those categories that have employment implications (see Table 6.6), the treaty trader or investor category (i.e., E visa holders) was expanded to include trade in services and technology industries; the foreign student category (i.e., F visa holders) was liberalized for a three-year period to permit work outside the students' field of study as long as the students maintain good academic standing and their employers attest to the fact that they have sought to recruit citizens and that the wages and working conditions are the same as those offered to citizens; the temporary nonagricultural worker category (i.e., H-1B visa holders) was redefined to apply to "specialty occupations" whose applicants are admitted on the basis of professional education, skill, or experience and, for the first time, a cap of 65,000 visas a year was applied to skilled workers (i.e., H-1B visa holders) and a cap of 66,000 visas was applied for unskilled workers (i.e., H-2B visa holders); and the intracompany transfers category (i.e., L visa holders) was expanded to include international accounting firms; and the procedures required to process all such applications were made easier. Three new nonimmigrant categories were created of which two have direct employment implications. A new O visa is created for aliens with "extraordinary ability" in the sciences, arts, education, business, and athletics. A new P visa was created for aliens who perform as athletes or entertainers for specific performances and it is capped at 25,000 visas a year. Both of these new categories were formerly included in the H-1 visa category, which has now been more narrowly defined to exclude these groups.

In the case of those nonimmigrant categories that have employment consequences, the new law has greatly added to their legalistic nature. Throughout the legislation there are numerous provisions for filing petitions and appeals, all of which virtually assure that lawyers will become even more involved in the application and review processes than they already are.

The Grounds for Exclusion are Extensively Recodified

The Immigration Act of 1990 made some important changes in the area of immigrant exclusions. As noted in earlier chapters, Congress began in the 1870s to add various categories for which persons are "excludable" from consideration to become immigrants to the United States regardless of what country they may be citizens. By 1990, there were thirty-three such grounds and they pertained to such broad issues as moral turpitude, political ideology, health, and economic self-sufficiency. The new legislation recodified these into nine categories. Some exclusions were modified (i.e., those pertaining to former members of totalitarian regimes or former prostitutes); some were eliminated (i.e., those pertaining to homosexuals and most of those that had barred persons with physical or mental disabilities); some were expanded (i.e., the power to exclude terrorists) and some were altered (i.e., provisions that shifted the authority to determine whether a person has a communicable disease that is of "a public health significance," like AIDS, to the U.S. Department of Health and Human Services from the INS).

The Congressional Retreat from Economic Reality

Despite its numerous changes in procedures and the extensive media hype that exalted its alleged virtues, the Immigration Act of 1990 is essentially an expansion in scale of the previously existing immigration system that had been in effect since 1965. Its most important characteristic is that it increases legal immigration levels by about 35 percent over the previously authorized levels. Like the law it replaced, the new law gives short shrift to the specific human capital endowments of those to be admitted and to the general labor market conditions that prevail within the country at any given time. Thus, the new legislation largely perpetuates the illusion that immigration policy—despite is magnitude—has minimum economic consequences.

As with its predecessor, the Immigration Act of 1990 is inflexible with respect to the total number of immigrants it admits each year. The 700,000 immigrants (675,000 beginning in fiscal year 1995) will all come each year regardless of whether the economy is in a period of prosperity, recession, or depression. The level of admissions is functionally independent of the state of the domestic economy. Indeed, its implementation on October 1, 1991 could not have been more poorly timed. The U.S. economy was struggling out of a lengthy recession at the time, only to reel back again into a deeper recession in the Fall of 1991. Certainly the last thing that the slumping economy needed was an infusion of an additional inflow of immigrant job-seekers of this enlarged magnitude.

The increase in the level of immigration meant that both the number of family-related and the number of employment-related visas could be increased and they both were. The addition of the new entry route for "diversity immigrants" means that another noneconomic admission route has been added to the nation's immigration system. As a result, the 140,000 visas a year that are to be made available for employment-based reasons represent exactly the same percentage (20 percent) of the total legal admissions (700,000 visas) as was the case under the Immigration Act of 1965. Hence, there is no real change in policy emphasis; 80 percent of those admitted will enter without regard for their human capital attributes.

Even the use of the 140,000 slots to indicate the number of work-related immigrants to be admitted each year is a gross overstatement of what the law actually provides. This is because the figure includes not only the eligible workers themselves but also their "accompanying family members."

As a result, the number of actually needed workers admitted under the work-related provisions will be far fewer—perhaps only one-third of the total annual figure of 140,000 admissions. It is likely that the majority of those admitted under the work-related provisions will actually be admitted only because they too are family members. Moreover, any work-related slots that are not used in any given year are to be added to those slots available solely for family-related admissions.

The retention of family reunification as the dominant characteristic of the immigration system means that the human capital attributes are not involved in the entry decisions for the vast majority of those persons who are legally admitted. The same is true for the diversity immigrants whose only human resource requirement is that they must have a high school diploma or its equivalent. Thus, all of the contemporary labor market research that stresses the need to raise the skill, education, and communication abilities of labor force entrants are largely ignored when it comes to the issue of labor force entry via legal immigration.

In addition, the emphasis given to family reunification assures that most new immigrants will settle in the same geographic labor markets as have their relatives whose family ties were the basis for their admission. This means that kinship, rather than labor market needs, will still be the primary basis for settlement. The effect is that most new immigrants settle in central cities of a selected number of metropolitan areas where earlier immigrants established enclaves of persons from the same ethnic background.[15] The anticipated result is that ethnic networking will continue to be a major feature of the hiring process in these markets.[16]

Ethnic network hiring was a distinguishing feature of the urban labor markets of the earlier waves of mass immigration of the nineteenth and early twentieth centuries. But since the passage of the Civil Rights Act of 1964, hiring practices were supposed to be changed so that it is illegal to hire (or to exclude) job applicants on the basis of their national origin. But such practices have again become common in those urban labor markets where immigrants have congregated. The casualties often are the native-born citizens who also reside in these cities (a disproportionate number of whom are minorities, youth, and women) who are denied the opportunity to compete for such jobs on an equal access basis. In a 1987 study of immigration in New York City, for example, Elizabeth Bogen noted the phenomenon when she candidly wrote: "there are tens of thousands of jobs in New York City for which the native-born are not candidates."[17] The reasons she cites are that "ethnic hiring networks and the proliferation of immigrant-owned small businesses in the city have cut off open-market competition for jobs."[18] Quite perceptively, she strongly suggests that the blatant "discrimination against native workers is a matter for future monitoring." Given the mounting racial tension in many urban communities between citizens (especially black Americans) and recent immigrants, the need for such research on this subject is long overdue. Likewise, research in those rural labor markets where immigrant workers have become a significant factor (e.g., in the agriculture industry of the Southwest) has also noted the widespread use of ethnic networking in the hiring process.[19] The negative effect on the employment of native-born workers for these rural jobs is the same in its results as it is in urban labor markets. The concept of networking is highly praised by many scholars who study the current immigrant experience.[20] But what is overlooked in these studies is that most of these practices—especially those of ethnic employers—are absolutely illegal. What is the difference between "ethnic networking" (often lauded) and "the old boy system" of hiring which is roundly condemned by all antidiscrimination advocates?

In earlier waves of immigration, networking served to aid in the adjustment process of immigrants. But those immigrants entered the United States prior to the passage of the Civil Rights Act of 1964. Times in the United States have changed—hopefully for the better. Since 1965, any employment practice that purposely excludes opportunities for native born workers on the basis of national origin is illegal conduct, and it should be stopped. Unfortunately, the current politics associated with immigration policy at the federal, state, and local level has caused elected officials to be reluctant to address this critical local issue despite the fact that it is often a primary cause of racial tension in their communities.[21]

As for the new admission category of "diversity immigrants," it not only ignores the whole issue of human capital characteristics of immigrants but it introduces an array of highly questionable practices to the nation's immigration system. To begin with, it resurrects the use of national origin as a criterion for legal entry. It was, after all, the primary goal of immigration reform in the 1960s to rid the immigration system of this very feature. It is shocking to see it reintroduced in such a devious manner. The transitional program that is in effect through 1994 turns the entire issue of diversity, as it is discussed elsewhere in U.S. society, on its head. For in every context except in the area of immigration policy, "diversity" is used to mean efforts to broaden the spectrum of participation to include members of groups other than non-Hispanic whites. But as the concept is explicitly implemented in this program— especially with its mandated reservation of 40 percent of all the available visas for the first three years reserved only for immigrants from Ireland, diversity is intended to favor non-Hispanic whites (see Appendix C). Indeed, one immigration lawyer aptly described the program as being "a kind of white person's lottery."[22] Aside from the implied racism of the "diversity immigrant" provisions, the whole concept of using a lottery as the mechanism for admitting immigrants is itself the antithesis of rational policymaking. It is a surrender of accountability for consequences that can only make sense to politicians. As a former Commissioner of the INS, Allan Nelson, said of the use of the lottery, "it sort of cheapens the immigration process."[23] Indeed, the only other group to benefit from this program were the nation's immigration lawyers and consultants—many of whom received substantial fees from their clients "essentially to stamp and mail envelopes containing very simple application letters."[24]

As for the new "investor immigrants" category, the entire concept should be viewed as a source of shame. It introduces the principle that the rich of the world can buy their way into the United States. Never before has such a concept been embraced by U.S. immigration law. But as one immigration consultant boasted, "I believe we have done a great job with boat people [i.e., Southeast Asian refugees] and I think that a few yacht people are not going to hurt America."[25] Aside from the fact that it will be almost impossible to enforce, this category represents a reward of privileged status for "yacht people" that is unworthy of legal protection. The other major beneficiaries of this new entry standard are the nation's immigration lawyers and consultants who were its chief proponents. Rewarding personal greed should have no place in the nation's immigration system.

Another dubious provision of the legislation is the "special immigrants" category that gives priority to "religious workers." While there may be some legitimate purposes for such a preference, it is a vague concept that begs for opportunistic abuse.

In addition to what Congress has already done in the name of immigration reform, other actions under consideration simply defy reason. To be specific, Senators Orrin Hatch (R-Ut.) and Edward Kennedy jointly introduced a bill in June 1990 and again in September 1991 to repeal the employer-sanctions provisions of IRCA. As discussed in Chapter 6, employer sanctions were the heart of the legislative effort to restrict illegal immigration. Stopping illegal immigration was supposed to be the *quid pro quo* for increasing legal immigration. To be sure the employer-sanctions program has had its problems but the major reason that it has failed to curtail illegal immigration is that the identification issue was not adequately addressed under IRCA. With illegal immigration again soaring and with charges being made that employer sanctions have caused discrimination against some ethnic minorities, the momentum to repeal the sanctions program should not be taken lightly.[26] But if it succeeds, it will mean the IRCA was one of the biggest hoaxes that Congress has ever perpetrated on the American public. Several million persons who illegally entered the United States were given amnesties at the price of trying to prevent future illegal entry. If repealed, this entire effort will have been in vain. As Senator Alan Simpson, who strongly opposes the repeal effort, has warned,

> If this bill passes a very clear message will go out to the world: "Well, the U.S. no longer is serious about controlling its borders. Come on in, the more the merrier. You can go to work and be pretty well exploited because there is no way to penalize employers."[27]

The legislative need is to make employer sanctions enforceable. To do so, Congress needs to establish a uniform worker-identification system which is not subject to being counterfeited; increase the funding that INS needs to enforce the sanctions program; add financial penalties for those apprehended illegal entrants who successfully find jobs; and expand the enforcement of the antidiscrimination provisions of IRCA. Making employer sanctions work is what should concern Congress—not the repeal of the only real deterrent that public policy now has.

The Kennedy–Hatch bill would replace sanctions with provisions that would double the authorized size of the U.S. Border Patrol, increase the size of the Wage and Hour Division of the U.S. Department of Labor, and add U.S. attorneys to prosecute smugglers of illegal aliens into the United States. All of these actions are needed but, given the severe federal budget restrictions of the early 1990s, it is doubtful that any of these programmatic authorizations, if passed, would ever be matched by companion appropriations. After all, IRCA called for increased border enforcement in 1986 but the funds for such purposes are yet to be forthcoming.

Senator Hatch has promised to keep introducing the bill if it is not acted upon in 1992. He has tried to broaden support for repeal by appealing to Hispanics (on the issue of alleged discrimination), and to business groups (on the issue that sanctions are a burden), and by alleging that all that the sanctions program has done is to spur a "cottage industry" in the production of fraudulent documents.[28]

Synchronization and the National Interest

The employment trends associated with the transformation of the nation's labor market are patently clear. The occupations that stress skill and educational achievement are expanding and those that do not are contracting. From the standpoint of efficiency, the nation's immigration policy must be tailored accordingly. The so-called "preparedness issue" of the U.S. labor force is a quality issue, not a quantity issue. Immigration policy should be primarily designed to admit a limited number of those workers who, in the short run, are needed to meet identifiable labor shortages while keeping out most of those who are not already qualified to fill such labor shortages.

Congress should set an overall ceiling that embraces all forms of immigration and which could not be annually exceeded. The ceiling should include legal immigrants, refugees, and asylees who will be legally permitted to enter the United States in a given year. The legislative ceiling should be seen as a maximum number allowed to enter but not an annual goal to be achieved. Within the context of the permissible legislative ceiling, the actual level on immigration for any given year should be set administratively by an agency of the executive branch of the federal government. The number could be anywhere from zero up to the authorized annual ceiling.

Permitting the annual number of admissions to be set administratively would provide the necessary flexibility to respond to different economic circumstances that is currently absent from the nation's immigration system. The administrative agency could be required to defend its decision each year at public hearings before the appropriate committees of Congress. But the decision should not be a subject of political negotiation or change by Congress. The check of the agency's power would be the fact that, if the agency's decisions cannot be defended in a credible manner, Congress always has the power to change the law in the future.

The specific agency responsible for setting the annual immigration level and for the daily administration of all facets of immigration policy should have an employment mission. Since most immigrants and their family members will enter the labor force, such an agency is best suited to judge how many immigrants should be admitted and under what entry guise. It also would be better equipped to enforce internally the laws that apply to immigrants at the workplace (for example, employment sanctions and antidiscrimination protections for resident aliens that are derived from the employment relationship).

Ideally, such an agency would be the one that is accountable for the major human resources development efforts of the nation. Such an agency, in addition to its immigration duties, would also be responsible for education, training, labor market information, and equal employment opportunity policies. At the present time, of course, such a superagency does not exist. As a consequence, the next best option would be to return responsibility for immigration policy to the U.S. Department of Labor which had such a mandate from the time it was founded in 1914 until 1940 (see Chapter 4).

Being an employment-oriented agency, it could best identify the specific occupational needs that immigration might be able to address. It is better qualified to debate how overall employment levels could adjust to specific numbers of new immigrants regardless of the criteria under which they are admitted. Moreover, because it also has enforcement responsibilities for wage and hour violations, child labor laws, occupational health and safety laws, and migrant farmworker protections, it could easily add enforcement of employer sanctions and antidiscrimination against aliens to its duties. To be sure, the laxity of enforcement activities of the Department of Labor in these areas in recent years is an embarrassment, but so has been enforcement of immigration laws by the Department of Justice. In all of these situations, enforcement must be increased through the provisions of additional funds and staff, or no policy reforms will have any meaning. Indeed, the chronic inattention to the enforcement of employment laws—especially those pertaining to low wage workers and children—is one of the seamier aspects of contemporary life in the United States.

The issue of refugee and asylee accommodation, of course, is more complicated to incorporate in this administrative structure. Advisory roles with the U.S. Department of State and the Department of Justice with certain delegated responsibilities to each agency could be built into the proposed administrative structure but the U.S. Department of Labor should still bear the ultimate responsibility for what takes place.

The primary objective should be to establish a targeted and flexible immigration policy designed primarily to admit persons who can fill job vacancies for which qualified citizens and resident aliens are unavailable. At this juncture, this means jobs that require significant skill preparation and educational investment. The number of immigrants annually admitted, however, should be far fewer than the number actually needed. Immigration should never be allowed to dampen two types of market pressures: those needed to encourage citizen workers to invest in preparing for vocations that are expanding; and those needed to ensure that government bodies provide the requisite human resource development to prepare citizens for the new types of jobs that are emerging.

Because it takes time for would-be workers to acquire skills and education, immigration policy can be used on a short-run basis to target experienced immigrant workers for permanent settlement who already possess these abilities. But the preparedness, or lack thereof, of the domestic labor force is the fundamental economic issue confronting the United States. Over the long haul, citizen workers must be prepared to qualify for jobs that have the greatest growth potential.

This philosophy may seem harsh on its surface but it is nothing more than applying to would-be immigrants the same standard that John F. Kennedy once asked of citizens in 1961 before the "fourth wave" of mass immigration began; namely, the guiding principle should be what immigrants can do for this country, not what this country can do for them.

Legal entry should be restricted to skilled and educated immigrants because the United States has an abundance of unskilled and poorly prepared would-be workers. With job prospects for unskilled and semiskilled workers becoming dimmer by the day, long-term human resource strategy must be predicated on ways to enhance the employability of workers facing reduced demand for their services and to prevent future would-be workers from facing such dismal prospects. That too many of those persons lacking sufficient skills and education are from the nation's growing minority populations only adds urgency to this domestic challenge.

A shift in admission preference away from family reunification toward employment-based criteria can be expected to encounter fierce opposition despite the fact that the rationale for establishing the priority for family reunification in 1965 was anything but noble in its original intentions (see Chapter 5). As the eminent authority on immigration, John Higham, has written in 1991,

> This [the elimination of family preference] will be as difficult to change as were the earlier anomalies and deficiencies in American immigration policy. Like those earlier deficiencies, the family preference scheme will have a stubborn constituency in the ethnic groups that believe they benefit from it. Just as the national origin quotas suppressed variety in the alleged interests of the older American population, so the current law does the same in the supposed interest of the groups that have recently dominated the incoming stream.[29]

The most obvious component of the family reunification system to be eliminated is the preference for adult brothers and sisters of U.S. citizens. Under the Immigration Act of 1990, this preference is given 65,000 visas a year (a slight increase over what had existed since 1965). No other major immigrant-receiving nation in the world provides such an admission category. Indeed, the original version of the Simpson-Mazzoli bill in 1982 called for its total elimination but the proposal did not survive the subsequent deliberations over the bill's terms. If adult brothers and sisters of U.S. immigrants wish to immigrate to the United States, they should be required to qualify on the same grounds as any other would-be immigrant. The other three family-related categories should be reduced significantly. Whatever purpose family reunification may have played in the past, it should have only a minor future role in any serious immigration reform effort.

Given the unprecedented forces that are reshaping the occupational, industrial, and geographic employment patterns of the nation, the United States can ill afford an immigration policy that runs counter to its best interests. As the discussion in Chapter 7 sought to make clear, the nation is at an economic crossroad. It must choose between being a nation of high wages, made possible by a highly productive labor force, or becoming a nation of low wages, the consequence of a low productive labor force. In other words, does the nation seek to rank with countries like Japan and Germany or does it seek to move in the direction of Third World countries?

The necessity to choose the former of these two options is made more imperative by the changes that are reconstituting the composition of the nation's labor force. As the world's first advanced industrial society to have a multiracial and multicultural labor force, it is mandatory that the society not polarize along racial and ethnic lines over who is employed in the growth occupations and industries and who is left to flounder in the declining employment sectors or forced into the underclass of the economy. Thus, equity considerations and the need for domestic tranquility demand that every effort be made to incorporate those segments of the population that are experiencing difficulties qualifying and preparing themselves for the job sectors that are expected to expand. The design of immigration policy, therefore, must not be allowed to increase the competition in the existing low-wage labor markets nor be allowed to diminish in any way the pressures needed to develop and upgrade the latent talents of those citizen groups who are already disproportionately vulnerable to the rapidly changing employment trends.

As immigration policy can influence the quantitative size of the labor force as well as the qualitative characteristics of those it admits, it can shape labor market conditions as well as respond to its changes. As matters now stand, there is little synchronization of immigrant flows with the demonstrated needs of the labor market. While there is no prospect for a general labor shortage in the 1990s, there is a likelihood of serious spot shortages of qualified labor. These shortages will be most apparent in the range of occupations that require extensive training and education preparation. There is no shortage now nor any prospect of a future labor shortage for jobs that require little in the way of human capital for job applicants. In the technologically driven and internationally competitive economic setting of the 1990s, no industrialized nation with as many functionally illiterate adults as in the United States need have any short-run fear of a scarcity of unqualified workers. Moreover, if only to make matters worse, immigration—especially that of illegal immigrants, recent amnesty recipients, and refugees—has itself become a major contributor to the growth of adult illiteracy in the United States.[30] To this degree, immigration, by adding to the surplus of illiterate adult job seekers, is serving to diminish the limited opportunities for poorly prepared citizens to find jobs or to improve their employability by on-the-job training. It is not surprising, therefore, that the underground economy is thriving in many urban centers. Moreover, the nature of the immigration and refugee flow is also contributing to the need to expand funding for remedial education, basic training, and language literacy programs in many urban communities that have been impacted by their arrival. Too often these funding choices cause scarce public funds to be diverted from programs to upgrade the human resource capabilities of the citizen and resident alien labor force.

In addition to the high incidence of adult illiteracy that currently exists, there should be no fear about any future shortage of the unskilled when the nation is experiencing a national high school dropout rate averaging 25 percent. The dropout rate is 40 percent for blacks and over 50 percent for Hispanics (the two most rapidly growing component groups in the youth population). And these grim statistics do not take into account the additional somber fact that the quality of education provided for many of these minorities who do graduate from high school "does not even meet the standard of a rising tide of mediocrity."[31]

It is also important to note that the decline in the number of youths in the labor force that began in the 1980s is just about over. Beginning in 1996, this group will begin to increase again in absolute numbers so that by the year 2005 it is projected to be larger by about 2.8 million people than it was in 1990.[32] Thus, as the U.S. Department of Labor has reported, "the worry about lack of entry level workers, which was of consequence in the late 1980s and early 1990s, should ease considerably, if not disappear entirely, as we progress through this decade [the 1990s]."[33]

In this economic environment, an immigration policy designed to admit a flexible number of highly skilled and educated workers is what is required. The Immigration Act of 1990 was ostensibly intended to move public policy in this direction. But, as has been shown, it actually expands the nepotistic family reunification focus that had been the predominant feature of the law it replaced and only marginally increases employment-based immigration. It is the inordinate adherence to this principle of family reunification, the continuing entry of illegal immigrants, and the admission of substantial numbers of Third World refugees that is a major contributor to this worsening mismatch between the qualifications of many job seekers and the actual needs of the U.S. labor market.

Already having an abundance of unskilled or poorly educated adults, the last thing that the nation needs is to continue to allow unskilled and poorly educated persons to immigrate into the United States. It is always possible for more highly skilled and educated persons to do unskilled work. Hence, in the unlikely case that all of the experts on labor force trends and projections are wrong and the future demand is for unskilled workers with a contraction of need for skilled workers, the operation of normal market forces should be able to guide the excess supply of skilled workers to vacant unskilled jobs. This assumes, of course, that the operation of the market is not sabotaged by an immigration policy designed either to admit unskilled nonimmigrant workers or to continue to tolerate the massive illegal entry of unskilled workers. But the reverse is not possible. If skilled and educated workers are needed, they cannot readily be created. Unskilled workers cannot fill skilled jobs except at great financial cost associated with significant time delays for retraining and relocation or with significant productivity losses for the economy due to inefficient operations. Moreover, the lack of sufficient educational foundations will prevent many currently unskilled adults from ever being trained for the types of jobs that are projected to be most in demand in the next decade.

On the positive side, immigration can be used as a means of providing the types of experienced workers that are actually needed. Under present circumstances, these workers are those that already have skills and education and, for whatever reason, voluntarily wish to leave their homelands. Such is especially the case of workers who are in fields that involve computer technology; conduct scientific research; and provide higher education itself. It is in this capacity that immigration can find a justifiable purpose in this new era. Immigration policy can serve as a short-run method to fill these types of jobs until the nation can enact the quality human resource development policies capable of meeting this emerging demand.

Largely by means of circumvention, the current immigration system is trying to perform this function despite the self-defeating burdens imposed on it. The nonimmigrant system is becoming a significant avenue into the country's labor market for skilled and educated workers. Indeed, it is very likely that the topic of the use nonimmigrant foreign workers will emerge as a major domestic labor policy issue of the 1990s. Nonimmigrant policy is supposed to allow for the admission of foreign workers to fill temporary spot shortages. Eventually, the nonimmigrants are expected to return to their homelands and, over time, market forces combined with public and private training should generate a domestic labor supply. It is not intended to be an avenue for permanent immigration or a means of long-term worker dependency by U.S. employers. But because 80 percent of the available visas each year are restricted to family-related admissions and because, in the past, there have been lengthy backlogs of applicants or country ceilings that have affected the availability the employment-based visas, many employers have turned to the nonimmigrant system to find experienced workers that are otherwise unavailable or for whom they do not wish to compete, hire, or train from the citizen-born pool. This is, of course, a perversion of this element of immigration policy. For most of the relevant nonimmigrant categories, there are no annual ceilings and some categories permit workers to remain in the country for many years. Thus, it is conceivable that nonimmigrant workers could soon become as or more important than the existing legal immigrant system in terms of its annual labor supply implications.

A shift from a family-based to a labor market-oriented immigration policy, of course, does have its dangers. For even the use of immigration as a source of experienced workers should be viewed as a policy of last resort, not immediate recourse. It should be used only in consort with other public policy measures intended to develop the employment potential of the nation's human resources. Labor shortages, should they develop, should not be viewed as a problem to be solved immediately by immigration. Rather, labor shortages should be viewed as an opportunity to educate youth; to retrain adults; to eliminate discriminatory barriers; and to introduce voluntary relocation programs to assist would-be workers to move from labor surplus to labor shortage areas.

As matters now stand, the incidence of unemployment, poverty, and adult illiteracy is much higher and the educational attainment levels significantly lower for blacks and Hispanics than for non-Hispanic whites and most Asians. In addition, blacks and Hispanics are disproportionately employed in industries and occupations already in sharpest decline—the goods-producing industries and blue-collar occupations. Thus, the most rapidly increasing groups in the labor force are precisely those most adversely at risk from the changing employment requirements. Unless public policy measures are targeted to their human resource development needs, many members of both groups, as well as other vulnerable segments of the general population, will have dim employment and income prospects in the emerging postindustrial economy. The United States cannot allow its labor force to continue to polarize along racial and class lines if it hopes to prosper and persevere.

If the prevailing policy of mass and unguided immigration continues, it is unlikely that there will be sufficient pressure to enact the long-term human resource development policies needed to prepare and to incorporate these citizen groups into the mainstream economy. Instead, by providing both competition and alternatives, the large and unplanned influx of immigrant labor will serve to maintain the social marginalization of many citizen blacks and citizen Hispanics. If so, the rare chance afforded by the employment trends of the 1990s to reduce significantly the economically disadvantaged population and the underclass will be lost for another generation. It will also mean that job opportunities will be reduced for the growing numbers of older workers who may wish to prolong their working years and for the vast pool of disabled citizens who were only recently extended employment protection by the Americans with Disabilities Act of 1990. In other words, a substantial human reserve of potential citizen workers already exists. If their human resources development needs were addressed comprehensively, they could provide an ample supply of workers for most of the labor force needs of the 1990s and beyond.

The national interest dictates that priority must always be to prepare citizen and resident alien workers for jobs in the expanding employment sectors of the economy. To respond to labor shortages by using immigration policy to fill jobs in an economy that is not at full employment is analogous to choosing to take a shortcut through quicksand. Immigrants can fill the jobs, but the social cost to the nation is a loss of opportunities to prepare the citizens and resident alien labor force for such opportunities with all of the attendant social and human costs.

It goes without saying that an employment-based immigration system is predicated on the assumption that every effort is made to reduce illegal immigration. It is probably impossible in a free society to stop illegal immigration entirely but the goal should be to pursue actively every possible means to reduce its incidence. Illegal immigration, aside from the competition it often provides with other low-wage citizen and resident alien workers, is a major explanation for the revival of "sweatshops" and the upsurge in child labor violations that have occurred since the mid-1980s in many urban areas.[34] Existing fair labor standards laws, child labor laws, and occupational health and safety laws should be vigorously enforced to end such practices regardless of whether or not such illegal aliens and their children are actually displacing citizen or resident alien workers. U.S. employers should not be permitted to use Third World wages and working conditions to employ workers formerly from Third World countries under any circumstance—although this is exactly what is happening.

The entire presumption that the nation can have a realistic immigration policy is predicated on the notion that its terms can be enforced. But the scale of illegal immigration over the years has completely undermined this premise. Employer sanctions must remain the core of the deterrence posture of the nation but its loopholes with regard to the use of fraudulent documents and the absence of a counterfeit proof identification system must be corrected. Also financial penalties should be imposed on illegal immigrants themselves just as they are on any other offender of federal law. More attention should be paid to addressing the push factors in the major source countries. Forms of assistance should be tailored to the particular factors in any single country that cause so many of their citizens to leave their homelands. These may involve one or more of such concerns as excessive population pressures, mass poverty, corrupt governments, or widespread human rights violations. U.S. assistance could take the form of family planning assistance, limited trade concessions, economic development assistance, or technical assistance. Additional funds and staff should be devoted to border enforcement activities and inland investigations of "visa overstayers." It may mean that stronger physical barriers need to be established at those points along the border where massive illegal entry is known to occur. The message that illegal immigration to the United States is no longer an option must be made a fact of life.

With regard to refugee policy, the goal should be to make the treatment of refugees ideologically neutral. To this end, the Cuban Adjustment Act of 1966 should be repealed. All political refugees should be treated the same. The refugee concept should be applied to individuals and not generalized to groups. Certainly the United States is obligated to participate in worldwide efforts to assist legitimate political refugees but there is more to be done than simply admitting them for permanent settlement. Attention should be given to other policy alternatives. Aside from the standard efforts to resettle refugees in other regional countries near their homelands when it is feasible, or to provide financial aid to support refugees in camps while they remain in neighboring third-party countries (if conditions in their homelands are expected to change in the near future), the United States should link its foreign policy, foreign aid, and foreign trade policies to adherence to human rights principles in those countries that generate mass numbers of political refugees. Nonetheless, when there is no other recourse, those refugees and their family members who have sustained persecution for their individual actions should—as now—be admitted on a limited basis. But the admission of refugees should explicitly mean that fewer family-related visas are available in any given year. There must be some element of "trade-off." The legal link between the legal immigration system and refugee policy must be re-established (as was the case from 1965 to 1980). Otherwise, the political temptation is (as has been the case) for the federal government to act in piecemeal fashion that results in significant total inflows of refugees for which local and state governments eventually bear most of the costs. Indeed, it would be preferable if the federal government would absorb all of the financial costs associated with preparing refugees for employment and their families for settlement and employment. Refugees are admitted to the United States as a direct result of federal policy decisions. Consequently, all of the people of the United States should share the costs of refugee policy and not just those who live in the local communities that are heavily impacted by their presence.

The political asylee issue raises the same questions as does the refugee issue. There needs to be an expedited method to separate the legitimate claims for political asylum from the claims by persons who are simply using it as a pretext to enter the country for personal economic gain. The original Simpson-Mazzolli bill of 1982 proposed that negative decisions of asylee adjudication cases be only appealable to courts on the basis of procedural errors. Substantive rulings on the merits of the decisions would not be appealable. These provisions were bitterly opposed by immigration lawyers and by some civil rights organizations. But the current system of lengthy appeals, protracted cases, and high legal costs simply cannot be sustained. A way of bringing rapid closure to these cases must be found. The new corps of asylum officers that was established in 1990 who are specially trained for these purposes should be empowered with a limitation of any appeal of their negative decisions to procedural violations alone. Likewise, if such expedited decision-making procedures could be established, the practice of keeping asylee applicants in detention while their cases are resolved could be applied uniformly. Otherwise one is confronted with the present mockery to common sense whereby many applicants simply make an asylum request, are released on their own recognizance, and disappear before their adjudication hearing or soon after a hearing in which they receive a negative decision.

The United States needs to adopt an immigration policy that is consistent with its rapidly changing labor market trends. If congruent, immigration policy can provide a valuable tool to national efforts to enhance economic efficiency and to achieve societal equity. If contradictory, immigration policy can present a major barrier to the accomplishment of either or both goals. The luxuries of allowing immigration policy to continue to be determined on purely political criteria (i.e., to placate special interest groups) and to achieve idealistic social dreams (i.e., to pursue diversity simply for its own sake) can ill be afforded. Making immigration policy a human resource development policy would give immigration policy what it now lacks: economic accountability for what it does.

Notes

1. See George Borjas, *Friends or Strangers: The Impact of Immigrants on the U.S. Economy* (New York: Basic Books, 1990), pp. 18-22. See also Barry Chiswick, "Is the New Immigration Less Skilled Than the Old?" *Journal of Labor Economics* (April 1986), pp. 192-196.

2. See David North and Marion F. Houstoun, *The Characteristics and Role of Illegal Aliens in the U.S. Labor Market: An Exploratory Study* (Washington, D.C.: Linton and Co., 1976), p. 104 and Maurice D. Van Arsdol, Jr., Joan Moore, David Heer, and Susan P. Haynie, *Nonapprehended and Apprehended Residents in the Los Angeles Labor Market* (Washington, D.C.: U.S. Government Printing Office, 1979), p. 69.

3. Marta Tienda, George Borjas, Hector Cordero-Guzman, Kristen Neuman, and Manuela Romero, *The Demography of Legalization:*

Insights from Administration Records of Legalized Aliens Report to the U.S. Department of Health and Human Services (Chicago: Population Research Center Discussion Paper Series, October, 1991), Table 8, and discussion on pp. 34-36; see also U.S. Immigration and Naturalization Service, Statistics Division, *Provisional Legalization Application Statistics* (December 1, 1991), p. 2.

4. For example, see *Report to the Congress*, "Proposed Refugee Admissions for fiscal year 1992" (Washington, D.C.: Coordinator for Refugee Affairs, 1991), pp. 33-34 and 39-40.

5. Among these are George J. Borjas, *Friends or Strangers: ..., op. cit.*; Elizabeth Bogen, *Immigration in New York* (New York: Praeger Publishers, 1987); Thomas R. Bailey *Immigrant and Native Workers: Contrasts and Competition* (Boulder: Westview Press, 1987); Leon F. Bouvier and Vernon M. Briggs, Jr. *The Population and Labor Force of New York: 1990 to 2050* (Washington, D.C.: Population Reference Bureau, 1988), Chapter 6; David Card, "The Impact of the Mariel Boatlift on the Miami Labor Market," *Industrial and Labor Relations Review*, (January, 1990), pp. 245-257; F. Ray Marshall and Leon F. Bouvier, *Population Change and the Future of Texas* (Washington D.C.: Population Reference Bureau, 1986); Thomas Muller and Thomas J. Espenshade, *The Fourth Wave: California's Newest Immigrants* (Washington, D.C.: The Urban Institute Press, 1985); and Leon F. Bouvier, *Fifty Million Californians* (Washington, D.C.: Center for Immigration Studies, 1991).

6. Kevin McCarthy, and R. Burciago Valdez, *Current and Future Effects of Mexican Immigration in California: Executive Summary* (Santa Monica: The Rand Corporation, 1985) and Thomas Muller and Thomas Espenshade, The Fourth Wave, op. cit.

7. Ray Marshall, "Immigration in the Golden State: The Tarnished Dream," in *U.S. Immigration in the 1980s: Reappraisal and Reform*, edited by David E. Simcox (Boulder: Westview Press, 1988), p. 195.

8. Ibid.

9. Robert Reinhold, "In California, New Talk About a Taboo Subject," *New York Times* (December 3, 1991), p. A-20, and "Business Abandons Paradise," *Rocky Mountain News* (July 18, 1991), p. 65.

10. Michael Fix, *The Paper Curtain* (Washington, D.C.: Urban Institute Press, 1991), p. 304.

11. Congressional Research Service, "Memorandum: S. 358, the Immigration Act of 1990, as Approved by Congress," (November 9, 1990), p. 1.

12. Robert Pear, "Lawmakers Agree on Immigration Rise," *New York Times* (October 21, 1990), p. A-26.

13. Seth Mydans, "For Skilled Foreigners, Lower Hurdles to U.S.," *New York Times* (November 5, 1990), p. A-12.

14. Seth Mydans, "For Winners in Visa Lottery, Round 2," *New York Times* (November 29, 1991), p. A-22.

15. Alejandro Portes and Ruben G. Rumbaut, *Immigration America: A Portrait* (Berkeley, University of California Press, 1990), Chapter 2.

16. Philip Martin, "Network Recruitment and Labor Displacement" *U.S. Immigration Policy in the 1980s*, edited by David E. Simcox (Boulder: Westview Press, 1988), pp. 67-91. See also Donatella Lorch, "Ethnic Niches Creating Jobs that Fuel Immigrant Growth," *New York Times* (January 12, 1992), pp. A-1 and A-20.

17. Elizabeth Bogen, op. cit., p. 91.

18. Ibid.

19. Martin op.cit.; see also Richard Mines and Philip Martin, "Immigrant Workers and the California Citrus Industry," *Industrial Relations* (Spring, 1984) pp. 139-1949.

20. Portes and Rumbaut, op. cit., Chapter 2.

21. E.g., see Joseph N. Boyce, "Struggle Over Hospital in Los Angles' Pits Minority Versus Minority," *The Wall Street Journal* (April 1, 1991), p. A-1 and p. A-4 and David Gonzales, "Criticisms Aimed at Statements on Immigrants," New York Times, (October 5, 1990), p. B-3.

22. Seth Mydans, "40,000 Aliens to Win Legal Status in Lottery," *New York Times* (September 25, 1991), p. A-1.

23. Ibid., p. A-19.

24. Ibid.

25. Seth Mydans, "Foreign Millionaires in No Rush to Apply for Visas, U.S. Finds," *New York Times* (December 22, 1991), p. A-18.

26. See, Michael Fix, *The Paper Curtain ..., op. cit.*; U.S. General Accounting Office, *Immigration Reform: Employer Sanctions and the Question of Discrimination* (Washington, D.C.: U.S. Government Printing Office, 1990); and Vernon M. Briggs, Jr., "Employer Sanctions and the Question of Discrimination: The GAO Study in Perspective," *International Migration Review* (Winter 1990), pp. 803-815.

27. "Employer Sanctions Repeal Bills Introduced," *Immigration Report* (November 1991), p. 1.

28. "Bills Introduced in House and Senate to Repeal Immigration Employer Sanctions," *Daily Labor Report* (June 28, 1990), p. A-5.

29. John Higham, "The Purpose of Legal Immigration in the 1990s and Beyond," *Social Contract* (Winter 1990-91), p. 64.

30. "Hearings Accent Problem of Work Force Illiteracy," *Daily Labor Report* (August 2, 1985), p. A-10.

31. U.S. Congress, Joint-Economic Committee, "The Education Deficit," *Staff Report Summarizing the Hearings on "Competitiveness and the Quality of the American Labor Force"* (Washington D.C.: U.S. Government Printing Office, 1988), p. 1 and 16.

32. Ronald E. Kutscher, "New BLS Projections: Findings and Implications," *Monthly Labor Review* (November 1991), p. 6.

33. Ibid.

34. For example, see, "ILGWU Expands Campaign Against Sweatshops," *AFL-CIO News* (May 14, 1990), p. 7.; Constance Hays, "Immigrants Strain Chinatown's Resources," *New York Times* (May 30, 1990), p. B-1 and B-4; Peter T. Kilborn, "Tougher Enforcing of Child Labor Laws Is Vowed," *New York Times* (February 8, 1990), p. A-22; Peter T. Kilborn, "Widespread Child Labor Violations," *New York Times* (March 16, 1990), p. A-10; and Lisa Belkin, "Abuses Rise Among Hispanic Garment Workers," *New York Times* (November 28, 1990), p A-16; and Donatella Lorch, "Immigrants From China Pay Dearly to be Slaves," *New York Times* (January 3, 1991), p. B-1.

APPENDIX

Appendix A The Preference System Created Under The Immigration Act of 1965 (in effect until 1980)		
Preference	**Category**	**Maximum Proportion of Total Admitted**
First	Unmarried adult sons and daughters of U.S. citizens	20%
Second	Spouses and unmarried adult sons and daughters of aliens lawfully admitted for permanent residence	20% plus any not required by first preference
Third	Members of the professions, scientists, and artists of exceptional ability	10%
Fourth	Married sons and daughters of U.S. citizens	10% plus any not required by first and third preferences
Fifth	Brothers and sisters of U.S. citizens	24% plus any not required by first four preferences
Sixth	Skilled and unskilled workers in occupations for which labor is in short supply	10%
Seventh	Refugees	6%
Nonpreference	Any applicant	Numbers not used by preceding preferences

Source: Immigration and Naturalization Service.

Appendix B The Legal Immigration System And Its Preference Allocations That Were In Effect From 1980 To 1991		
Preference	Category	Maximum Proportion of Total Admitted
First	Unmarried adult sons and daughters of U.S. citizens	20%
Second	Spouses and unmarried adult sons and daughters of aliens lawfully admitted for permanent residence	26% plus any not required by first preference
Third	Members of the professions, or persons of exceptional ability in the sciences and arts	10%
Fourth	Married sons and daughters of U.S. citizens	10% plus any not required by first and third preferences
Fifth	Brothers and sisters of U.S. citizens, 21 years of age and over	24% plus any not required by first four preferences
Sixth	Skilled and unskilled workers in occupations for which labor is in short supply	10%
Nonpreference	Any applicant	Numbers not used by preceding preferences

Source: Immigration and Naturalization Service.

Appendix C. The Thirty-four Countries Whose Nationals Are Eligible for the Transitional Program for Diversity Immigrants, 1992-1994

Albania	Indonesia
Algeria	Ireland
Argentina	Italy
Austria	Japan
Belgium	Lativa
Bermuda	Liechtenstein
Czechoslovakia	Lithuania
Denmark	Luxembourg
Estonia	Monaco
Finland	New Caledonia
France	The Netherlands
Germany	Norway
Gibralter	Poland
Great Britain	San Marino
Guadeloupe	Sweden
Hungary	Switzerland
Ireland	Tunesia

Index

About The Author

Vernon M. Briggs, Jr. is a labor economist on the faculty of the School of Industrial and Labor Relations at Cornell University. He has written extensively on a variety of issues pertaining to the preparation of the nation's labor force for employment. Aside from previous work on all aspects of the nation's immigration policy, he has also published books and articles on apprenticeship training, public service employment, the employment and training of youth and minorities, and rural labor market analysis. He was formerly a member of the National Council on Employment Policy from 1977 to 1987 and served as its chairman from 1985 to 1987.